Praise for FoodFest 365!

"Yvan is a talented and creative young chef. Since our time together at Le Cirque 2000, Yvan has continued to pursue his passion for food and cooking with a sense of humor and style. Whether you are looking for a delicious dessert or fun ideas for refreshing cocktails, they can be found within these pages. Filled with fun, easy, and imaginative recipes, *FoodFest 365!* is a must for any cook's library. Strap on your rollerblades and race—don't walk—to get your copy. I know I am!"

—Jacques Torres, M.O.F. (*Meillure Ouvrier de France*);
Chocolate Executive Officer, Jacques Torres Chocolate, New York

"Food should be fun! To make food fun every day you need a secret weapon and *FoodFest 365!* is it. Yvan the 'chefologist' gives us ideas, twists, fun stories, chef tips, pictures, and recipes so awesome you want to lick 'em off the pages! Explore, experiment, and make food fun and delicious with Yvan as your guide."

—Keegan Gerhard, Chef/Owner, D Bar Desserts;
Host, *Food Network Challenge*

"I have had the pleasure of watching (and judging) Yvan when he competed on the Food Network show *Chopped* and it was such a pleasure watching this chef demonstrate his passion and creativity in such a difficult setting! Yvan proved not only his skills as a cook, but showed that a true artist lives inside him, and manifests itself in his playful, whimsical, and 'outside-the-box' dishes. I have no doubt Yvan [and his company iFood Studio] is going to go a long way and reinvent many, many dishes in the process, and that *FoodFest 365!* is just the first look at what this talented chef can do. Kudos!"

—Chris Santos, Executive Chef/Partner, The Stanton Social;
Judge on *Chopped*

"*FoodFest 365!* is an amazing book chock full of fun and playful recipes and ideas. I love how Yvan really captures the essence of spirited youth. *FoodFest 365!* is sure to bring the family together both in the kitchen and at the table."

—Johnny Iuzzini, Executive Pastry Chef, Jean Georges Restaurant;
Author of *Dessert FourPlay: Sweet Quartets from a Four-Star Pastry Chef*

Praise for FoodFest 365!

"Beautiful, happy recipes, a masterpiece from Yvan! Love the Little Devils and the juicy burger. A must in your kitchen!"

—Cyril Renaud, Chef/Owner, Bar Breton

"*FoodFest 365*! is easy to follow, caring, and happy, just like Yvan, who's always on your side!"

—Akiko Katayama, Food Writer; Judge on *Iron Chef America*

"[Mr. Lemoine's] desserts . . . verge on spectacular."

—*New York Times*

"Yvan Lemoine is one of the most talented chefs in the country. His fanciful couplings of flavor and texture put him in a league of his own."

—Carmen Marc Valvo, Fashion Designer

"It's refreshing to find a cookbook that really has so much fun with food and invites the entire family to participate and enjoy the process of cooking and eating together. Yvan's simple and delicious recipes will teach you proper technique and have you looking forward to holidays you've never before heard of (like Jelly-Filled Doughnut Day) for years to come. It's a book that will have you smiling from the beginning of the recipe until the very last bite."

—Andrea Strong, Writer and Founder of the Popular Food Blog *The Strong Buzz*

"Yvan is a talent that is rarely seen. He creates masterpieces that satisfy not only the palate but the eye as well. He puts heart and soul into his work, and as you can see from this book, it shows. I commend him to the fullest extent, and always look forward to experiencing his future endeavors."

—Jonathan Pogash, NYC Beverage Consultant, *www.thecocktailguru.com*; President NY Chapter, United States Bartenders Guild

Praise for FoodFest 365!

"We all know about the big food holidays like Thanksgiving, Easter, Passover, Chanukah, Christmas, and July 4th, but this book gives us a valid excuse to celebrate food each and every day. Yvan's enthusiasm for food comes through loud and clear in this energetic book, and his passion for enjoying food is only matched by his skill in preparing it. He has put the fun back in our mouths by celebrating the things he—and we—love to eat. Each recipe is a cooking history lesson and a reassurance of kitchen success for seasoned chefs and home cooks who haven't been to cooking school, but can handily prepare the foods they love to eat and try some new ones, too. As an added bonus, this book offers a perfect explanation for when you're indulging. Need to explain to your personal trainer why you had salted caramel flan for breakfast? Once he knows that it's National Caramel Day, he'll simply have to forgive you. Of course he may make you drop and give him twenty, but it's well worth it if you followed Yvan's delicious recipe."

—Francine Cohen, Editor-in-Chief,
Inside F&B (www.insidefandb.com)

"This book is exactly what you need for inspiration every day of the year. It's fun, fab, and fascinating."

—Gary Regan, ArdentSpirits.com

"I had the pleasure of preparing food and drinks with Yvan in my studio. The recipes were not only easy enough to follow for a beginner cook such as myself, but they tasted delicious and looked amazing."

—Diana Falzone, TV Personality and Host of Cosmolicious Radio

"I have known Yvan since his high school days when he showed signs of independence, imagination, and creativity. His talents are many and his accomplishments to date are truly amazing. His *first* book (for I believe there will be many more) is filled with recipes that show his joy for life, knowledge of food, and his desire to have fun in the kitchen. Enjoy!"

—Richard Grausman, President/Founder, C-CAP
(Careers through Culinary Arts Program)

Praise for FoodFest 365!

"Yvan is a genius. Nothing more, nothing less. His recipes are simple and full of his voice. Reassuring, playful, encouraging and inventive—all at once. Buy this book if you want each day to be a festival celebrating food, family, life, and love. These are recipes that will give you reason to be at the table sharing with loved ones without fuss and with much aplomb."

—Suvir Saran, Chef/Owner, American Masala and Devi;
Author of *American Masala* and *Indian Home Cooking*

"Every day for me IS a food fest so the fact that Yvan D. Lemoine created this cookbook titled *FoodFest 365!* pretty much makes him my soul mate. I mean, National Jelly-Filled Doughnut Day? I was already observing that high holy day on my own, and now, thanks to Yvan's recipe for PB&J Doughnuts, his gourmet guidance gathers my fellow food followers as one. His foodie words of wisdom serve as a pied piper of sorts . . . and make me want to eat pie."

—Allison Hagendorf, TV Personality; Food Writer and Enthusiast

"'Y' is an energetic presence to the culinary world with his undying quest for new techniques, exotic ingredients, and anything fun!"

—Kevin Lasko, Executive Chef, Park Avenue Restaurant

"A true free spirit."

—*Food Arts Magazine*

A YEAR-LONG PARTY WITH A RECIPE A DAY!

September 26: Pancake Day

January 4: Spaghetti Day

December 10: Lager Day

FOOD FEST 365!

November 10: Vanilla Cupcake Day

THE OFFICIALLY FUN FOOD Holiday Cookbook

Yvan D. Lemoine

BEER

Adamsmedia
Avon, Massachusetts

Published by
Adams Media, a division of F+W Media, Inc.
57 Littlefield Street, Avon, MA 02322. U.S.A.
www.adamsmedia.com

ISBN 10: 1-4405-0619-1
ISBN 13: 978-1-4405-0619-2
eISBN 10: 1-4405-1000-8
eISBN 13: 978-1-4405-1000-7

Printed in China

10 9 8 7 6 5 4 3 2 1

Library of Congress Cataloging-in-Publication Data
is available from the publisher.

Readers are urged to take all appropriate precautions before undertaking any
how-to task. Always read and follow instructions and safety warnings for all tools
and materials, and call in a professional if the task stretches your abilities too far.
Although every effort has been made to provide the best possible information
in this book, neither the publisher nor the author are responsible for accidents,
injuries, or damage incurred as a result of tasks undertaken by readers. This
book is not a substitute for professional services.

Many of the designations used by manufacturers and sellers to distinguish their
product are claimed as trademarks. Where those designations appear in this
book and Adams Media was aware of a trademark claim, the designations have
been printed with initial capital letters.

Photos by Patricia Koo

This book is available at quantity discounts for bulk purchases.
For information, please call 1-800-289-0963.

I dedicate this book to my friend Michael Batterberry,
the eternal flame.

With special thanks to my family: Mom, Dad, Beatriz,
Johnny, Bas, Jesse, and Grandma for your patience and love,
and to my dog Lucas for eating everything I dropped on the
floor while cooking.

I love you all.

Acknowledgments

As they say, "We all walk on the shoulders of giants who came before us." That's why I'd like to take a mcment to thank the people who have helped me along the way. The ones who paid when I was broke and didn't have any money to buy the food to test these recipes. The ones who helped me clean the kitchen after I dropped the flour all over the floor. The ones who help me wash the dishes, pots, and crusted stuck-to-the-pan cheese casseroles. The ones who helped me clean pasta sauce from the walls, wipe up spilled soup inside the fridge, and got rid of the burnt cookies. The ones who tasted all the stuff I made and told me whether it was any good or not. Everyone who has taken the time out and had the patience to teach me how to cook. I apologize to all who gained 20 pounds from tasting all the food—I promise, I'll make it up to you. To Suvir, my good friend and guiding light, without you, this book would not have been possible. Diane, you rock. Wendy, my editor, I'm sorry for all the missing recipes, gram-ounce conversions, and ramblings you had to rifle through to produce this cookbook. My community of butchers, farmers, fishmongers, and supermarket staff. Thank you Cyril Renaud, my friend and mentor. Michael and Ariane Batterberry, my friends and guiding light, for always believing in me when sometimes I didn't. Joe and Dhanny Palma for their love and nurture since I was a little irresponsible rugrat. Ifeta and Gigi for letting me shoot at Diwine. A big shout out to John of Brooklyn Bagel in Astoria and Martha's Bakery. Thank you to Sarah and Ryan Koo for letting me use their babies and to Patricia Koo, the talented photographer of all these delicious food shots. To a special family of food websites: Eater, Chowhound, Serious Eats, Food Network, Dorie Greenspan, DavidLebovitz.com, Lynne Olver's Foodtimeline.org, and finally to TheNibble.com because that's where I got the idea for a food holiday cookbook. Thanks!

Introduction

This book is about our national foods holidays—delicious, frivolous, and daily food holidays. Because if there's something we all love celebrating, it's food! When you think about all the other holidays, how do you remember them? Christmas = ham. Thanksgiving = turkey, cranberry sauce, and stuffing. The Fourth of July = burgers and hot dogs, of course. I think all these holidays were created as an excuse to get together and eat! So why not cut out the middleman and go straight to the food? Well, my friends, in this book, we do just that. Inside, you'll find a celebration of festive food holidays, from simple to extravagant recipes for meals, snacks, cocktails, and desserts . . . the kind of recipes the whole family can do together. The recipes range from simple fudge to an elaborate Spanish paella, which might lead you to ask, "What's up with paella? That's not American." You're right. But when you think about it, what *is* American food? We are a nation of nations, a jumbled up mess of immigrants from all over the world, and our food reflects that. Consider our great "American" treasures—burgers, hot dogs, and even apple pie aren't technically native to the United States. We have immigrant-Americans to thank for bringing over an incredible array of culinary wonders that have become an integral part of our everyday menu. American food is nothing but a big mish-mosh of the world's greatest edible treasures, and that treasure is ours to gobble up. This book aims to remind you of what great American food is all about and to celebrate its delicious and colorful history. Eat well, my friends.

Cook's Note

Food holidays are as valid as Mother's Day, Valentine's Day, or Cinco de Mayo. They come about as the result of a group petitioning the government to commemorate a particular food on a particular day. The president then approves or denies them. From there, it's up to us to promote it and celebrate it!

THE HOLIDAYS

January

JANUARY 1
Bloody Mary Day | 2

JANUARY 2
Cream Puff Day | 3

JANUARY 3
Cherry-Filled
Chocolate Day | 3

JANUARY 4
Spaghetti Day | 4

JANUARY 5
Whipped Cream Day | 5

JANUARY 6
Shortbread Day | 5

JANUARY 7
Tempura Day | 6

JANUARY 8
English Toffee Day | 6

JANUARY 9
Apricot Day | 7

JANUARY 10
Bittersweet Chocolate
Day | 8

JANUARY 11
Hot Toddy Day | 8

JANUARY 12
Curried Chicken Day | 10

JANUARY 13
Peach Melba Day | 11

JANUARY 14
Hot Pastrami
Sandwich Day | 11

JANUARY 15
Strawberry Ice Cream Day | 12

JANUARY 16
Fig Newton Day | 12

JANUARY 17
Hot Buttered Rum Day | 13

JANUARY 18
Peking Duck Day | 14

JANUARY 19
Popcorn Day | 15

JANUARY 20
Cheese Lover's Day | 16

JANUARY 21
New England Clam
Chowder Day | 16

JANUARY 22
Blonde Brownie Day | 17

JANUARY 23
Rhubarb Pie Day | 18

JANUARY 24
Peanut Butter Day | 19

JANUARY 25
Irish Coffee Day | 19

JANUARY 26
Pistachio Day | 20

JANUARY 27
Chocolate Cake Day | 20

JANUARY 28
Blueberry Pancake Day | 21

JANUARY 29
Corn Chip Day | 21

JANUARY 30
Croissant Day | 22

JANUARY 31
Brandy Alexander Day | 23

February

March

April

May

June

July

August

September

October

OCTOBER 1
World Vegetarian Day | 228

OCTOBER 2
Fried Scallops Day | 228

OCTOBER 3
Caramel Custard Day | 229

OCTOBER 4
Taco Day | 230

OCTOBER 5
Apple Betty Day | 231

OCTOBER 6
Noodle Day | 232

OCTOBER 7
Frappe Day | 233

OCTOBER 8
Fluffernutter Day | 233

OCTOBER 9
Submarine-Hoagie-Hero-
Grinder Day | 235

OCTOBER 10
Angel Food Cake Day | 235

OCTOBER 11
World Egg Day | 236

OCTOBER 12
Gumbo Day | 237

OCTOBER 13
Yorkshire Pudding Day | 238

OCTOBER 14
Chocolate-Covered Insects
Day | 238

OCTOBER 15
Chicken Cacciatore Day | 239

OCTOBER 16
Liqueur Day | 239

OCTOBER 17
Pasta Day | 240

OCTOBER 18
Chocolate Cupcake Day | 241

OCTOBER 19
Seafood Bisque Day | 242

OCTOBER 20
Brandied Fruit Day | 243

OCTOBER 21
Caramel Apple Day | 244

OCTOBER 22
Nut Day | 244

OCTOBER 23
Boston Cream Pie Day | 245

OCTOBER 24
Bologna Day | 245

OCTOBER 25
Greasy Foods Day | 246

OCTOBER 26
Pumpkin Day | 246

OCTOBER 27
Potato Day | 247

OCTOBER 28
Wild Foods Day | 247

OCTOBER 29
Oatmeal Day | 249

OCTOBER 30
Buy a Doughnut Day | 249

OCTOBER 31
Trick or Treat for
UNICEF Day | 250

November

December

DECEMBER 1
Pie Day | 277

DECEMBER 2
Fritters Day | 277

DECEMBER 3
Apple Pie Day | 278

DECEMBER 4
Cookie Day | 278

DECEMBER 5
Sacher Torte Day | 279

DECEMBER 6
Gazpacho Day | 280

DECEMBER 7
Cotton Candy Day | 280

DECEMBER 8
Chocolate Brownie Day | 281

DECEMBER 9
Pastry Day | 282

DECEMBER 10
Lager Day | 283

DECEMBER 11
Noodle Ring Day | 283

DECEMBER 12
Cocoa Day | 284

DECEMBER 13
Ice Cream and
Violins Day | 284

DECEMBER 14
Bouillabaisse Day | 285

DECEMBER 15
Cupcake Day | 286

DECEMBER 16
Chocolate-Covered
Anything Day | 288

DECEMBER 17
Maple Syrup Day | 288

DECEMBER 18
Roast Suckling Pig Day | 289

DECEMBER 19
Hard Candy Day | 289

DECEMBER 20
Fried Shrimp Day | 290

DECEMBER 21
Hamburger Day | 291

DECEMBER 22
Date Nut Bread Day | 292

DECEMBER 23
Pfeffernuesse Day | 292

DECEMBER 24
Egg Nog Day | 293

DECEMBER 25
Pumpkin Pie Day | 294

DECEMBER 26
Candy Cane Day | 294

DECEMBER 27
Fruit Cake Day | 295

DECEMBER 28
Chocolate Candy Day | 296

DECEMBER 29
Pepper Pot Day | 296

DECEMBER 30
Bicarbonate of Soda Day | 297

DECEMBER 31
Champagne Day | 298

JANUARY

JAN. 1

Bloody Mary Day

Mmmm . . . the Bloody Mary . . . what a great way to start the book! Originally believed to have been created by George Jessel around 1939 when he mixed vodka with tomato juice, the modern Bloody Mary didn't actually get its wings until Fernand Petiot started adding spices and Worcestershire sauce while at the St. Regis in New York. At this point the recipe had no horseradish! Today, you'll find more variations on this recipe than any other cocktail—from a "Bloody Caesar" with clamato juice, to a "Bloody Maria" with tequila, to a "Chelada" with beer, or a "Steaming Mary," served hot with a dollop of butter on top. Here's a classic recipe to get you started.

ALREADY READY BLOODY MARY

Makes 2 morning eye-openers

3 cups tomato juice

½ teaspoon celery salt

Juice of ½ lemon

3 tablespoons Worcestershire sauce

20 turns of fresh pepper

5 dashes of hot sauce

1 cup good-quality vodka

2 tablespoons freshly grated horseradish (optional)

1 Combine ingredients and pour back and forth between two glasses.

2 Strain into highball glass, garnish with celery, and enjoy!

Cook's Note

The trick is to leave it in the fridge overnight with your liquor of choice. Alcohol absorbs flavors and by the time this is ready you won't taste the booze, but just a wonderful infusion of flavors.

JAN. 2 — Cream Puff Day

Cream puffs are made with a special dough called choux, *in which flour is added to boiling water and butter and cooked, then piped and baked. The steam created is used to leaven these little gems. The term* choux *means "cabbage" in French, and once you've baked these you'll see how they resemble* petit choux!

"CABBAGE" CREAM PUFFS

Makes 1 dozen

1 cup water

1 tablespoon sugar

Pinch of salt

6 tablespoons butter

5¾ ounces all-purpose flour (sifted)

4 large eggs and 1 egg white

Pastry Cream (Feb. 20)

❶ Combine water, sugar, salt, and butter in a pot and bring to a boil. When butter has melted, add sifted flour and stir with a wooden spoon until dough is formed. Cook on medium heat for 1 minute, stirring constantly.

❷ Remove pot from heat, pour dough into stand mixer. Let cool until it's warm. Mix on medium-high, adding one egg at a time until you have a smooth mixture. Pipe or spoon mixture onto a greased baking sheet. Bake for 10 minutes at 400°F then lower temperature to 325°F.

❸ Glaze cream puffs with egg wash (1 egg and 2 teaspoons of water) and return to oven until golden (10 minutes). Remove from oven and leave out until cool (do not refrigerate). Cut pastries in half, fill with chilled cream (using a pastry bag), and enjoy!

JAN. 3 — Cherry-Filled Chocolate Day

From Shirley Temples to sundaes, banana splits, and—of course—these chocolates, cherries add an elegant yet playful touch to any food they meet. To make the melty-gooey syrup encasing the cherry inside the chocolate shell, confectioners use the age-old trick of making fondant and letting it sit for about a month, which turns it into liquid sweetness. This recipe features a chocolate filling!

CHERRY CHOCOLATES

Makes about 2 dozen candies

1 jar maraschino cherries

3 tablespoons butter (softened)

3 tablespoons light corn syrup

1½ cups powdered sugar

¼ teaspoon salt

½ cup dark cocoa powder

8 ounces good-quality dark chocolate (melted)

8 ounces good-quality white chocolate (melted)

❶ Drain cherries. Place on paper towel until dry.

❷ To make fondant: Combine butter, corn syrup, powdered sugar, salt, and cocoa powder and stir. When dough comes together, knead with your hands until smooth, then place in Ziploc bag to keep it from drying out.

❸ Take a tablespoon of dough, flatten into thin disk, and gently wrap around cherry, leaving stem exposed. Place on plate dusted lightly with powdered sugar, and refrigerate until fondant is hard.

4 To temper dark chocolate, melt ¾ of chocolate in microwave until it's liquid, then stir in remaining chocolate until melted.

5 Coat cherries in chocolate and allow to cool. Decorate cherries by drizzling with white chocolate. Cover and keep at room temperature for about a month; this will make fondant melt.

Spaghetti Day

By law in Italy, all spaghetti is made from 100 percent semolina flour. But spaghetti is consumed all over the world with a thousand different varieties. Growing up, one of my favorite meals was a plate of piping-hot spaghetti with ketchup and Parmesan on top. It might sound odd, but this is one of the dishes that always makes me feel like a kid. As an adult, I've graduated to this easy and delicious sauce.

SIMPLE PASTA SAUCE

Makes 3 cups

Olive oil

1 medium onion (chopped)

2 cloves garlic (chopped)

1 stalk celery (chopped)

1 carrot (chopped)

Sea salt and freshly ground black pepper

2 (32-ounce) cans crushed tomatoes

2 dried bay leaves

4 tablespoons unsalted butter (optional)

1 In large casserole pot, heat oil over medium-high heat. Add onion and garlic and sauté until soft and translucent, about 5 to 10 minutes. Add celery and carrots and season with salt and pepper. Sauté until all vegetables are soft, about 5 to 10 minutes.

2 Add tomatoes and bay leaves and simmer uncovered on low heat for 1 hour or until thick. Remove bay leaves and check for seasoning. If sauce tastes acidic, add unsalted butter, 1 tablespoon at a time, to balance flavors.

3 Add ½ the tomato sauce into food processor. Combine until smooth. Continue with remaining tomato sauce. Serve on al dente spaghetti with plenty of freshly grated Parmesan cheese.

Cook's Note

If you're not using all the sauce, allow it to cool completely and pour 1- to 2-cup portions into freezer plastic bags. This will keep in the freezer for up to 6 months.

Whipped Cream Day

Shortbread Day

Whipped cream refers to cream that contains at least 30 percent fat and has air incorporated into it by whipping. Chantilly, a whipped cream with vanilla, is said to have been created by Francois Vatel, chef at the Chateau de Chantilly in France. Whipped cream can be savory as well as sweet and used as the base for simple mousses and to thicken soups.

Shortbread cookies are some of the easiest and most versatile you can make as you only need four ingredients: vanilla, butter, sugar, and flour. I use this dough as the base for pies or when I'm working with kids, because you can press this dough into pans and molds instead of rolling it out. And because the dough has no eggs or leavening ingredients, it won't melt or slide in the oven, making it unnecessary to use pie weights. You've gotta love the simplicity and the buttery texture!

PERFECT CHANTILLY CREAM

Makes 2 cups cream

2 tablespoons powdered sugar

2 cups heavy cream

1 teaspoon vanilla extract (or ½ vanilla pod, scraped)

❶ Combine sugar, heavy cream, and vanilla extract (or scraped pod) into metal bowl.

❷ Set bowl over another bowl with ice. Whip cold and slow to get the smoothest and most stable cream.

❸ Serve on practically anything!

Cook's Note

Cooking is all about intuition. When you think something's done, it probably is; when you think it's too hot, it probably is. *Trust your senses.*

SHORTIES

Makes 2 dozen

½ cup unsalted butter (softened)

½ cup margarine (softened)

¾ cup powdered sugar

2 teaspoons vanilla extract

1 teaspoon lemon juice

Zest of 1 lemon

2 cups all-purpose flour (sifted)

Pinch of salt and granulated sugar

❶ Cream butter, margarine, sugar, vanilla, lemon juice, and zest for about 2 minutes. Sift flour and salt, and add slowly to butter mixture. Blend until smooth.

❷ On top of a piece of plastic wrap, mold dough into a log, wrap, and refrigerate for 2–3 hours.

❸ Remove from fridge and slice into thin disks with a knife dipped in warm water. Place disks into baking cups, sprinkle with salt and granulated sugar, and bake at 375°F for 15–20 minutes or until golden.

Tempura Day

Reportedly brought over by the Portuguese, tempura is a light batter commonly made from sparkling water and kept chilled in order to produce a crispy crust when dropped in hot oil. Initially only served from street carts, it was later adopted into everyday Japanese cuisine. I tested a dozen different tempura recipes, with disastrous results, until I came up with this one, which is the epitome of simplicity with an explosion of flavor! (If you want a simple tempura batter, simply omit the spices. . . .)

TANTALIZING VEGGIE TEMPURA

Serves 2

½ tablespoon egg white (chilled)

5 teaspoons all-purpose flour, plus extra for dredging veggies

7 teaspoons seltzer water (chilled)

Pinch of dried chili flakes

1 fresh rosemary or thyme sprig (leaves only)

Salt for sprinkling

1 small eggplant (thinly sliced)

1 small zucchini (thinly sliced)

3 cups vegetable oil

❶ Add egg white to flour and whisk well. Slowly add seltzer and whisk in well, then add chili flakes and herbs.

❷ Salt sliced veggies, and let sit for a minute so some water drains from them. Pat veggies dry, dredge in flour, then dip in batter and fry at 375°F until golden. Remove from oil and set veggies on paper towels. Make sure to salt and pepper as soon as they come out.

English Toffee Day

Toffee is made from boiling sugar or molasses with water and butter until a caramel is formed. Depending on the temperature and the addition of different ingredients, results will vary from a sauce to a hard candy. English toffee is a very buttery form of toffee to which almonds are often added. This is an easy toffee that you can make at home since it doesn't require a sugar thermometer. Just be careful, because this stuff is hot!

SUPER-EASY TOFFEE

Makes 2 cups

1 cup granulated sugar

1 cup white chocolate (melted)

½ teaspoon coarse salt

❶ Place Silpat on cookie tray that is at least ½" deep (otherwise you run the risk of very hot toffee spilling over).

❷ In a deep and heavy pot, melt sugar over medium-high heat. Stir constantly with a wooden spoon. As sugar begins to melt, little clumps will form. Break them up with wooden spoon and continue stirring until sugar is dissolved. Reduce heat to low-medium. Cook sugar until it starts to smoke slightly and begins to foam.

❸ Turn heat off and add melted white chocolate. Stir well until mixture is thoroughly combined. Pour molten toffee onto Silpat or into individual candy molds. Sprinkle with salt and let cool.

Cook's Note

A Silpat is a relatively inexpensive rubber reusable heat-proof mat available online or in most baking stores.

Apricot Day

When ripe, apricots are extremely sweet and packed full of vitamin A. Their growing season is short in California, but they also come from Turkey, Greece, France, and even Japan. Apricots are believed to have originated in China but migrated to the Mediterranean, where they thrived in the continental climate. We can thank the Spanish for planting them in missions when they came to the new world—San Francisco was the perfect climate for them to flourish! I use canned apricots for the filling of this tart. Of course, you can use fresh apricots, but canned ones work great in a pinch.

APRICOT-ALMOND TART

Serves 6–8

½ (14-ounce) package frozen puff pastry

1 7-ounce box almond paste (cut into small cubes)

⅓ cup sugar

2 tablespoons unsalted butter (melted)

Pinch of salt

2 eggs (beaten)

2 tablespoons all-purpose flour

2 cups canned (or fresh) apricot halves

½ cup sliced almonds

❶ Thaw one pastry sheet at room temperature for 20 minutes, then unfold and with a fork mold into a tart pan with a removable bottom. Prick bottom of tart, and set aside.

❷ In a stand mixer, combine almond paste with sugar, butter, salt, and eggs. Beat on medium until mixture is smooth. Add in flour and beat on medium for another minute. Pour filling into about ½ of tart.

❸ Drain canned apricots and place seed-side down onto filling. Sprinkle with sliced almonds.

❹ Bake for 15 minutes at 400°F then turn heat down to 350°F. Bake for 10 more minutes until golden and set.

❺ Serve with powdered sugar and whipped cream.

JAN. 10
Bittersweet Chocolate Day

I first learned to make this from Jacques Torres, Mr. Chocolate himself! Traditional chocolate mousse calls for only eggs, chocolate, and sugar; however, most recipes require a little bit of whipped cream, too. Normally you have to whip the yolks, then the whites, and incorporate everything together with the chocolate, which takes a while and dirties several bowls. So when I found out that you could do it with only whipped cream and chocolate, I was sold! This dessert is rich yet light. It's bound to disappear fast!

CHOCOLATE VAMOUSSE

Makes 6 cups

14 ounces bittersweet chocolate (melted)

1 quart heavy cream (chilled)

1 teaspoon powdered sugar

1 Melt chocolate over low-medium heat.

2 Whip cream with powdered sugar to very soft peaks.

3 Add ⅓ of cream into warm chocolate and fold in well and fast using a rubber spatula

4 Transfer mixture into remaining soft cream and fold in fast. (Don't worry if there are a few chocolate swirls and pockets of whipped cream still white in the mix; when you eat it, it creates layers of flavor.)

5 Scoop into cups or a large container and it's ready to eat, or refrigerate to enjoy later.

Hot Toddy Day

JAN. 11

The traditional toddy recipe can be made with whiskey, brandy—or even sake!—but the traditional recipe simply calls for sugar, hot water, and the spirit. I decided to share my mom's recipe for her heal-all toddy. Every time any of us gets sick she makes it. I don't know if it heals or not, but it tastes awesome and I always feel better afterwards.

MY MOM'S TODDY

Heals 4 "sick" people

2 Red Delicious apples (peeled, cored, and sliced)

3 tablespoons honey

2 cinnamon sticks

Juice and peel of 1 lemon

1 quart water

2 cups applejack (or apple brandy like calvados)

1 Heat all ingredients in a pot, and boil for 15 minutes.

2 Add the applejack and serve piping hot!

Hot Toddy Day, January 11

Curried Chicken Day

Green curry is an incredible paste made by pounding or grinding green chilies, galangal, fresh turmeric, ginger, garlic, shallots, and shrimp paste. This is the main flavoring for the curry, along with some coconut milk. There are many types of curries, spanning from Thai to Indian cuisine, and it's eaten all over the world. This particular dish comes from Thailand, and I know some of the ingredients may sound a little obscure, but if you go to an Asian market you should be able to find everything. If not, try ordering online. I promise—it's worth the effort!

GREEN CURRY CHICKEN

Serves 4

2 (14-ounce) cans unsweetened coconut milk

1 teaspoon salt

½ teaspoon fresh pepper

¼ cup fresh ginger (sliced into matchsticks)

1 lemongrass stalk (cut in two, bottom half reserved and cut in two lengthwise)

Peel of 1 lime

2 tablespoons green curry paste

2 cloves garlic (thinly sliced)

1½ pounds boneless and skinless chicken (cut into thin strips)

2 tablespoons vegetable oil

½ large Spanish onion (thinly sliced)

1 large green pepper (thinly sliced)

½ can bamboo shoots (sliced into matchsticks)

Handful fresh cilantro

Handful fresh Thai basil

❶ Combine 1 can coconut milk, salt, pepper, ginger, lemongrass, lime peel, green curry paste, and garlic in a bowl. Whisk well and add sliced chicken. Pour mixture into a Ziploc bag and marinate for at least 1 hour.

❷ While chicken marinates, prep veggies.

❸ After chicken marinates, take out two sauté pans, one deeper than the other. Put about 1 tablespoon of oil in each on high heat. Drain chicken, reserving liquid, and pat dry with paper towels. In one sauté pan, drop chicken (gingerly!) and partially cover with a lid (to cut down on splatter, which makes cleanup no fun).

❹ In the other pan, sauté remaining veggies, adding a little salt and pepper. When veggies have wilted, add remaining can of coconut milk, remaining liquid from the marinade, and heat up.

❺ When chicken is done on one side, flip and continue to cook on other side until almost done, about 30 seconds.

❻ Pour chicken into pan with veggies and coconut milk and cook for another minute. Add cilantro and Thai basil, then taste to check seasoning.

❼ Cover and let steep for another 5 minutes. Serve with jasmine rice and sliced green onions.

Cook's Note

I *always* forget ingredients in recipes. Don't sweat it. Just organize yourself. I like putting all my ingredients on a tray or bowl as I am measuring them. This way when I start to cook, I know everything in the tray has to go in. Compartmentalize and conquer!

Peach Melba Day

Peach Melba was created by renowned Chef of Chefs, Auguste Escoffier, while working at the Savoy hotel in London. Escoffier created the dessert in honor of the beautiful Australian soprano Nellie Melba. Even though the name connotes a complicated and elaborate dessert, it's actually quite simple—a combination of peaches, vanilla ice cream, and raspberry sauce. The original dessert was served on an ice swan, but you can omit this if you don't have an ice swan lying around somewhere. (Or do you?)

PEACH MELBA

Serves 6–8

2 cups canned peaches in syrup (preferably halves; you can also use fresh)

3 cups Homemade Vanilla Ice Cream (July 23)

1 cup frozen raspberries

Granulated sugar to taste (depending on the sweetness of berries)

Juice of 1 lemon

Shortbread cookies or toasted almonds

❶ Warm peaches in the microwave for about 1 minute.

❷ Place a couple into a goblet and top with two scoops of vanilla ice cream.

❸ Blend raspberries with a little lemon juice and add sugar a little at a time until sauce is sweet, then drizzle over the Melba.

❹ Serve with shortbread cookies or sprinkle with toasted almonds.

Hot Pastrami Sandwich Day

Legend has it pastrami was brought to the States by Jewish immigrants in the nineteenth century. There's dispute over who created the first pastrami sandwich in NYC—Sussman Volk or the 2nd Ave Deli, which both opened in 1887. Truth is, it doesn't matter as they were both serving a sandwich that had been created decades earlier! What matters is that your sandwich has a ginormous portion of meat served on rye with thick mustard and crunchy pickles. My fave? Katz's Deli.

PASTRAMI

Serves 4

2 tablespoons black peppercorns

3 bay leaves

2 tablespoons mustard seeds

1 tablespoon juniper berries

½ teaspoon allspice

½ cup crushed garlic (fresh)

½ cup brown sugar

½ cup kosher salt

4 cups water

2 pounds trimmed beef brisket

2 tablespoons coriander seeds

2 tablespoons black peppercorns

1 tablespoon yellow mustard seeds

½ tablespoon white peppercorns

⅛ cup kosher salt

⅛ cup paprika

4 cloves garlic (minced)

1. Make brine by combining first nine ingredients in a bowl and whisk well.

2. Place the brisket in a large Ziploc bag and pour in the brine. Allow mixture to sit in your refrigerator undisturbed for three weeks.

3. You now have corned beef. To make pastrami, soak corned beef in cold water for about 2 hours, and get ready to make the rub.

4. To make the rub, combine remaining ingredients in a mortar and crush until coarse. Coat brisket with rub and place it in a roasting pan with a rack that is at least 1" from the bottom of the pan. Place a few ice cubes at the bottom along with a little water—this will turn your smoker or grill into a cold smoker for a little while. Smoke corned beef in smoker or grill to 225°F, and smoke for about 1 hour per pound until it reaches an internal temperature of 150°F. Remove from the smoker and serve right away.

JAN. 15
Strawberry Ice Cream Day

My friend Franca is an angel. She owns a berry farm called Burried Treasures, in which she raises (and I do mean raises) the most magical little strawberries you will ever taste in your life. They are heaven-sent, which is why I call her an angel and her strawberries angelberries. I have a hard time coming up with anything to do with these berries because they need nothing more. In January when I am craving them and still need to wait a few months for fresh ones, I console myself by grabbing a pint of frozen berries and make this ice cream.

FRANCA'S STRAWBERRY ICE CREAM

Makes 6 cups

Homemade Vanilla Ice Cream (July 23)

2 cups strawberry purée

1. Prepare Homemade Vanilla Ice Cream.

2. When base is chilled, add strawberry purée and freeze according to ice cream maker's instructions.

Fig Newton Day
JAN. 16

Figs are a popular fruit in many countries and are used in a variety of desserts as well as served dried or in candy to accompany cheeses and charcuterie plates. The Fig Newton cookie came to life in 1891 by Philadelphia baker Charles M. Roser when he created a patent over a machine that inserted a fig cream into dough. I like to serve these with blue cheese as soon as they come out of the oven or cool them down and enjoy.

COUNTRY FIG NEWTON–LIKE BARS

Makes 2 dozen

3 cups all-purpose flour

½ cup brown sugar

¾ teaspoon baking powder

¼ teaspoon baking soda

½ teaspoon salt

½ teaspoon ground cinnamon

½ teaspoon grated nutmeg

8 tablespoons butter

4 tablespoons margarine

3 whole eggs

❶ Sift all dry ingredients. Knead 1 tablespoon butter at a time until it is all incorporated, followed by margarine. Add the eggs one at a time, incorporating well each time.

❷ When the dough comes together, roll into a ball, place inside a Ziploc bag, and refrigerate overnight.

FIG FILLING

2 cups dried or fresh figs (de-stemmed and cut into small chunks)

2 cups red wine

4 whole cloves

1 tablespoon of vanilla or 1 vanilla bean

½ cup brown sugar

Zest and juice of 1 lemon

1 egg for wash

❶ Cut figs and bring to a boil with red wine, spices, brown sugar, lemon zest, and juice. Simmer until most of the red wine has evaporated and you have semi-dry figs.

❷ Place in food processor and purée, then place in container and chill. When both the filling and dough are cold, assemble bars.

❸ Flour a clean surface and rolling pin. Grab ⅓ of dough and roll ⅛" thick and 4" wide. Spoon fig filling into the middle, about a ¼" thick and about 1" thick wide. Use egg wash to brush the edges of the dough and overlap the edges on top to create a log-shaped pastry. Flip log so that overlapping sides are face down, and refrigerate for 10 minutes.

❹ Brush with remaining egg wash and, using a sharp knife, slice 1" marks, making sure to only cut though the top layer of the dough. Sprinkle with brown sugar and a dash of salt. Bake at 350°F for 15 minutes until golden.

Hot Buttered Rum Day

Around 1860, the country was divided into rye drinkers, whiskey drinkers, and rum drinkers, and cold toes in New England were begging for warmth. Right before Prohibition, New England was guzzling up a ton of rum, up until it was no longer allowed. After that, they administered rum as medicine and it is said that's how Hot Buttered Rum was born. Why the butter? Apparently, it's only there to keep your mustache nice and lubricated. Here is my favorite recipe, mustache not included.

HOT BUTTERED RUM

Serves 1

2 ounces dark rum (Goslings, Santa Teresa, Myer's)

1 teaspoon dark brown sugar or molasses

1 ounce hot water

½ tablespoon butter

Whole cloves

Grated nutmeg

❶ Put rum and sugar in a coffee mug. Add about 1 ounce of hot water and stir well.

❷ Cut a pad of butter, about ½ tablespoon. Stud pad with a few cloves. Drop butter into rum.

❸ Sprinkle a little nutmeg on top and enjoy!

Peking Duck Day

Peking duck is an Imperial dish hailing from Beijing—one of the quintessential culinary representatives of the great red nation. Peking duck is made with a special breed of duck (Pekin), and after an intensive drying-out process and multiple cornstarch baths the skin becomes a glossy film of crackling glass begging to be roasted. Traditionally, the ducks hung in ovens fired by wood coals, which imparted a fragrant taste and caramel color, but you can make it in a regular oven, no problem. It takes a while, but it's an awesome showstopper!

PEKING DUCK

Serves 4

1 5–6 pound Pekin duck

Salt and pepper

4 tablespoons maltose syrup (or honey)

2 tablespoons honey

1 scallion, sliced thin (plus more for serving)

6 cups water

3 tablespoons fresh ginger (chopped small)

1 tablespoon salt

2 tablespoons sherry

2 tablespoons soy sauce

2 tablespoons cornstarch

Cook's Note

If you have no patience, or are a little creeped out by the sight of a head-on duck hanging from your kitchen cabinet, then perhaps this is not the project for you. It takes a while to prepare. Are you game? Then read on! The most crucial part of this dish is a hairdryer. Yes, I said I use a hairdryer. You don't have to, but it will save you a ton of time.

❶ Call your butcher and asking him to order you a Pekin duck with the head on. Ask him to prep it for you.

❷ Rinse out duck and pat dry with paper towel. Season cavity and all around with salt and pepper. Place duck breast-side up on counter. Using both your hands, apply pressure to break middle breastbone. Take wings and twist them backwards (like duck is being arrested), then push them a little higher until they stay in place. Use butcher twine to close cavity with remaining skin. Make sure you tie it tightly; don't let any air escape. Take straw, piece of thin hose, or bicycle pump and stick it in hole in neck of duck. Pump air slowly while duck inflates. Push air through while pumping slowly to make sure duck puffs up nicely. Once duck is plump, remove hose while keeping pressure by squeezing with your hand in order to prevent air from escaping. Take another piece of twine, tie it around neck, and secure with a few knots, sealing in air. Hang duck feet-side down from string around neck.

❸ Place hairdryer on high about 2 feet from duck and position so it hits duck directly. Dry on one side for 1 hour. Flip around and do the same to other side.

❹ While duck's drying, bring remaining ingredients except cornstarch to a boil in wide pot. Allow to simmer for 10 minutes to infuse flavors. Dissolve cornstarch in some water, then whisk back into simmering liquid. Whisk until thickened (it will still be liquidy, resembling warm Jell-O).

5. Hang duck over pot and ladle hot mixture over duck. Do this for about 3 minutes, coating every inch of duck. Return duck to where you had it before for a little more drying, placing a plate underneath to collect drippings. Set hair dryer on high again and dry each side for 15 minutes. Reglaze duck and dry for another 15 minutes on each side. Glaze a third time and dry for 30 minutes on each side.

6. Heat oven to 350°F. Place large roasting pan lined with aluminum foil and ½" of water at bottom and set up roasting rack on top. Cook duck breast-side up for 15 minutes, turn to one side and cook for 15 more minutes, then to the other side for another 15. Finally place duck breast side down and cook for a final 15 minutes for a total of 1 hour.

7. Serve with plenty of scallions, hoisin, duck or soy sauce, and Chinese pancakes. Or blend a little ginger into olive oil and scallions for a traditional dressing.

JAN. 19 — Popcorn Day

Some popcorn was found in a cave in Utah that was more than 1,000 years old, making it one of the oldest American snacks! Popcorn became the official movie snack during the Depression; vendors would line up outside movie theaters selling little 5 cent bags to crowds of moviegoers. It didn't take long for theater owners to realize the money they could be making, so they invited the vendors inside until they realized they didn't need them at all. This super snack is indeed a favorite, gobbled up at more than one billion pounds a year. That's close to 70 quarts of popcorn per American per year!

SALTED CARAMEL POPCORN

Serves 2

¼ cup granulated sugar

¼ cup brown sugar

Water

1 teaspoon butter

3 cups popcorn, popped

Coarse salt to taste

1. In a deep pot, pour sugar and a little water until the sugar looks like wet sand.

2. Bring sugar to a boil, then cover with a lid. Cook for 2 minutes on medium heat until large bubbles form.

3. Take a spoon and dip into pot of sugars (caramel) and put in the freezer. Remove after a few seconds and touch caramel. If it's hard, it's ready.

4. Turn off the heat and drop the butter in. Stir well, then drop in popcorn. Using a wooden spoon stir, coating all kernels with caramel.

5. Pour popcorn onto a cookie sheet that has been lightly covered with a nonstick spray.

6. Sprinkle salt all over popcorn, then allow to cool.

7. Once cool, pop in a movie and enjoy with your popcorn.

Cheese Lover's Day

Technically all cheese starts out the same, but that's where the similarities stop. Different cheeses are made depending on what animal the milk comes from, their diet, plus the bacteria, mold, or acid that is introduced to the milk. Today the same methods are used that were used thousands of years ago but on a much larger scale. Our fascination with cheese is so strong, there are literally thousands of different varieties from all over the world available at your local market. And the stats don't lie. On average, we consume more than 30 pounds of gooey, meltidy, creamy goodness a year.

QUESO FRESCO

Makes 2 cups

- ½ gallon whole milk
- 2 cups buttermilk
- ¼ cup white vinegar
- 1 teaspoon salt

1. Heat whole milk to 185°F, stirring constantly and scraping the bottom of the pot, and keep it there for 10 minutes.

2. Turn off heat, add buttermilk and vinegar, and stir well. You will start seeing little lumps in the water. Allow mixture to sit for 15 minutes.

3. Pass through a fine cloth (I use a clean pillow-case) and hang for 30 minutes over another container to collect dripping whey.

4. Remove cheese from cloth and place in a bowl. Season with salt and stir with a spoon.

5. Press cheese into a plastic container. Refrigerate overnight.

New England Clam Chowder Day

During one beach outing with my family, my Dad collected clams all afternoon and by the end of the day had a bag full of them. We got home, showered, and came down to my Dad cooking up a storm—intense garlic, olive oil, herbs, and fresh clams with spaghetti perfumed the house! We sat down to eat, when all of a sudden, "Crunch, Crunch, Crunch!" In all his excitement, Dad had forgotten to soak the clams and rinse them out properly. The moral of the story? Don't forget to clean the clams!

NEW ENGLAND CLAM CHOWDER

Serves 5–6

- 8 cups littleneck clams (or 2 cups already-cleaned clams)
- 3 tablespoons salt (depending on salinity of clams)
- Olive oil
- 2–3 sprigs fresh thyme
- 4 cups Spanish onion (½" slices)
- 1 cup celery (½" slices)
- 1 cup bacon (½" chunks)
- 5 garlic cloves (thinly sliced)
- 3 tablespoons butter
- Black pepper and salt to taste
- 4 cups potatoes (peeled, ½" cubes)
- 2 cups clam juice
- 2 bay leaves
- 1 cup water
- 2 cups half-and-half
- ½ cup scallions
- ½ cup fresh parsley
- ½ teaspoon white pepper

1. Clean clams with a small brush, place them in a pot, and cover with cold water and 2 table-spoons of salt. Let stand for 10 minutes. Change water and repeat the process.

2. Place a pot (big enough to hold clams and still leave a little head room) on high heat. Add 2 tablespoons olive oil, a few thyme sprigs, and a handful of sliced onions. When onions start sizzling, add clams and cover pot. Cook for 10 minutes, opening the pot and stirring once halfway through or until all clams have opened.

3. Line a pasta strainer with three coffee filters and place over another bowl. Pour clams and onion mixture into the strainer. The filters will catch any sand left in the clam stock. Reserve stock for later use.

4. While the clams are straining, in same big pot, sweat (sauté without any color) remaining onions, celery, bacon, garlic, and butter with black pepper and pinch of salt. Sweat mixture over medium-high heat for about 5 minutes until onions are translucent.

5. Add potatoes and stir for 2 minutes more. Add clam juice, clam stock, bay leaves, and water, then cover pot for about 15–20 minutes or until potatoes are almost cooked through.

6. While mixture is cooking, discard the coffee filters and place the clams, still in the pasta strainer, under running water to clean out any remaining sand. (Either leave clams in their shells or save the meat.) After you have cleaned clams, potatoes should still be a little underdone.

7. Add clams and half-and-half to pot and lower heat. Cook for another 10 minutes.

8. With a potato masher, mash chowder a little in the pot (this will thicken it up).

9. Chop scallions and parsley, add to chowder, and turn heat off.

10. Season with white pepper and serve piping hot with a dash of hot sauce and crusty bread.

Blonde Brownie Day

JAN. 22

The history of blondies predate our beloved brownies by what seems to be centuries. Ancient Romans, Greeks, and Egyptians made soft, unleavened cakes with honey, spices, flour, and nuts. Chocolate was not readily available or affordable for Americans until the twentieth century. By the 1950s, blondies or "blonde brownies" were popular all across America. I love these as they are easy to carry around, are jam-packed with flavor, and have a long shelf life.

BLONDIES

Makes 1 dozen

8 tablespoons butter (softened)

8 tablespoons margarine

1 cup light brown sugar

⅔ cup granulated sugar

½ teaspoon salt

2 teaspoons vanilla

2 whole eggs

2 cups self-rising flour

2 cups baking white chocolate chips

2 cups macadamia nuts or peanuts (coarsely chopped)

① In a large bowl, whip butter, margarine, and sugars. Add salt, vanilla, and eggs one at a time, incorporating thoroughly.

② With a wooden spoon, add sifted flour and combine well. Mix in chocolate and nuts.

③ Scoop batter onto a greased and floured baking sheet. Wet hands and press dough down into an even sheet.

④ Bake at 350°F for 35–40 minutes until golden. Cut while hot and eat warm!

Rhubarb Pie Day

Rhubarb is a delicious vegetable that comes into season mid to late spring to early Fall. However, hothouse rhubarb is available almost all year round. It looks like pink celery and tastes like strawberries and plums combined. It is good to note that although rhubarb is acidic and delicious, the leaves are toxic. When cooked with a little sugar, rhubarb turns into amazing spreads and make an incredible filling for this pie. I use a shortbread crust at the bottom and top it with a crumble for a little extra fun.

RUSTIC RHUBARB PIE

Serves 5–6

5 cups of fresh rhubarb (¾" chunks)

1 cup granulated sugar

3 tablespoons water

½ teaspoon cornstarch

① Place rhubarb in a deep pan, cover it with sugar, cover with aluminum foil, and bake at 300°F for 30 minutes.

② Remove from oven, remove aluminum foil, and allow to cool.

③ When it is cool, combine the water with cornstarch to make a slurry, then add to rhubarb.

Crumble

1 cup granulated sugar

¼ teaspoon salt

1 cup all-purpose flour

1 cup instant oats

1 cup unsalted butter (melted)

½ teaspoon vanilla extract

① In a bowl, sift sugar, salt, and flour, then add oats.

② Melt butter with vanilla and add to oat mixture. Mix well with a wooden spoon until crumbly.

Pie

Shortbread dough (Jan. 6)

① Press shortbread dough into pie shell. Trim edges and score the bottom with a fork.

② Pour in rhubarb mixture and top with crumble, making sure it meets the edges of the crust.

③ Bake at 350°F for 35 minutes or until crumble is golden brown.

④ Allow the pie to rest for 15 minutes and serve warm with Perfect Chantilly Cream (Jan. 5) or Homemade Vanilla Ice Cream (July 23).

Peanut Butter Day

The first patent for peanut butter was given to Marcellus Epson in Montreal, Quebec, in 1884, so in a way this day honors him! I love peanut butter. Everything about it reminds me of being a kid. There's something comforting and simple about the nutty smell and the creamy buttery taste that makes everything okay. Mix peanut butter with cheesecake and it becomes a double whammy. Put it inside a cone? Jackpot!

PEANUT BUTTER CHEESECAKE CONES

Makes 6–8 cones

1 cup chunky peanut butter

1 cup (8-ounce package) cream cheese

½ cup milk

2 cups heavy cream

6 tablespoons powdered sugar

6–8 sugar cones

Peanuts for garnish

❶ Whip peanut butter and cream cheese until light and fluffy. Add ¼ cup milk and continue whipping until light.

❷ In another bowl, combine heavy cream and remaining milk with powdered sugar and whisk until soft whipped cream forms.

❸ Separate cream into two batches, reserving a little to top cones later on. Mix remaining cream with peanut butter mixture by hand until smooth. Scoop into cones and refrigerate until set, about 1 hour. Top with remaining cream and a few peanuts. Serve right away.

Irish Coffee Day

The original Irish coffee is said to have been invented by a Joseph Sheridan, the head chef at Foynes in Limerick, Ireland. One night in the 1940s, disgruntled American passengers landed from a terrible flight on a bitterly cold evening. Sheridan spiked their coffee with Irish whiskey, and when the passengers asked if they were drinking Brazilian coffee, he told them it was Irish coffee. The trick to this recipe is to use soft whipped cream as opposed to stiff cream. This creates a creamy-frothy head similar to that of a properly poured pint of Guinness.

IRISH COFFEE

Serves 1

3 ounces strong coffee

1 shot Irish whiskey

1 teaspoon brown sugar

Nata or Perfect Chantilly Cream (Jan. 5), but not completely whipped, just so it resembles soft custard

❶ Combine hot coffee, whiskey, and brown sugar in a sturdy glass mug.

❷ Top with the soft whipped cream.

Pistachio Day

Pistachio trees were first introduced to California in 1904 but were not promoted as a commercial crop until 1929. Pistachios can be traced back to western Asia where they originated before making a huge impact on the Mediterranean world by way of Iran. Pistachios are a green nut packed full of vitamins and minerals and make an awesome snack. Here I incorporate them into sweet crispy meringue with a dash of salt to make a super-yummy snack.

SALTED PISTACHIO MERINGUES

Makes 2 dozen little meringues

3 egg whites

¼ teaspoon cream of tartar

⅔ cup granulated sugar

½ teaspoon coarse salt

1½–2 cups shelled pistachios (roasted, chilled, and coarsely chopped)

½ cup powdered sugar

❶ Whip egg whites with cream of tartar until you have soft peaks. Gradually add granulated sugar until it has been incorporated, and whip on high until stiff peaks form.

❷ In another bowl, combine salt, pistachios, and powdered sugar, and toss to coat the pistachios well. Add the nut mixture to whites and fold in thoroughly.

❸ Spoon mixture onto greased aluminum or parchment paper lightly sprayed with vegetable oil, and cook at 225°F for about 45 minutes, checking them in the last 15 minutes to make sure they don't get browned.

Chocolate Cake Day

This is my favorite type of cake. Come to think of it, it's my family's favorite too, and probably yours. Here's a simple recipe for a buttery-light chocolate cake. Top it with chocolate frosting and you have the makings of an incredibly delectable dessert. I like to make this for birthdays—especially kids' birthdays . . . but then again, aren't we all just kids at heart anyways? When it comes to chocolate cake we are.

CHOCOLATE CAKE

Serves 8–10

1 cup water or coffee (I prefer coffee)

1 cup Dutch processed cocoa powder

1 cup buttermilk

1½ cups cake flour or 1½ cups plus 3 tablespoons all-purpose flour

2 teaspoon baking soda

½ teaspoon baking powder

Pinch of salt

1 cup unsalted butter (softened)

1¼ cups granulated sugar

4 large eggs

2 teaspoons vanilla extract

❶ Bring water or coffee to a boil and whisk in cocoa powder. Let mixture cool then mix with buttermilk.

❷ Sift together flour, baking soda, baking powder, and salt; set aside.

❸ In a large bowl, cream butter and sugar until light and fluffy. Beat in eggs one at a time, then stir in vanilla. Add flour mixture alternating with cocoa mixture.

4 Spread batter evenly between 2 or 3 greased 9" round cake pans. Bake for 25–30 minutes at 350°F. Allow to cool before frosting and serving.

JAN. 28 Blueberry Pancake Day

True to their name, pancakes contain all the ingredients you'd find in a regular cake you cook in the oven. The difference is that pancakes are rapidly cooked and browned stovetop in a pan, hence "pan-cakes." They are mostly leavened with either baking powder or whipped egg whites, although yeast is sometimes used. The earliest written account of a pancake actually dates back to 1430. The most popular variation of pancakes are blueberry pancakes and chocolate chip pancakes. Here is killer recipe that can be eaten anytime—day or night!

VERY BERRY BLUEBERRY PANCAKES

Serves 2–3

1 tablespoon sugar

¼ teaspoon salt

1½ cup all-purpose flour

3½ teaspoons baking powder

2 tablespoons maple syrup

1 egg

3 tablespoons butter (melted)

1¼ cup whole milk

1 cup fresh or frozen blueberries

1 Sift sugar, salt, flour, and baking powder into a large bowl. With your hand, make a small well in the middle and drop maple syrup, egg, and melted butter.

2 Whisk slowly, incorporating the flour a little at a time while slowly adding the milk to create a smooth batter. Add blueberries and stir well.

3 Cook on a hot pan or on a griddle sprayed with a little nonstick spray.

Corn Chip Day

Corn chips seem to be the most natural American snack since we are so wealthy in corn. They come in many shapes and sizes but they are mostly fried and served with dip. Corn chips and tortilla chips are both made from corn flour, but their difference is that corn chips are fried from pure dough whereas tortilla chips are fried, precooked tortillas.

CORN CHIPS

Makes about 3 dozen

1 cup masa harina (corn flour, not corn meal)

1¼ cup warm water

1 tablespoon all-purpose flour

1 teaspoon salt

½ teaspoon crushed red pepper

1 teaspoon dried oregano

½ teaspoon ground pepper

3 cups vegetable oil

1 Combine all ingredients in a bowl and knead well. Roll into a log, cover with aluminum foil, and refrigerate until hard.

2 Using a string, cut very thin strips of the dough and fry in 350–375°F oil until golden. Remove from oil and drain on paper towels before you dig in!

Croissant Day

Buttery delicious French croissants evolved from the Austrian Kipferl, which was made in honor of a crescent moon. Croissants take a bit of effort, planning, temperature control, and plenty of patience. My friend Dorina owns a bakery called ORO in NYC, and I think she makes the best croissants I've ever tasted. (If the bakery was any closer I would probably weigh 5 million pounds!) Here is an adaptation of her recipe you can try at home, or if you need inspiration and are in New York, swing by the bakery and have one of her amazing croissants. Make sure to have an almond one, too!

ORO BAKERY CROISSANTS

Makes 2 dozen

2¾ cups plus ¼ cup unsalted butter (soft)

1½ ounces fresh or 3¾ teaspoons dry yeast

½ cup sugar

1¼ cups plus ½ tablespoon (10½ ounces) water at 100°F

3 cups all-purpose flour

5¼ cups whole-wheat flour

1¾ tablespoons salt

1 cup whole milk (room temperature)

¼ cup unsalted butter (soft)

2 eggs (mixed with 1 tablespoon water)

❶ Take 2¾ cups butter and mold into a 10" square butter pad about 1" thick.

❷ In a bowl, combine yeast, sugar, and water, cover with plastic wrap and leave in a warm place for 5 minutes to activate yeast. After 5 minutes, transfer to standing mixer with paddle attachment.

❸ Sift both flours and salt and add slowly to yeast mixture so it starts coming together. Switch to hook attachment and finish adding remaining flour along with milk, finishing with the remaining ¼ cup butter.

❹ Knead dough for 3 minutes on medium-high speed until it becomes elastic. Wrap bowl with plastic wrap and let dough rest for 20 minutes.

❺ Flour your clean surface and roll out dough to a 13" square. Place butter pad so it forms a diamond inside dough. Close all corners of dough in, overlapping all edges and making sure there isn't too much flour on edges so they will seal when rolled out. Refrigerate for 10 minutes.

❻ Roll out dough into a long rectangle, flouring the surface so it doesn't stick. Fold in one side at a time, overlapping and creating a square. Refrigerate for 20 minutes. Repeat process two more times.

❼ Roll out dough ¼" thick on a large piece of parchment paper. Refrigerate for 30 minutes.

❽ Take a ruler and measure out every 6" on top and bottom. Cut across, creating triangles. Make a small slit at the bottom of every triangle. Roll croissants and place on parchment paper on a double cookie sheet, otherwise when baked the bottoms will burn. Spray with nonstick spray, cover with plastic wrap, and let rest in a warm place for 30 minutes to an hour until double in size.

9 Combine egg with water to make wash and brush tops of croissants.

10 Bake, uncovered, for 25–30 minutes at 400°F until golden. Allow to cool before eating.

Brandy Alexander Day

The Brandy Alexander is a twentieth-century sensation created for the wedding of Mary Princess Royal and Countess of Harewood in London in 1922. Cream based and chocolate flavored, it played a big role in movies during its heyday. It is based on an older gin based drink simply called "Alexander."

BRANDY ALEXANDER

Makes 1 drink

2 ounces brandy

½ ounce dark crème de cacao

½ ounce heavy cream

Ice

Whole nutmeg for garnish

1 Combine ingredients in a shaker, fill with ice, and shake well for 5 seconds.

2 Strain into a chilled cocktail glass and garnish with freshly grated nutmeg.

FEBRUARY

Baked Alaska Day

Bombes can be traced back to Renaissance times when ice cream was simply placed on top of cakes. Then, in the nineteenth century, Charles Ranhoffer, then chef at Delmonicos, served this to commemorate the purchase of Alaska. Regardless of its origin or the countless people that collaborated to bring us the modern incarnation, Baked Alaskas are fun and festive toasted meringue bombes that are often served flaming for a more grandiose effect. Here, you will find my infamous Carrot Baked Alaska recipe.

CARROT BAKED ALASKA

Serves 6–8

Carrot Cake (Feb. 3)

1 quart rum raisin ice cream

4 egg whites (carefully crack eggs; rinse and reserve eggshell halves)

⅛ teaspoon cream of tartar

½ cup granulated sugar

½ teaspoon vanilla extract

Bacardi 151

1. Cut cake into 3" circles with a ring cutter or a can. Place cakes on cookie sheet and top off with 1 or 2 scoops of the ice cream. Place in the freezer for 30 minutes.

2. While waiting, make meringue. Whip egg whites with cream of tartar and ⅓ of the sugar on medium high until they form soft peaks.

3. Add another ⅓ of the sugar and continue whipping until it returns to soft peaks. Add the remaining sugar and continue to whip until you have stiff and glossy peaks. Add vanilla and whip in well.

4. Remove the cakes with the ice cream and cover with meringue, using a pastry bag fitted with a flat tip or just with a small spatula, and place 1 egg shell on top of every Alaska.

5. Bake at 400–425°F for 3–5 minutes or until golden brown.

6. When ready to serve, fill egg shell with about 1 tablespoon of Bacardi 151 and ignite. It will burn for about 30 seconds, so serve immediately while still flaming.

Heavenly Hash Day

Heavenly Hash is a combination of dreams and fantasies transformed into chocolate, marshmallows, caramel, and almonds with ice cream and fudgy swirls. My friend Cherin wrote to me one day asking me to create a dessert with a list of things she likes. I included them all in this pie. I warn you, this is a messy but extremely yummy and simple pie that will get devoured the minute you place it on the table!

CHERIN'S HEAVENLY HASH PIE

Serves 5–6 (or Cherin on a good day)

Shortbread dough (Jan. 6)

Homemade Vanilla Ice Cream (July 23)

Chocolate Ice Cream (June 7)

Store-bought caramel sauce

Perfect Chantilly Cream (Jan. 5)

Store-bought pie shell

1 cup mini marshmallows

1 cup slivered almonds (toasted and chilled)

1 cup chocolate chips

1 cup salted pretzels (crushed coarsely)

❶ Prepare dough, ice creams, sauce, and whipped cream.

❷ Bake pie shell at 350°F for 10–15 minutes until the crust is golden, then allow to cool.

❸ Combine all other ingredients except whipped cream in a plastic bowl (reserve a little bit of each for decoration); leave streaks of each, do not overmix.

❹ Press into pie crust with a spoon or spatula. Spread whipped cream on top and sprinkle on reserved bits.

❺ Serve with strongly brewed espresso.

Carrot Cake Day

Back in the day, carrots (which contain more sugar than any other veggie aside from sugar beets) were popular for sweetening cakes, pies, and puddings because sugar was scarce. The first American reference dates back to 1783 when George Washington was served a piece of carrot cake at Fraunces Tavern in lower Manhattan. Carrot cakes use raw carrot, which bakes along with the batter creating a semidense yet extremely moist cake. My trick is to use a little yogurt and baby food to enhance the carrot flavor.

CARROT CAKE

Serves 6

3½ cups all-purpose flour

2 teaspoon baking powder

2 teaspoon baking soda

½ teaspoon salt

1 cup granulated sugar

½ cup light brown sugar

2 teaspoon ground cinnamon

¾ cup low-fat plain yogurt

3 eggs

5 ounces carrot baby food (about 2 jars)

3 cups finely shredded carrot

1 cup pecans (toasted and chopped)

¾ cup vegetable oil

1. Sift all dry ingredients except pecans. Make a well in the middle and pour in remaining ingredients except oil. Combine everything, then add oil and mix well.

2. Oil and flour a 9" x 12" pan and pour in batter. Bake at 350°F for 45 minutes or until a knife comes out clean when inserted in the middle. Serve warm.

Stuffed Mushroom Day

Mushrooms can be stuffed with everything from crab to sausage and even cheese. They are mouthwatering treats, often served in Italian restaurants as appetizers. My problem with stuffed mushrooms is that they're never big enough! I have one bite and it's gone, so I created a giant, satisfying stuffed mushroom. I also have a thing for sausage and peppers so I decided to stuff portabellas with sausage and peppers and top them with a mountain of cheese. Hopefully they will fill you up!

SAUSAGE AND PEPPER STUFFED MUSHROOMS

Serves 3

2 teaspoons olive oil

4 sausage links

½ Spanish onion (thinly sliced)

1 red pepper (thinly sliced)

3 portabella caps

Salt and pepper

Lots of mozzarella and Cheddar (shredded)

Fresh parsley (chopped)

1. In a big pot over high heat, drizzle olive oil and allow it to start smoking.

2. Using a sharp knife, cut sausage out of the casings and spread meat onto the pan. Allow sausage to brown, stirring with a wooden spoon.

3. Add onions and peppers and sauté over high heat until they are caramelized and slightly charred.

4. Rinse and clean out the portabella caps. Using a spoon, scoop the gills of the portabellas and place caps on aluminum-lined pie pan or sizzle platter.

5. Sprinkle with salt and pepper, then scoop sausage and peppers on top.

6. Drizzle with olive oil and pour about 3 tablespoons water at the bottom to prevent the mushrooms from drying out and sticking to the pan.

7. Cook at 350°F for 5 minutes. Remove from the oven and cover top of each mushroom with a handful of cheese.

8. Place in the broiler for 3–5 minutes or until all the cheese is beautifully bubbling.

9. Sprinkle with chopped parsley and serve immediately.

Chocolate Fondue Day

Nutella Day

Fondue is a Swiss dish traditionally served in the middle of a table that is meant to be shared. Stemming from the French fondue, meaning "melted," fondues vary from cheese to chocolate and even meat. The pot is normally served suspended with a wick underneath to keep the contents hot and melted. Though the first fondues appear as far back as Homer's Iliad, the modern chocolate fondues began appearing in the 1960s. Nowadays there are whole restaurants devoted to this obsession.

Crepes originated in Brittany in the northwest of France. They are basically a super thin, eggy pancake without any leavening ingredients. The word comes from the Latin "crispa" meaning "curled," since they curl at the edges when you cook them. They are delicious whether savory or sweet, warm or cold. My good friend and mentor Cyril Renaud owns Bar Breton in NYC and makes by far the best crepes anywhere here or in France. I've worked with him for many years, and the one recipe we've always gone back to and tweaked over the years is this one. Technique truly is the most important thing in making the perfect crepe.

CHOCOLATE FONDUE

Serves 2

¾ cup evaporated milk

¼ cup condensed milk

1¾ cups bittersweet chocolate (chopped)

❶ Bring milk to a boil. Add chocolate and stir well.

❷ Serve hot with chunks of pound cake, marshmallows, berries, and anything else you can get your hands on!

NUTELLA AND BANANA CREPES

Serves 3

2¼ cups all-purpose flour

8 large eggs

3½ tablespoons melted butter

1 quart whole milk

¼ teaspoon salt

1 tablespoon granulated sugar

1 banana, sliced

Nutella

❶ Sift flour into a bowl. Make a well in the middle with a ladle and add the eggs. Slowly whisk the eggs together, incorporating the flour little by little. Let the eggs pull in the flour, don't force it in. When the batter starts getting thick, add the melted butter then drizzle in the milk, little by little. Whisk until all the flour has been incorporated.

❷ Add salt and sugar, then strain the batter. Let the batter rest overnight so the gluten relaxes and all the flour particles hydrate and absorb the milk. This will create a smooth batter for a paper-thin crepe.

❸ Spray Teflon pan with nonstick spray. Place over medium-high heat and wait until the pan starts smoking a little. Ladle crepe batter into middle of pan. Rotate pan handle so batter spreads evenly all around.

❹ Cook until surface is dry, flip with spatula, and cook for another 10 seconds. Remove from pan, and place crepe on a plate.

❺ Spread with Nutella and sliced bananas, fold over, and dust with powdered sugar.

❻ Serve hot, and maybe with a little vanilla ice cream or whipped cream.

FEB. 7 Fettuccine Alfredo Day

Fettuccine Alfredo is the epitome of phenomenal cuisine, simply done. It was created in Italy by Alfredo de Lelio at his restaurant Alfredo Alla Scrofa around 1914 as a variation of Fettuccine al Burro (fettuccine with butter). This is an easy but decadent recipe—and as long as you have quality ingredients, this dish should be done in about 15 minutes! The secret here is the fresh pasta and the egg yolks that you stir in at the end.

EASY-BREEZY FETTUCCINE

Serves 2

3 tablespoons butter

1 tablespoon extra-virgin olive oil

4 garlic cloves (sliced thin)

Water for boiling

Salt and olive oil for water

9 ounces fresh fettuccine

⅔ cup heavy cream

½ cup Parmigiano-Reggiano

⅛ teaspoon white pepper

Pinch of nutmeg

2 egg yolks

Fresh parsley

❶ Heat butter and olive oil over medium heat in a sauté pan big enough to hold the pasta. Add garlic and cook on low-medium for about 1 minute, making sure garlic doesn't color. Turn off heat and allow garlic to perfume the oil and butter.

❷ Fill a big pot with water, add salt (about 1–2 tablespoons) until water has the salinity of the ocean, and a good drizzle of olive oil. Over high heat, allow it to come to a rolling boil.

❸ Drop pasta in, detangling it as you drop it to make sure strands don't stick together. Boil for about 2 minutes, stirring occasionally.

❹ While pasta is cooking, bring garlic-infused oil to a sizzle over medium-high heat. When sizzling, add cream and bring to a boil, then add cheese and reduce heat to low-medium. Add pepper, nutmeg, and ½ cup pasta water, and stir well.

❺ Strain pasta and add to sauce. Add 2 egg yolks and combine well. Sprinkle chopped parsley on top and serve immediately.

Molasses Bar Day

Molasses is the base for a lot of my favorite rums. It is created as a byproduct from the manufacturing of sugar from sugarcane or sugar beets. Yes! Did you know 30 percent of the world's sugar comes from beets? Molasses has a homey kind of caramel and spice to it that makes it perfect for holiday cooking. It's Feb. so not particularly the holiday season, but who cares? Make them anyway, I promise you'll love them.

NUTTY MOLASSES BAR

Serves 6

1 cup walnuts

½ cup butter (softened)

¾ cup light brown sugar

1 large egg

½ cup molasses

1 teaspoon vanilla extract

1 teaspoon baking powder

1 teaspoon baking soda

1 ½ cup all-purpose flour

1 teaspoon cinnamon

½ teaspoon grated nutmeg

½ teaspoon ground ginger

½ teaspoon cloves

5 anise stars

❶ Place walnuts on a cookie sheet and roast for 5 minutes at 350°F, then let cool.

❷ While walnuts are roasting, cream butter with sugar until smooth. Add egg, then molasses and vanilla. Combine until smooth.

❸ Sift all dry ingredients and add slowly into batter. Mix until smooth.

❹ Line a deep 10" pan with Reynolds Wrap Release nonstick aluminum foil (I bake everything on this), give a quick spray with nonstick spray around the edges and scoop dough in. Spray a little more cooking spray on your hands and press the dough evenly in the pan.

❺ Dot with star anise and bake for 20 minutes or until a small knife comes out clean in middle.

❻ Cool and serve at room temperature or serve chilled with a glass of cold milk.

Bagels and Lox Day

NYC is the capital of this day! Russ and Daughters on the Lower East Side in particular has an incredible array of smoked, cured, and flavored types of salmon from all over the place. But the essential part of Bagels and Lox is a good, NY–style water-boiled bagel. Bagels can be traced back to Krakow, Poland, around the 1600s. Jewish immigrants brought over this delightful bread when they migrated to NY, quickly forming Bagel Bakers Local 338 and canvassing the city with their high-quality product. Here, I'll show how to make your own savory sandwich.

LOX

Serves 3–4

½ cup salt

1 teaspoon ground white pepper

1 cup sugar

½ pound good-quality salmon filet (skin on, cleaned, scaled, and bones removed)

1 lemon

1 garlic clove (sliced thin)

1 bunch of dill

Cook's Note

This lox comes from the Swedish gravlax, which is normally cured. The only difference with this and smoked salmon is that after the salmon has been cured it is then smoked.

❶ Combine salt, pepper, and sugar in a bowl.

❷ Rinse salmon under cold water and pat dry very well with a paper towel.

❸ Take a container about the size of the salmon that leaves about one finger of space on all sides. Pour ½ of the salt mixture into that container.

❹ Slice the lemon in thin slices and arrange on top of the salt, creating a little bed for the salmon. Top with garlic pieces and a good handful of dill to cover.

❺ Place salmon flesh-side down on the dill; this allows the flesh to absorb the flavor.

❻ Add remaining salt-sugar mixture, covering the entire salmon. Cover tightly with a lid or plastic wrap and allow to sit at room temperature for about 5 hours while all the sugar and salt melt.

❼ Place another container of about the same size on top of salmon and fill with either 1 pound of rocks, pie weights, or marbles, and leave in the fridge for 2 days.

❽ After 2 days, remove the salmon from the fridge and rub it dry.

❾ If the salmon was never frozen or sushi quality, freeze it for at least 2 days to kill any remaining bacteria. If it was previously frozen, toast a bagel, shmear it with some scallion cream cheese, top with thinly sliced lox, a slice of tomato, thinly sliced red onions, a teaspoon of capers, the other half of the bagel, and enjoy!

Bagels and Lox Day, February 9

Cream Cheese Brownie Day

These brownies are dense, fudgy, creamy, and sweet with a hint of saltiness added from the cream cheese. It is one of the most flavor-packed dessert bars you can make. Although brownies have a long, delicious history, cream cheese brownies are pretty modern. You can also substitute berry-flavored cream cheese if you want extra zing.

CREAM CHEESE BROWNIES

Serves 6–8

8 ounces semisweet chocolate (chopped)

1 cup unsalted butter (softened and cut into small pieces)

2 cups light brown sugar

4 large eggs

1¼ cup all-purpose flour

½ teaspoon baking soda

½ teaspoon baking powder

¼ cup cocoa powder

½ cup cream cheese

2 tablespoons milk

1 teaspoon vanilla extract

❶ Melt chocolate in a microwave 1 minute at a time, stirring in between minutes to melt evenly.

❷ Add butter and 1½ cups sugar, then whisk until smooth. Add 3 eggs, one at a time, whisking in between to incorporate well.

❸ Sift in flour, baking soda, baking powder, and cocoa powder.

❹ In another bowl, whisk cream cheese, milk, vanilla, remaining egg, and remaining sugar until smooth.

❺ Spray a 10" square pan with nonstick cooking spray and line bottom with Reynolds Release nonstick aluminum foil.

❻ Pour in chocolate mixture first and then swirl in cream cheese mixture with a butter knife.

❼ Bake at 350°F for 35–40 minutes, until a toothpick inserted in center comes out a little moist. Cut with a sharp knife while still warm and allow to cool.

Peppermint Patty Day

Peppermint patties are simple fragrant mint disks covered in dark chocolate. I make this recipe even easier by using bought fondant (used to cover wedding cakes and such) to which I add a little water and strong peppermint oil. In case you want to make the fondant from scratch, here is a cool recipe using powdered sugar and mini marshmallows.

MINT-MARSHMALLOW FONDANT PATTIES

Makes 2 dozen patties

2 cups mini marshmallows

4 tablespoons water

2 cups powdered sugar (sifted)

Vegetable shortening

1 teaspoon or more mint oil

1⅛ cups bittersweet chocolate

Small, fresh mint leaves

1. Melt marshmallows with water in a large bowl in the microwave for 1 minute. Give it a quick stir and melt for another minute.

2. Sift ¾ of the powdered sugar into the bowl and begin to stir until all sugar has been incorporated and it has turned into a Play-Doh-like consistency.

3. Grease your hands and work surface with vegetable shortening. Sift remaining sugar onto work surface and place fondant on top. Work remaining sugar into fondant until it is smooth. Add peppermint oil and work it in until everything smells refreshing.

4. Roll fondant between two pieces of parchment paper until about ¼" thick. Place on cookie sheet and then in the freezer for about 30 minutes until fondant hardens. Use a ring cutter to cut disks out and place back in freezer for another 3 minutes.

5. While fondant is freezing, melt 1 cup chocolate in a microwave on high heat, 1 minute at a time, stirring in between.

6. When all chocolate is melted, add remaining chocolate and stir until that has completely melted in. (This will temper the chocolate and give you a better crisp when patties are coated.)

7. Using a chocolate dipping fork (or barbecue fork), dip patties in tempered chocolate, gently shake off excess, and place back on parchment.

8. Top each with a mint leaf and refrigerate for at least 2 hours before enjoying.

Plum Pudding Day

Plum pudding is a fragrant steamed pudding traditionally served on Christmas day. Originally from England, this pudding is packed full of delicious spices and spiked with just enough brandy to lighten the mood during the holidays. This is akin to our much-feared fruitcake, but moist and smooth with all the aromatics of orange and spice. What's really cool about this is that you can douse it with Grand Marnier and ignite it for a festive presentation.

PLUM PUDDING (A.K.A. CHRISTMAS PUDDING)

Serves 6–8

3 cups white egg bread (potato or challah, any of these work)

1 cup apricots

1½ cups prunes in syrup

½ cup all-purpose flour

1 cup brown sugar

2 tablespoon granulated sugar

1 teaspoon ground cinnamon

½ teaspoon ground nutmeg

¼ cup molasses

½ cup Grand Marnier

¼ teaspoon ground cloves

1 cup butter (melted)

½ cup applesauce

½ cup orange marmalade

Zest of 1 orange

4 large egg whites

1. Toast bread and pulse in a food processor until it turns to bread crumbs.

2. Cut dried fruit to ¼" cubes and sift dry ingredients.

3. Combine all ingredients in a large bowl except for egg whites and 1 tablespoon sugar.

4. In separate bowl, whip egg whites with remaining sugar until soft peaks form. Fold whites into pudding batter and mix well.

5. Butter and sugar a bowl to cook pudding in.

6. Wrap bowl tightly in plastic wrap, and poke a few holes on the top.

7. Cook in microwave on "defrost" for 30 minutes, then cook on high for 6 minutes or until set.

8. Allow pudding to cool to room temperature, then remove plastic wrap and unmold it onto a serving platter.

9. When ready to serve, pour a few tablespoons of Grand Marnier in a pan and heat. Bring the pan close to the pudding, and pour over.

10. Ignite and serve immediately.

Cook's Note

Steaming the pudding allows flavors to really develop, so if you have time, steam for 5 hours over a double boiler instead of cooking it in the microwave. If you don't have time, don't sweat it, the pudding will be great anyway!

Tortellini Day

FEB. 13

The legend of the tortellini is based on pure love and adoration. It's believed to have been created in Castelfranco Emilia, when a countess checked into an inn. The host, infatuated with her beauty, couldn't resist peeking through the keyhole of her room. The room being low lit with only a sprinkling of candles, the innkeeper could only gaze at her navel. This vision inspired the innkeeper to create the pasta in her honor.

HOMEMADE CHEESE TORTELLINI

Serves 2

Pasta Dough

1¾ cups all-purpose flour

¼ cup semolina flour

½ teaspoon salt

3 eggs

1 teaspoon extra-virgin olive oil

Filling

1 cup ricotta cheese

1 tablespoon chopped basil

1 teaspoon olive oil

Salt and pepper

⅛ cup Parmesan cheese

1 egg white

1. Sift flour into a bowl. Add semolina flour and salt. Make a well in the middle and add the eggs. Mix slowly until a dough is formed. Add olive oil. Add a little more flour if dough is too sticky.

2. Wrap in plastic wrap and allow dough to rest for 30 minutes at room temperature. (This will relax the gluten in the dough, making it more tender and allow the flours to absorb all the moisture.)

3. While the dough is resting, make filling. Combine all ingredients except egg white in a bowl and refrigerate.

4. Roll out dough as thin as you can, flouring the clean work surface and rolling pin well. Use a dough roller if possible; it will work much better and tortellini will be more delicate.

5. Drop ½ teaspoon of filling with about 1" of space in between each. Brush space between the filling with an egg white. Cut into 2" squares, and fold over creating a triangle, then fold it again, making the classic tortellini shape.

6. Boil in salted water until al dente and serve with Simple Pasta Sauce (Jan. 4) and a sprinkling of Parmesan.

FEB. 14 Crème-Filled Chocolates Day

Crème-filled chocolates are a favorite amongst Americans and range in sizes from bite-sized hearts for your honey to egg shapes for Easter. They can be filled with a myriad of creams from smooth to chunky, from healthy to liquor-laced. Making chocolates requires a few tools that make the process a lot easier and make the results much prettier. For this recipe, you'll need a simple chocolate mold and a pastry brush.

CREAMY CHOCOLATE BITES

Makes about 2 dozen chocolates

1 cup bittersweet chocolate (Valrhona or El Rey)

Sweet Dream Butter Cream (Apr. 22)

1 Melt all but 1 tablespoon chocolate in microwave for 30 seconds on high. Remove and stir.

2 Add remaining chocolate and stir until melted.

3 Make sure chocolate mold is super clean and dry. Using a pastry brush, cover inside of mold with chocolate and let set for 1 minute.

4 Brush again with chocolate and refrigerate until hard, about 20 minutes.

5 Fill ⅔ with Sweet Dream Butter Cream and place in the freezer until hard, about 30 minutes.

6 Pour more chocolate on top of buttercream, and using a spatula, scrape extra chocolate from tops. Refrigerate until chocolate has set, at least 2 hours.

7 To remove chocolates, flip mold and twist while gently tapping on the table.

Gumdrop Day

FEB. 15

Brightly colored gumdrops are usually covered in granulated sugar, which gives them a crispy sugary crunch at the beginning, giving way to a chewy center. Here, I make them with pectin, which is a gelling agent derived from fruit that makes them a bit healthier than those with high fructose corn syrup, and a little softer. I also add some vitamins, which is completely optional! I just figured this would be a cool way of getting kids to take their vitamins.

GUMDROPS

Makes about 1 dozen

1 cup granulated sugar

1 cup applesauce

Juice of ½ lemon

¼ cup fruit pectin

2 Airborne tablets (orange flavor)

8 drops red food coloring

1 In a heavy-bottomed pot, combine all ingredients, except food coloring and Airborne tablets, and bring to a boil while whisking continuously for 3 minutes.

2 Crush Airborne tablets and add to syrup along with the food coloring. Whisk until completely dissolved.

3 Pour into a 9" loaf pan that has been lightly sprayed with nonstick spray.

4 Allow to cool overnight, then cut in cubes and roll in granulated sugar. Keep in sugar in the fridge in an airtight container.

FEB. 16 Almond Day

Native to the Middle East, almonds are a delicious nut in the same family as peaches. There are two types of Almonds: one with white flowers producing sweet almonds, the other with pink flowers producing bitter almonds. Almonds are considered to be healthy for the brain and nervous system, and 1 ounce of almonds is equal in nutrients to ½ cup of broccoli—and we all know how good broccoli is for us! Nowadays, if you're eating almonds, more than likely they came from California where almond trees thrive. They are pollinated by close to 1 million hives!

ALMOND MADELEINES

Makes about 2 dozen

2 large eggs

⅛ cup sugar

½ teaspoon vanilla extract

¼ teaspoon almond extract

⅓ cup all-purpose flour

3 tablespoons almond flour

¼ teaspoon salt

4 tablespoons (½ stick) unsalted butter (melted and cooled)

1 Combine eggs with sugar and whip on high speed until thick, about 6 minutes.

2 Add vanilla and almond extracts. Sift dry ingredients and add until incorporated. Using a rubber spatula, fold in melted butter.

3 Oil and flour a Madeleine pan, fill ⅔ of the way up with batter. Bake at 375°F for 10 minutes or until golden.

4 Remove from oven and tap pan on the counter to release the little cakes. Dust with powdered sugar and serve immediately.

FEB. 17 Indian Pudding Day

Indian Pudding is an elaborate hasty pudding. Stemming from New England, it is made with cornmeal much like polenta and then baked with nuts and dried fruit. The resulting baked pudding is smooth and earthy with touches of spices and dark sugars. I make this pudding for my grandma and she loves it. Though not as common as it once was, Indian Pudding is a wonderful way to end a meal in the middle of winter. Its warmth and depth of flavor satisfies every time.

INDIAN PUDDING

Serves 4–5

1½ cup evaporated milk

4½ cups milk

½ cup butter

3 tablespoons granulated sugar

1 teaspoon ground cinnamon

½ teaspoon ground nutmeg

¼ teaspoon ground cloves

½ cup yellow cornmeal

1 cup molasses

¼ cup flour

½ teaspoon salt

3 eggs

1 Bring milks, butter, sugar, and spices to a boil.

2 Whisk in cornmeal with the molasses, flour, and salt, then cook over medium heat until it thickens, about 2 minutes.

3 Break eggs into a bowl, add a few table-spoons of corn mixture into eggs and whisk. (This is called tempering the eggs and it prevents them from curdling when added to the pudding.)

4 Pour egg mixture into corn mixture and whisk for 10 seconds.

5 Turn the heat off and pour the pudding into a loaf pan. Place the loaf pan inside a roasting pan and fill the roasting pan with hot water until the water rises halfway up the sides of the loaf pan. Bake at 350°F in a water bath for 1 hour. Serve warm with Homemade Vanilla Ice Cream (July 23).

Crab-Stuffed Flounder Day

FEB. 18

Flounder is a wonderful whitefish with a mild texture and a light ocean salinity that pairs perfectly with a little spice. I stuff this flounder with mango and jalapeños—technically just a crab cake filling—then it's breaded and fried. This is a great way to get your kids to eat fish and a great way for you to enjoy a little taste of the tropics.

TROPICAL FLOUNDER

Serves 2

2 10-ounce flounder fillets (cleaned)

Filling

1 cup fresh crabmeat

1 scallion (sliced thinly)

1 tablespoon mayonnaise

2 tablespoons red pepper (finely chopped)

2 tablespoons green peppers (finely chopped)

1 teaspoon lemon juice

2 tablespoons fresh mango (in small cubes)

2 eggs

1 teaspoon jalapeño pepper (finely chopped)

Salt and pepper

Bread crumbs

All-purpose flour for dredging

Vegetable oil for frying

1. Combine first nine filling ingredients, using just ½ egg, in a bowl. Add enough bread crumbs so you have a stuffing that's not too sticky but still holds its shape.

2. Season fillets with salt and pepper on both sides, then place half the filling in each of the filets. Roll tightly.

3. Dip the roll into flour then remaining eggs and bread crumbs. Set aside.

4. Fill a skillet ½" with oil. Fry fillets until golden, flip, and cook on other side. Serve with lemon wedges and tartar sauce.

Chocolate Mint Day

FEB. 19

You know when you leave a restaurant and as you're walking out they have that little bowl by the exit or the cash register filled with plastic-wrapped mints that say "Thank You" on them? Well, this is the spruced-up version of those. Chocolate with mint is a classic combination normally left until after dinner, earning the moniker "after-dinner mints."

ANYTIME MINTS

Makes about 2 dozen

⅛ cup heavy cream

½ cup white chocolate

3 tablespoon powdered sugar

½ teaspoon peppermint oil

4 drops green food coloring

1 cup milk chocolate (melted)

1 cup powdered sugar

1. Bring cream to a boil and add white chocolate. Allow chocolate to melt and whisk until incorporated.

2. Add sugar and whisk until it forms a smooth paste, add the mint oil and food coloring then mix again, and pour into a bowl.

3. Place in the fridge or freezer until hard, about 30 minutes.

4. Use a melon baller to create bite-sized ball portions of mint chocolate.

5. Put bowl of melted chocolate and bowl of powdered sugar next to each other. Using a fork, dip each ball in melted chocolate, then drop into powdered sugar. Toss around with the fork until evenly coated.

6. Freeze until hard, about 20 minutes. Enjoy!

Cherry Pie Day

If I said you could eat a delicious piece of pie while walking, what would you say? These are the kinds of thoughts that cross my mind all day long. So, I came up with Pie Cones. A little kooky? Yes. Difficult? Not at all. You merely take store-bought sugar cones and fill them with cherry pie filling. The end result is a delicious pie you can eat with one hand and carry while walking. Try this with apple pie, or banana cream pie, or, well you get the point. . . .

CHERRY PIE CONES

Serves 5–6

1 package store-bought sugar cones (about 12 cones)

1 (14-ounce) can cherry pie filling

Perfect Chantilly Cream (Jan. 5)

Pastry Cream

4 cups whole milk

2 vanilla beans (or 1 tablespoon vanilla extract)

8 egg yolks

1 cup granulated sugar

4 tablespoons cornstarch

2 tablespoons unsalted butter (soft)

1 In a metal pot (not aluminum), bring milk and vanilla to a boil. Turn off heat, cover, and steep for 10 minutes.

2 While the milk is steeping, whisk egg yolks with sugar and cornstarch.

3 Add some hot milk to the egg yolks. (This is called tempering; it warms the yolks to prevent curdling when added back to the hot milk.)

4 Add egg mixture to pot and cook on medium-high while whisking rapidly. Cook for 3 minutes until pastry cream is nice and glossy. Taste it and make sure it doesn't taste starchy; if it is, cook another minute.

5 Remove from heat and whisk in butter until smooth.

6 Pour into a bowl and cover with a piece of plastic wrap that touches the cream. This creates a barrier that prevents cream from forming a skin on top.

7 Refrigerate until cold.

8 Fill cones halfway up with pastry cream, top with cherry pie filling, and finish with a dollop of whipped cream and a cherry garnish on top.

Sticky Bun Day

Sticky buns, a.k.a. cinnamon rolls, seem to have started with the Pennsylvania Dutch. Eighteenth-century settlers recreated a German pastry called Schnecken, loosely translated into "Snail," because when rolled the pastries resembled snails. In Venezuela, where I was born, we make a variation of these with fresh cheese on top called golfeados. I've actually changed the syrupy gooey sticky caramel and made it with rum and a touch of molasses. I think they make the sticky buns extra sticky, which I love.

Making the Dough

❶ The trick to making this dough is making sure all of the ingredients are at room temp except for the warm water for the yeast and the milk. Combine the warm water with the yeast and about 1 tablespoon of the sugar. Cover with a warm towel and leave on top of the stove or in a warm place for 20 minutes until the mixture triples in volume.

❷ Sift all dry ingredients in a mixing bowl. With mixer on slow, and using paddle attachment, add milk slowly, then eggs, yeast mixture, vanilla, and butter. Combine until roughly mixed.

❸ Knead the dough for 7 minutes on medium speed. When the dough is elastic and smooth, spray with nonstick spray, place warm towel on it, and allow it to proof (when the yeast eats and makes little air bubbles) for 1½ hours or until it doubles in volume.

Preparing the Filling

❶ In the meantime, prepare Filling by combining brown sugar, cinnamon, and salt. With your fingertips, crumble little pieces of clumped-up brown sugar with cinnamon and salt. Set aside.

Preparing the Topping

❶ To prepare Caramel Topping, prep a 10–12" springform pan by lining the bottom disk with aluminum foil before placing the ring around the disk, then secure. Spray the sides with nonstick spray.

❷ Combine all ingredients except cheese in a pot and bring to a boil. Simmer for 1 minute and pour into prepared pan. Let cool on a counter.

GOOEY STICKY BUNS WITH CHEESE

Serves 8

¼ cup water (warm)

1½ teaspoon dry yeast

⅛ cup granulated sugar

1 teaspoon salt

4 cups all-purpose flour

¾ cup whole milk (warm)

3 egg yolks

1 teaspoon vanilla extract

4 tablespoons unsalted butter (cubed at room temp)

Filling

1 cup brown sugar

1 tablespoon ground cinnamon

¼ teaspoon salt

5 tablespoons unsalted butter (melted)

Caramel Topping

1 cup brown sugar

3 tablespoons light corn syrup

2 tablespoons dark rum

2 cups pecans (chopped)

1 tablespoon molasses (optional)

¼ teaspoon salt

2 cups queso blanco or mozzarella (shredded)

Rolling the Buns

1 When dough has proofed, lightly flour a clean work surface and roll out to about 18" x 15".

2 Brush dough with all but 1 tablespoon melted butter and evenly spread brown sugar mixture.

3 Roll dough a little at a time by starting at bottom left corner and rolling up, moving across as you roll up. The seal of the roll should be facing down when you get ready to cut to prevent it from coming undone. With a sharp knife using a sawing motion, cut the roll in half, then cut that in half, and cut that in half again until you have about 8 1½" thick portions.

4 Brush portions with remaining melted butter and arrange them face up in prepared springform pan. Cover pan with plastic wrap and refrigerate overnight, or at least 6 hours.

Baking the Buns

1 When ready to bake, take buns out of the fridge and allow them to come to room temperature for 30 minutes.

2 Preheat oven to 375°F, spray buns with nonstick spray, and bake for 30–35 minutes.

Finishing Up

1 When buns are done, position a plate at least 1" bigger than the springform pan on top and carefully invert the buns onto the plate. Release the springform lock and remove the ring, then carefully remove the disk and aluminum foil from buns.

2 Top warm, gooey sticky buns with the shredded cheese, pop back in oven for a few minutes to melt cheese, then serve immediately!

Margarita Day

The margarita is one of the most versatile cocktails out there. Hailing from Mexico, it's traditionally served in its own glass (a variant of the Champagne coupe) and must be made with tequila, orange liqueur, and lime juice. But that's just where it starts! The drink can be blended, served on the rocks or straight up, with salt, without salt, with fruit, champagne, etc.! I kept this one simple, with fresh lime juice, premium orange liqueur (Cointreau or Combier), 100 percent agave silver tequila (like Patron Silver), grated lime zest, and a glass rimmed with coarse salt.

MISS MARGARITA

Serves 1

2 ounces Patron Silver tequila

1 ounce orange liqueur

1 ounce fresh lime juice

4 grates lime zest

Ice

Coarse salt and lime slices for garnish (optional)

1 Shake all ingredients in a cocktail shaker.

2 Fill with fresh ice (*not* the ice in the back of the freezer with the film of moldy snow; ice made with clean water and frozen the night before) and shake well for at least five Mississippis. I like mine on the rocks or frozen. I also like rimming the margarita glass with the wedge of a lime and dipping it in coarse salt.

3 Pour into glass and enjoy!

Banana Bread Day

Banana Bread falls into the category of a quick bread, which uses baking powder or baking soda instead of yeast as a leavener. It was made popular in the eighteenth century when American housewives began making the bread with Pearlash, a modern ancestor to chemical leaveners. I like making this banana bread with overripe bananas and letting it rest wrapped in a bag overnight before warming up in the morning and devouring!

BANANA BREAD

Serves 4–6

1½ cups self-rising flour

1 teaspoon baking soda

½ teaspoon salt

3 overripe bananas

1 teaspoon vanilla extract

¼ cup butter

2 eggs (beaten)

1 Sift dry ingredients.

2 Mash bananas with a fork or potato masher, add vanilla, and set aside.

3 Melt butter over medium heat and whisk continuously until butter turns brown and it looks like oil and bread crumbs.

4 Remove from heat immediately and pour into banana mixture. Stir well and add eggs, then mix everything together.

5 Add banana mix into flour mix and combine slowly. Do not overmix. Butter and flour a 9½" loaf pan, then pour in batter.

6 Bake at 350°F for 40–50 minutes until a toothpick inserted into the middle comes out clean. Remove from oven, allow it to cool down until it's just warm, then store in plastic wrap or plastic bag and leave out until the next day. The flavors will marry and bread will soften. Serve warm with fresh, sliced bananas.

FEB. 24 Tortilla Chip Day

Tortilla chips are a requisite when eating Mexican food. They are also indispensable when watching a football game, or any other game come to think of it. They are simple chips made by cutting corn tortillas in triangles and then frying them until crispy. Traditionally served with salsa and guacamole, they are crispy little snacks that in my book should always be made into nachos.

TORTILLA CHIP NACHOS

Serves 4

1 pack corn tortillas (10–14 tortillas)

4 cups vegetable oil

Salt

Cheddar or Monterey jack cheese (shredded)

1 In a 2 quart (or bigger) heavy pot, heat oil to 375°F. Cut tortilla chips into triangles and fry in oil until golden and crispy.

2 Remove from oil and place on paper towels to drain. Season with salt as soon as they're out.

3 Top with shredded Cheddar and melt in microwave. Dig in!

Chocolate-Covered Nuts Day

FEB. 25

Chocolate-covered nuts are an easy snack that can be oodles of fun. They can be given out as little presents or just eaten as a snack throughout the day. I learned how to make these from Jacques Torres, Mr. Chocolate himself, so you know they're going to be good!

NUTTY CHOCOLATE MIX

Makes roughly 3 cups

1 cup good milk chocolate (finely chopped)

2 cups mixed toasted and salted nuts

½ cup cocoa powder

1 Heat chocolate in microwave 1 minute at a time until melted.

2 Place nuts in a large metal bowl. Add in a few tablespoons of melted chocolate and coat nuts using a wooden spoon.

3 Place bowl in the fridge for 30 seconds. Remove. Using the wooden spoon, stir nuts until the chocolate has cooled and dried. Repeat process two more times.

4 Coat nuts one last time with chocolate, but this time instead of putting bowl in the fridge, add cocoa powder. Stir well until nuts are fully coated.

5 Place bowl in fridge so chocolate nuts solidify and cocoa sticks.

6 Sift nuts to remove excess cocoa powder and serve.

FEB. 26

Pistachio Day

When thinking about what to do with this day, I turned to Facebook. With so many of my friends being foodies, chefs, and writers, they are always full of ideas, so when I needed to brainstorm, I just posted and waited. My friend, Francine Cohen, editor in chief of Inside F&B, *suggested I make a pistachio pesto and that inspired me to create this one.*

PISTACHIO PESTO

Makes ½ cup

⅛ cup fresh mint leaves (packed)

½ teaspoon white vinegar (rice vinegar or white balsamic)

5 tablespoon olive oil

⅛ cup pistachios (shelled)

¼ cup Parmigiano-Reggiano (grated)

¼ teaspoon ground pepper

❶ Clean mint and pick only the green leaves from stems. Combine mint, vinegar, and oil in a blender. Pulse for 3 minutes until well blended, stopping periodically to scrape down sides.

❷ Add pistachios, cheese, and pepper. Blend until pistachios are coarsely ground. Serve with chicken or lamb meatballs.

Kahlua Day

FEB. 27

Kahlua is a delicious coffee-flavored liqueur first made in 1936 in Veracruz, Mexico. When I first met my friend, Joey Florio, the first thing he asked me was to make an espresso martini. Unbeknownst to me, he had been nicknamed "Mr. Espresso Martini." Mine is good, but his is better, so here's his recipe, with a little twist . . . I make my own vanilla vodka by placing three vanilla beans scraped into a bottle of good-quality vodka and allow it to sit in a cool place out of the sun for a few days.

ESPRESSO MARTINI

Serves 1

1 ounce Kahlua

2 ounces vanilla vodka

1 ounce espresso

3 espresso beans

❶ Combine all ingredients except espresso beans in a shaker. Fill with ice and shake for 5 Mississippis, then strain into a chilled martini glass.

❷ Garnish with 3 espresso beans and enjoy.

FEB. 28 — Chocolate Soufflé Day

The word Soufflé is the past participle of the French verb souffler, which means "to puff up." Soufflés can be extremely temperamental but are also extremely easy to prepare, and once you master the art you can make them from anything—from cheese and chocolate to berries and even chestnuts! I learned to make soufflés during my internship working with Pastry Chef Laurent Richard at La Caravelle restaurant in Manhattan.

CHOCOLATE SOUFFLÉ

Serves 5–6 (8–10 ounce ramekins)

½ cup bittersweet chocolate (melted)

Half of Pastry Cream recipe (Feb. 20)

4 egg whites

2 tablespoons superfine sugar

Semisweet chocolate chips

Canola oil

❶ Combine melted chocolate with Pastry Cream and allow to cool.

❷ Whip egg whites on medium until frothy. Add sugar and whip on high until stiff peaks form. Fold a handful of chocolate chips along with egg whites into cream until incorporated.

❸ Oil and sugar soufflé molds and fill with batter. Bake at 375°F until it has risen above rim, about 5–8 minutes.

FEB 29 — Surf and Turf Day

(LEAP YEAR RECIPE!)

Surf and Turf is meant to be an extravagant meal in which you include two of the most expensive items you can order—and it's one of my favorite combos! A popular dish in British and Irish pubs as well as at American steakhouses, here I make what feels like the most over-the-top dish ever created. It is also probably one of the most complicated dishes in the book, but it's so worth the effort. I hope you enjoy.

YVAN'S SURF 'N' TURF

Serves 2

1 large 3–4 quart pot of water

Salt and pepper

Olive oil

1 2-pound live lobster

1 large Spanish onion

½ cup all-purpose flour

1 egg

1 cup bread crumbs

4 strips bacon

2 filet mignon steaks, 2" thick

4 tablespoons crumbled blue cheese

1 teaspoon butter

Wine Sauce

2 cloves garlic (thinly sliced)

Fresh rosemary sprigs

1 cup tomato sauce

1 cup red wine

1 tablespoon butter

1. Bring pot of water to boil, add salt and pepper, and a drizzle of olive oil.

2. Drop lobster in the boiling water, cover, and poach for 5 minutes. Remove lobster from water and place in an ice bath to cool. When cool enough to handle, twist tail and claws off the body. Wrap claws with a paper towel and crack with a nutcracker. Take a pair of scissors and cut from shoulder of claw through the elbow to the hard shell you just cracked. This should make the whole claw and arm pop out. (If it breaks into pieces, don't sweat it; lobster meat tastes great whether it's whole or in pieces.) Cut tail in half lengthwise and remove meat in two pieces. Set aside.

3. Peel onion and cut ¾" thick rings. Separate individual rings and toss in flour. Beat egg lightly and one by one dip rings into egg and then bread crumbs.

4. Fry rings in vegetable oil at 375°F until golden and crispy. Season with salt as soon as they come out of the oil and drain on paper towels.

5. Next, wrap 2 bacon strips around each filet and tie with butcher twine. Season both sides of meat with salt and pepper and heat a sauté pan over medium heat. Cook filets bacon-side down, and keep rotating 90 degrees every minute to give the bacon a little color.

6. After bacon is cooked, place filets meat-side down and cook for 3 minutes over medium heat. Flip filets and place sauté pan in 500°F oven for 3 minutes. Remove from oven and top both with crumbled blue cheese.

7. Drop butter in sauté pan with filets, and return to oven for 2 minutes or until cheese melts.

8. To prepare wine sauce, drizzle a little olive oil in a saucepan and sauté garlic with rosemary sprig over medium heat. When garlic is golden, add tomato sauce and wine. Cook for 5 minutes or until sauce has reduced by half.

9. Remove saucepan from heat and add butter. Stir sauce until butter melts and incorporates into sauce. Add salt and pepper to taste.

10. Cut string from filets and place on warm plates. Toss warm lobster with the melted butter and place one arm, one claw, and half a tail on top of each filet. Top filets with a little tower of onion rings and place a little bunch of rosemary sprigs in the hole of onion rings. Drizzle sauce around filets with a spoon and serve immediately! *Bon appétit!*

MARCH

Peanut Butter Lover's Day

Statistically, women tend to like smooth and velvety peanut butter; and men, well, if it's not super chunky, it's not even worth it. So how do you solve this culinary riddle when it comes to Peanut Butter Lover's Day? You rent a movie, snuggle up on the couch, and get a plate of these little nuggets.

PEANUT BUTTER BON BONS

Makes about 2 dozen

24 mini cupcake tin liners

2 cups bittersweet chocolate (melted and tempered)

Chocolate Pudding (May 1)

½ cup smooth peanut butter

½ cup chunky peanut butter

Whipped cream

Chopped peanuts

❶ Line mini muffin tins with liners and drop 1 tablespoon melted chocolate inside each. One by one, flip liners over bowl with melted chocolate to pour out excess and coat sides of liners with chocolate, then return to tins.

❷ Place in freezer for at least 5 minutes until hard. In the meantime, make sure prepared pudding is completely cold.

❸ With a small spoon, fill bottom of liners with about ½ teaspoon peanut butter (either chunky or smooth, but remember which is which—I split the tins up, making half and half).

❹ Top with pudding and freeze tins.

❺ When ready to serve, top Bon Bons with a little whipped cream and chopped peanuts (a little sprig of mint won't hurt, either).

Banana Cream Pie Day

When I think of a fun and light cream pie, this is what comes to mind. This simple pie is composed of a crispy shortbread crust that's pressed into a tart shell, with buttery banana pastry cream, light vanilla whipped cream, and fresh sliced bananas.

BANANA CREAM BONANZA

Serves 6–8

Shortbread dough (Jan. 6)

Pastry Cream (Feb. 20) or Vanilla Pudding (May 22)

2 ounces banana liqueur (99 Bananas liqueur)

2 ripe bananas

Perfect Chantilly Cream (Jan. 5)

Lemon Juice

❶ Prepare Shortbread Dough and rest for at least 2 hours. Press dough into a 1"-deep fluted tart pan making sure dough is about ¼" thick all around. Cut against rim of pan to remove excess dough.

❷ Prick bottom of tart shell all around and bake at 375°F for 15 minutes or until golden. Cool.

❸ Prepare Pastry Cream recipe, but before you remove cream from the pot to cool, add 2 ounces of 99 Bananas and cook for another 30 seconds.

④ Pour banana cream into a bowl and place plastic wrap directly on top to create a "skin," and cool in the fridge.

⑤ Fill tart shell with banana cream (whisk it a little to smooth if it turned chunky while cooling), then slice bananas and place all around on top of the cream, reserving about ½ banana to decorate top of the pie. Press bananas in a little so they are submerged in banana cream.

⑥ Prepare Perfect Chantilly Cream and scoop into a pastry bag with a medium star tip. (If you don't have a pastry bag or star tip, you can just spoon it on top of the pie.) Decorate top with rosettes of whipped cream about the size of a quarter.

⑦ Squeeze a little lemon juice on top of remaining banana slices. Coat them thoroughly with juice and decorate top of the pie with them. Serve immediately.

Cold Cuts Day

The term cold cut *refers to processed meats that are then cooked or cured and sliced thin for sandwiches. As I am a huge sandwich fan, I can't help but love cold cuts. Lyndsay Hatt, a friend of mine and pastry chef at Bar Breton, told me about this magical sandwich her mom used to for make her in which she'd take cold cuts and lay them on pizza dough then roll it and bake it in a loaf pan. This is my variation on her incredible idea—a fun sandwich that smells amazing and can feed a few people, easy. Thank you Mrs. Hatt!*

BAKED ITALIAN ROLL

Serves 4–5 (or 3 hungry teenagers)

Olive oil

Pizza dough (Sep. 5)

1 tablespoon dried oregano

3 tablespoons black olives (sliced)

Black pepper

¼ pound mortadella (sliced)

¼ pound cappicola (sliced)

¼ pound sopressatta (sliced)

¼ pound Genoa salami (sliced)

¼ pound provolone (sliced)

6–8 pepperocinis (sliced)

½ cup roasted red pepper (sliced)

1 egg

Sesame seeds

① Drizzle a little olive oil on a clean counter and your hands. Place the pizza dough—use my recipe or pick some up at your favorite pizza joint—on the oiled surface. Using your fingertips, press and spread the dough out to a rectangle as wide as your loaf pan, and about three times as long (the long side should be vertical to you). Make sure it's even.

② Sprinkle with the oregano, the sliced olives, and a little pepper (add any other spices that you want: garlic powder, chili flakes, etc. . . .).

③ Lay down the cold cuts one meat at a time, coating the surface of the dough. Stack the meats on top of each other as you lay each layer across the dough. Make the top layer the cheese, topped with pepperocinis and roasted red peppers.

4. To roll, start with the side closest to you and roll up, encasing all the delicious meats and cheese inside. Oil the inside of a loaf pan with a little olive oil and cover the dough with the pan. Sneak your fingers under the pan, grabbing the dough together with the pan, and flip it.

5. Drizzle with a little olive oil, cover with aluminum foil, and cook at 400°F for 30 minutes.

6. Remove from the oven and place on top of the stove.

7. Make an egg wash by whisking the egg, and brush the roll. Sprinkle with the sesame seeds and return to the oven for 3–5 minutes until golden all around.

8. Remove from the oven and allow to cool for 5 minutes. Run a knife around the edges and pop the roll out, cut using a serrated knife, and serve piping hot. I love this!

MAR. 4 Pound Cake Day

Pound cake is the great ancestor of all American cakes. The name stems from the recipe used to create it which uses 1 pound of butter, sugar, eggs, and flour. Nowadays chemical leaveners are added to make a lighter, moister cake. This recipe is extremely buttery and just dense enough to hold together. The trick here is to keep your ingredients at room temperature and whip everything well to incorporate as much air into the cake as humanly possible.

BUTTERY POUND CAKE

Serves 6–7

1 pound unsalted butter (soft)

3 cups granulated sugar

6 large eggs

1½ tablespoons baking powder

4½ cups all-purpose flour

½ teaspoon salt

1½ cups heavy cream

1 tablespoon vanilla extract

2 tablespoons lemon juice

Zest of 1 lemon

❶ Cream butter and sugar with mixer for about 10 minutes. Add one egg at a time, incorporating well in between additions.

❷ Sift dry ingredients. Add dry ingredients and heavy cream, alternating between one and the other while mixing.

❸ Add vanilla extract, lemon juice, and zest.

❹ Pour batter into 9" loaf pan or springform pan and bake at 325°F for 45–50 minutes or until a knife inserted in the middle comes out clean.

❺ Remove from pan and let cool on rack until it's just warm. Enjoy.

Cheese Doodle Day

Cheese doodles are crispy light corn puffs jam-packed with neon-orange cheese flavor. They just came out with a new "cheesier" version, which makes me happy, but I'm not satisfied, yet. Which brings us to my little brother, Johnny. . . . No one loves nachos as much as he does! He always wants me to make him nachos, so these cheese doodle nachos are for him.

JOHNNY'S NACHOS

Serves 2 hungry teenagers

1 large bag Cheese Doodles

1 cup salsa con queso (next to the salsa in your supermarket)

1 jalapeño

½ cup Cheddar cheese (shredded)

½ cup salsa

¼ cup Fresh Sour Cream (July 18)

2 tablespoons cilantro (chopped small)

❶ Pour Cheese Doodles on a plate.

❷ Microwave salsa con queso until boiling.

❸ Slice jalapeno thinly, seeds and all (unless you want it less spicy, in which case omit it altogether), making sure not to touch your eyes unless you want to cry like a baby. Wash your hands with soap thoroughly afterwards, soaping up twice.

❹ Sprinkle Cheddar cheese into bubbling salsa con queso, stir, and pour on top of Doodles.

❺ Top with spoonfuls of salsa all around Doodles, drizzle with sour cream, jalapeños, and sprinkle with cilantro. Serve immediately.

White Chocolate Cheesecake Day

The first cheesecake can be traced back as far as fifth-century Greece, where a physician by the name of Aegimus first recorded a recipe for making the delicacy. Cheesecake is made all over the world—in Germany and Poland with quark (a soft cheese), in Italy with ricotta—but in America, it's cream cheese all the way! All thanks to William Lawrence, who in 1872, along with other dairy farmers, discovered cream cheese while attempting to recreate the French Neufchâtel. Here, I incorporate white chocolate in the batter and browned butter in the crust. Yum!

WHITE CHOCOLATE CHEESECAKE

Serves 8

Crust

¼ cup butter (melted)

1½ cup your favorite cookie crumbs

1 tablespoon granulated sugar

⅛ teaspoon salt

Filling

1 pound (2 8-ounce packages) cream cheese (room temp)

⅔ cup granulated sugar

3 eggs

2 cups Greek yogurt or sour cream

½ cup white chocolate (melted)

1 teaspoon vanilla extract

1. Preheat oven to 325°F.

2. To make Crust, melt butter in a small pan over medium heat while whisking until it browns slightly.

3. Add cookie crumbs sugar, and salt. Using your hands, incorporate the butter into the crumbs. Take a springform pan and press the crust into the bottom using your hands.

4. To make Filling, whip cream cheese with sugar and eggs, adding one egg at a time and combining well.

5. Add yogurt, incorporate well, then drizzle in white chocolate while whisking.

6. Finish by whisking in vanilla. Wrap bottom of springform pan with aluminum foil so it covers the bottom, all the way around and up the sides. Place pan in a roasting pan and pour batter on top of crust.

7. Fill roasting pan with hot water so it rises halfway up the Springform pan; this will make a water bath for cheesecake to cook gently.

8. Bake at 325°F for 45 minutes; center will still be a little jiggly, then remove pans from oven and allow cheesecake to cool in water for at least 40 minutes. Refrigerate overnight or for at least 3 hours.

9. Run knife around the side of Springform pan and remove cake. Slice and serve.

Crown Roast of Pork Day

This dish is a showstopper! It is a large cut, anywhere from 9–15 chops or some-times more. This crown roast is traditionally served during the holidays or special celebrations. In my house, we're a big family, so it's just a great dinner! More importantly, it's impressive but still easy to prepare.

Preparing the Marinade

1. In a blender, combine all marinade ingredients until a smooth paste forms.

2. Rub paste all over crown roast, making sure to get into all the nooks and crannies. Use all of the rub. Place roast inside a large, clean garbage bag, tie closed, and refrigerate overnight, or for at least 3 hours.

Preparing the Stuffing

1. To make stuffing, in a large sauté pan over medium-high heat, cook bacon and potatoes, along with rosemary and garlic. Sauté for about 7 minutes until fat has rendered from bacon and everything starts to turn a pale golden color. Add olive oil, salt, and pepper, and continue to cook for another 3 minutes.

2. Transfer sauté pan ingredients into a large bowl and add apples. Allow to cool until you can handle with your hands without burning yourself. Toss everything together and set aside.

Preparing the Roast

1. Line a roasting pan with a sheet of aluminum foil so that there's a 2" lip all around (use two sheets if necessary). Remove marinated roast from plastic bag and place it in the middle of the roasting pan, then scrape the remaining marinade and coat the roast again.

2. Take 2 tablespoons of marinade and add it to the bowl with stuffing, toss everything together, and stuff it into cavity of roast. Try to stuff everything inside. This will support the roast and make it stand so it resembles a crown. Cover top loosely with aluminum foil to seal the roast.

KING'S ROAST

Serves 8

9 or more pork roast loin chops (tell your butcher you want to make a crown roast and ask to have it tied)

Marinade

½ cup honey

½ cup Dijon mustard

1½ tablespoons salt

2 teaspoons freshly ground pepper

½ cup fresh rosemary (sprigs only, no stem)

1 cup fresh garlic cloves (peeled)

Stuffing

1½ cups bacon (½" cubes)

4 cups red skinned potatoes (½" cubes)

3 tablespoons fresh rosemary (sprigs only, no stem)

½ cup fresh garlic cloves (peeled)

2 tablespoons olive oil

½ tablespoon salt

1 teaspoon pepper

3 cups Granny Smith apples (peeled, cored, and chopped into ½" cubes)

3 Bake at 350°F for 1½ hours.

4 Remove from oven, remove foil from top, and baste all around.

5 Cover center (where bones stick up and where stuffing is) with foil to prevent it from burning. (Note: If you see uneven color on the roast, it means your oven does not heat evenly. Simply rotate the pan 180 degrees.) Roast for another 30–45 minutes, basting every 20 minutes until a thermometer inserted in thickest part of roast reads 160°F. If you see parts of the roast getting too dark, cover that side with a piece of aluminum foil until the other side achieves the same color.

6 Remove from oven and allow to rest for at least 15 minutes. Slice and serve! Be sure to drizzle a little bit of the juices on top of every chop.

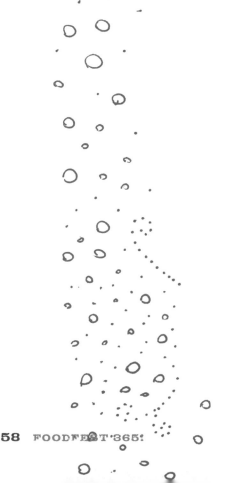

Peanut Cluster Day

MAR 8

Peanut clusters were the first step toward the modern candy bar. As most Americans love peanuts, it seems like a no-brainer that this is what we would add to our chocolate. Here, I simply add a little cream and powdered sugar to "soften" the bite of the cluster. You can also make this extravagant by adding some mini marshmallows, pretzel bits, caramels, or Rice Krispies . . . you get the picture!

PEANUT SOFTIES

Makes about 2 dozen

⅛ cup heavy cream

1 cup bittersweet chocolate (chopped small)

3 tablespoons powdered sugar

2 cups whole roasted peanuts

⅛ teaspoon coarse salt

1 Bring cream to a boil and add it to chocolate. Allow to sit for 1 minute, then whisk together, creating a ganache.

2 Sift sugar into ganache and whisk well.

3 Add peanuts. Combine with a wooden spoon.

4 Allow mixture to cool a bit until you can spoon it out. Spoon it out onto a baking sheet lined with parchment paper, wax paper, or aluminum foil.

5 Sprinkle with salt and refrigerate until hard, about 1 hour.

Crabmeat Day

Growing up we used to go crab hunting in the middle of the night. We would take rubber tubes (for tubing in the snow) and place a bucket inside that had holes to let some of the water through. Then we would walk around the shore with big flashlights and nets catching crab after crab after crab. I miss those good old days. Nowadays, you can find fresh crab all over the place. If I can't find crabs and can only get my hands on crabmeat, I always either make crab cakes or this crab dip.

CRAB DIP

Serves 4

 4 teaspoons fresh lemon juice

 ½ teaspoon salt (taste before adding salt, some crab meat is already salted)

 ⅛ teaspoon fresh black pepper

 2 tablespoons fresh ginger (grated or minced)

 1 cup cream cheese

 1 cup crabmeat

 2 scallions (sliced finely)

1 Combine lemon juice, salt, pepper, and ginger in a bowl. Using a fork or whisk, add cream cheese and combine until it is a smooth cream. Add crabmeat and scallions, then combine gently until it is roughly incorporated (don't break up the crab too much).

2 Serve in a bowl with a little paprika sprinkled on top. Delicious served with fried Tortilla chips made from Empanada Dough (Apr. 8). You can also make crab rangoon with this filling, using the same dough.

Blueberry Popover Day

Popovers are so named because they tend to pop when they cook. They are made with a light batter that puffs up and creates a hollow, light, and eggy pastry. Popovers use the same kind of batter as Yorkshire pudding and can be traced back to 1850. Here, I fill them up with fresh blueberries and glaze them with a little maple syrup for a perfect morning treat.

BLUEBERRY MAPLE POPOVERS

Makes 1 dozen

 1 cup all-purpose flour

 1½ tablespoons granulated sugar

 2 eggs (at room temperature)

 1 teaspoon kosher salt

 1 tablespoon unsalted butter (melted but just warm)

 1 cup milk

 1 cup fresh blueberries

 2–3 tablespoons maple syrup

1 Sift flour and sugar into a bowl. Make a well in the middle and add eggs, salt, and butter.

2 Whisk everything together slowly, allowing eggs to drag flour into the middle—do not force.

③ When batter starts to harden, add milk a little at a time while whisking. When milk has been completely incorporated and the batter is smooth, coat a cupcake pan with nonstick spray and pour batter in so it fills cups ⅔ of the way up. Add 5–7 blueberries to each popover and bake for 35–40 minutes at 400°F.

④ Remove pan from oven and glaze each popover with 1 teaspoon of maple syrup, then return to oven for 2 more minutes.

⑤ Allow to cool until they are warm and serve dusted with powdered sugar.

Oatmeal-Nut Waffles Day

Waffles are characterized by the waffle irons used to make these delicious delicacies. The word waffle comes from the Dutch wafel and has its origins in Medieval wafers. In those days, since there was no electricity, the cast iron pans were held together by a hinge and wooden handles, then placed on top of a fire to cook. There are dozens of varieties of waffles, but the biggest difference is the method used to leaven the waffles from fresh yeast in Belgian waffles to chemical leaveners in modern American ones.

OATMEAL-NUT WAFFLES

Serves 4

15 ounces buttermilk (room temperature)

3 whole eggs (beaten)

3 ounces unsalted butter (melted)

2 cups all-purpose flour

1 teaspoon salt

4 tablespoons sugar

½ teaspoon baking soda

1 teaspoon baking powder

1 teaspoon cinnamon

⅛ cup of your favorite flavored instant oatmeal

¼ cup walnuts (chopped)

① Combine all wet ingredients, and sift all dry ingredients, except oats and nuts.

② Add wet mixture to dry, then add oatmeal and walnuts and mix slowly until well combined.

③ Spray waffle iron with nonstick spray and cook until golden. Serve with honey.

Cook's Note

Storage conditions can affect the performance of your baking powder. Follow the expiration date on the package, and to test put ½ teaspoon of the baking powder into 3 teaspoons of room temperature water. If the fizz is strong, then it's still good to use.

Baked Scallops Day

Scallops are mollusks found in all of the world's oceans. They are delicate and white with a decorative shell that is usually sold as decoration. The word scallop is derived from the French escalope, meaning shell. Here I fill shell pasta with scallops, add a touch of meatiness with sausage, and top it all with a creamy mushroom sauce.

1 Bring large pot of water with salt and olive oil to a boil for shells.

2 Remove the little tough part attached to the scallop. Season well with salt, pepper, and garlic powder.

3 Coat bottom of a sauté pan with olive oil and place it over high heat. Allow oil to start smoking a little and place scallops in one at a time, flat-side down. Cook on one side for about 2 minutes, or until it turns golden and crusty. Flip and cook on other side for 1 minute more. Once cooked, chop scallops into four even pieces, so there will be several pieces in each pasta shell.

4 Invert sauté pan into a bowl that's big enough to hold 2 quarts. Return pan to heat, and lower to medium. Add more olive oil and add sausage chunks. Brown sausage, then add chopped garlic, pepper flakes, peas, and thyme. Cook until garlic is golden and peas are tender. Empty sauté pan ingredients into bowl with scallops.

5 In a separate bowl, mix ricotta, Parmigiano-Reggiano, ½ the parsley, salt, pepper, plus ½ cup mozzarella, and combine well. Adjust seasoning, then refrigerate until mixture is cool, about 20 minutes.

6 Drop pasta shells into boiling, salted water and cook for about 4–5 minutes until al dente, then strain and rinse with cold water. When pasta has cooled, drizzle with olive oil to prevent it from sticking together.

7 Drizzle casserole dish with olive oil. Stuff the shells with the scallop-sausage filling (you should be able to fill about 21 shells), layer cheese mixture on top, and place in casserole dish.

8 To make the Mushroom Sauce, drizzle olive oil into the same sauté pan and add butter. Let butter melt and sauté mushrooms with onions until cooked through.

SCALLOPS 'N' SHELLS

Serves 4–5

Large pot of water

½ teaspoon salt

Olive oil

1 pound diver scallops

½ teaspoon fresh ground pepper

Garlic powder

½ pound fennel sausage (small chunks)

5 garlic cloves (cut in sixths)

½ teaspoon red pepper flakes

½ cup peas

1 tablespoon fresh thyme (leaves only)

3 cups ricotta

2 tablespoons Parmigiano-Reggiano

4 tablespoons fresh parsley (chopped)

2 cups mozzarella (shredded)

Jumbo pasta shells (2 12-ounce boxes)

MUSHROOM SAUCE

Olive oil

2 tablespoons butter

1 cup button mushrooms

½ cup onions (finely chopped)

2 tablespoons flour

½ cup white wine (or vegetable stock)

1½ cups whole milk

9. Add flour and cook for about 1 minute. Add white wine and milk and whisk together. Cook on medium heat until you have a creamy sauce. Add salt and pepper to taste.

10. Pour sauce over the shells, top with remaining mozzarella, and bake at 350°F for 15–20 minutes or until cheese is bubbling and shell insides are hot. Garnish with remaining chopped parsley.

Cook's Note

Make sure you get your scallops from a reputable fish store. If they smell fishy, they're no good. If they smell sweet, you're in business.

1. Cream butter and sugar with mixer on high speed for about 8 minutes.

2. Sift flour and baking powder.

3. Break eggs into a separate bowl and add coconut milk. Add the remaining ingredients except the shredded coconut to the whipped butter, alternating between adding egg mixture and flour mixture and incorporating well between additions. Mix in coconut last.

4. Spray a 10–12" springform pan with nonstick spray and coat with flour. Pour batter into pan and bake at 350°F for 40 minutes or until a knife inserted in the middle comes out clean.

MAR 13 — Coconut Torte Day

In many recipes, coconut milk can be used as a substitute to heavy cream. The fat content is similar with an extra touch of the exotic. Here, I take a pound cake recipe and pump it with coconut milk to enhance the flavor of it then fold in shredded coconut for extra crunch.

COCONUT CRUNCH CAKE

Serves 6

1 pound butter (soft)

3 cups granulated sugar

4½ cups all-purpose flour

1½ tablespoons baking powder

6 eggs

1½ cups coconut milk

½ teaspoon salt

1 teaspoon vanilla

1 cup shredded coconut

Potato Chip Day

Potato chips are one of America's favorite snack and in all honesty couldn't be simpler to make! The original chip was created by Chef George Crum in New York around 1853. Irritated with a customer who kept sending his fried potatoes back because they weren't crispy enough, Crum sliced the potatoes very thinly so the customer would not be able to eat them with his fork. To George's surprise, the customer was ecstatic and soon became a regular at the lodge. This was the beginning of the potato chip, which came to be known as "Saratoga Chips."

PERFECTO POTATO CHIPPOS

Serves 3–4

4 Idaho potatoes

Large bowl of water

4 cups vegetable or canola oil

Salt to taste

1. Clean potatoes and slice very thinly. Using a mandolin will guarantee evenly thin chips, which means they'll be crispy and light.

2. Place in bowl with cold, salted water and soak for at least 10 minutes.

3. In large stockpot, heat oil to 375°F, using a thermometer to check temperature.

4. Drop a few chips in at a time and fry until golden. (It's okay if they brown a little.) Remove from oil and drain on paper towels.

5. Season with salt to taste as soon as they come out of oil. This way, the hot oil will melt the salt and cause it to stick. Make a bunch and keep them warm in the oven.

Pears Helene Day

MAR 15

This is another famous dish created by the great Chef Auguste Escoffier. It is composed of pears poached in syrup and served with chocolate sauce and crystallized violets. It is a classic dessert created in honor of the Operetta La Belle Helene. You can find crystallized rose petals at baking stores or online; this touch makes this simple dish the masterpiece that is was meant to be. If you can't find them, feel free to substitute with almonds.

PEARS HELENE

Serves 2–4

2 cups sugar

2 cups water

2 Bartlett pears (unripe and hard)

½ cup bittersweet chocolate (finely chopped)

¼ cup milk chocolate (finely chopped)

¼ cup heavy cream

Homemade Vanilla Ice Cream (July 23)

Crystallized violet petals

1. Combine sugar and water in a pot and bring to a slow simmer, making syrup.

2. Peel pears and cut then in half lengthwise. Using a melon baller, remove the seeds and drop halves into syrup mixture.

3. Poach pears until tender, about 15–20 minutes. Check by inserting a sharp knife into pears. When you feel no resistance, they're done.

4. Take ½ cup of the hot poaching liquid and add it to chocolate. Leave for 2 minutes so chocolate melts, then whisk everything together until a sauce forms. Add heavy cream and whisk until smooth.

5. Serve pears alongside vanilla ice cream drizzled with chocolate sauce and garnished with crystallized violet petals or almonds.

Artichoke Hearts Day

Artichokes are a perennial thistle originating in the Mediterranean. What you can actually eat in these is just the heart of the bud. But before you can get to the creamy center, you need to clean and remove a handful of bitter florets in the center called the "choke." Spinach and artichoke dip is a perennial favorite; here is my own tasty version.

SPINACH AND ARTICHOKE DIP

Serves 4–6

1 teaspoon olive oil

3 tablespoons butter

1 cup bacon (finely chopped)

1½ cups Spanish onion (finely chopped)

1 tablespoon fresh thyme (leaves only)

3 cloves garlic (chopped)

2 large bags of fresh spinach (chopped)

1 10-ounce can quartered artichoke hearts

1 cup ricotta cheese

1 cup cream cheese (8-ounce package)

2 cups mozzarella cheese (shredded)

½ teaspoon salt

¼ teaspoon fresh ground black pepper

❶ In a sauté pan over medium heat, drizzle olive oil and add butter until melted.

❷ Add bacon, onion, and thyme. Cook until golden. Add garlic, cook for 2 minutes, then add spinach and cook for 2 more minutes.

❸ Add artichokes and cook for 1 minute.

❹ Turn off heat and add remaining ingredients, reserving 1 cup of mozzarella to top the dip. (At this point you can blend everything together for a smooth dip, or leave it chunky.)

❺ Toss everything until ingredients are evenly distributed and pour into a casserole pan. Top with remaining mozzarella.

❻ Bake at 375°F for 15 minutes or until cheese is bubbly and golden. Serve with toasted rustic bread slices.

Corned Beef and Cabbage Day

Corned beef and cabbage is the quintessential Irish dish. It is tender and bright pink, typically served with boiled cabbage. The term corned has absolutely nothing to do with corn the vegetable, instead it refers to the "corns" or large salt grains used to cure the beef. Corned beef is made from brisket of beef that has been brined in salt and spices for about a three-week period. The meat is then boiled until fork-tender and then served with mustard.

CORNED BEEF

Serves 3–4

2 tablespoons olive oil

1 cup onion (sliced ¼" thick)

1 cup carrot (sliced ¼" thick)

1 cup celery (sliced ¼" thick)

1 teaspoon whole mustard seeds

1 teaspoon whole black pepper

1 teaspoon coriander seeds

1 teaspoon dried juniper berries

4 garlic cloves

4 tablespoons butter

1 3-pound flat cut (or first cut) corned beef

1 bay leaf

Handful fresh parsley (tied together with twine)

3 12-ounce bottles Sam Adams Irish Red beer, or any Irish beer

2 pound head Savoy cabbage

1. Heat the oven to 450°F.

2. In a 5–6 quart casserole dish or Dutch oven, drizzle 2 tablespoons olive oil. Place inside oven and heat for 5 minutes.

3. Add all vegetables, except cabbage, and spices and cook for about 7 minutes, stirring at the halfway point.

4. Remove from oven, lower heat to 300°F, and add 2 tablespoons butter, the brisket (fat-side up), bay leaf, parsley, and beer. Cover and cook for 3 hours.

5. At the end of the first hour, open dish and flip corned beef so the other side is submerged. Cook for another hour.

6. At the end of the second hour, a layer of white fat should be visible between two pieces of the corned beef. With a knife, cut right across

the middle of the fat, separating it into two parts. Lay both parts fat-side up.

7. Cut cabbage in half and remove the hard center. Slice into long strands about ¼" thick. Put inside casserole or Dutch oven. With a spoon, press down and spoon liquid on top so all the cabbage is wet from braising liquid. Cover and cook for remaining 30 minutes.

8. When ready to serve, add last 2 tablespoons butter to liquid and stir to dissolve. Slice corned beef thinly with a very sharp knife. Serve with thick mustard and spoon some of that delicious au jus on top!

Oatmeal Cookie Day

MAR 18

Oatmeal cookies incorporate either steel-cut oats or, in this case, instant oatmeal. Instant oatmeal is first cut into small pieces, then steamed and rolled, then dried. Oatmeal is a great way to get nutrition on the go, and it can help lower cholesterol at the same time.

OATMEAL RAISIN COOKIES

Makes 2 dozen

¾ cup butter (unsalted)

1 cup brown sugar

½ teaspoon salt

¾ cup all-purpose flour

½ teaspoon baking soda

½ teaspoon ground cinnamon

1 large egg

2 cups instant oats

1 teaspoon vanilla extract

Oatmeal Cookie Day, March 18

1. Cream butter and sugar in a mixer on high speed for about 8 minutes until nice and fluffy.

2. Sift all dry ingredients except oats. Slow mixer and add egg. Mix for 10 seconds, then add flour mixture in 2 parts. Combine thoroughly. Add oats, then vanilla. Combine well for at least 10 seconds.

3. Spoon mixture (if you have a small ice scream scoop of about 1–2 tablespoons, use that) about 1 tablespoon at a time onto a greased cookie sheet, leaving about 1" between cookies.

4. Bake at 350°F for 12 minutes.

MAR 19 Poultry Day

Poultry is a category of birds farmed for human consumption. They say you can judge the quality of a cook by the quality of his or her roasted chicken. So I present mine: simple, salty, crispy, and succulent.

YVAN'S ROASTED CHICKEN

Serves 2–3

1 2–3 pound chicken

Kosher salt

Fresh ground pepper

1. Rinse chicken in cold water.

2. Place cavity-side down over a few paper towels and prop it with a large can or container. Allow to drain for at least 5 minutes. Pat skin dry with paper towels.

3. Season the cavity liberally with salt and pepper and then fill it with a aluminum foil. (This will retain heat and allow the chicken to cook a little faster.)

4. Using twine, truss bird by twisting wings behind its back and locking them into place (kind of as if it was being arrested, just push wings up a little higher toward its neck) and tying legs together.

5. Sprinkle kosher salt and the pepper liberally all around bird.

6. Place chicken on a small rack inside a shallow roasting pan. Allow chicken to sit at room temperature for about 30 minutes. This will allow the inside of bird to warm up a bit and cook more evenly.

7. Cook chicken at 450°F for 45–50 minutes, rotating the pan if you notice uneven spots as it's cooking.

8. Remove from oven and allow the bird to rest for 5 minutes before you dig in! Enjoy!

MAR 20

Ravioli Day

Ravioli are little nuggets of filling surrounded by a layer of thin pasta. Culturally accepted as Italian, almost every nation in the world has a variation. From Asia we get wontons, gyoza, and jiaozi; from Turkey, Manti; the Germans refer to them as Maultaschen; and the Jewish kreplash. Ravioli, tortellini, and other Italian-stuffed pastas are referred as "Italian Wontons." Ravioli are simple to make but a bit time-consuming; however, they are a clever way to use leftovers! I make mine with an old-fashioned wonton dough recipe.

EGGPLANT AND GOAT CHEESE RAVIOLI

Serves 2

Pasta Dough (Feb. 13)

Filing

1 large eggplant

Salt and pepper

Olive oil

½ pound soft goat cheese log

Sauce

1 8-ounce jar of roasted red peppers

4 garlic cloves

1 sprig of fresh rosemary

3 tablespoons olive oil

½ teaspoon salt

½ teaspoon pepper

1 egg white

❶ Prepare Wonton Dough and place in fridge to rest for at least 15 minutes.

❷ Wash and slice eggplant lengthwise. Salt and pepper both sides of eggplant and allow to sit for 5 minutes. (The salt draws out moisture.)

❸ In a large sauté pan, drizzle about 3 tablespoons olive oil, covering bottom of pan on medium-high heat until oil begins to smoke. Place a few eggplant slices in, making sure not to crowd pan. Cook for about 2 minutes on each side until golden. Remove from pan and put aside in bowl. Repeat process with remaining eggplant slices, and allow to cool.

❹ To prepare sauce, line inside of a small casserole with aluminum foil. Drain liquid from peppers and place in casserole. Slice garlic cloves in half and add to casserole along with rosemary and olive oil. Season with salt and pepper, then cover with foil and bake in 400°F oven for 40 minutes or until garlic is golden. After 40 minutes, remove golden garlic from pepper mixture and add to reserved eggplant.

❺ Place peppers and remaining oil from casserole into a food processor and pulse until it becomes a coarse sauce. Taste, adjust seasoning if necessary, and set aside.

❻ Finely chop eggplant and garlic.

❼ With a very floured, clean surface and rolling pin, roll out dough until it's about as thick as a quarter. Brush entire surface with egg white and spoon out eggplant filling a tablespoon at a time, leaving about 1½" between each dollop.

❽ Cut ¼" thick disks off the goat cheese and place one on top of each portion of eggplant filling.

9. Roll out another piece of dough about the same size and place on top. With your fingertips, carefully press down on dough between ravioli, working your way from one side to the other, trying to release any trapped air between the layers and the filling. Using a ring cutter or small can, cut into circles.

10. Cook ravioli in salted boiling water and a little olive oil for about 2 minutes each or until almost transparent. Remove from boiling water with slotted spoon and transfer onto an olive oil drizzled plate, gently flipping and coating ravioli so they don't dry out and get nice and shiny. Serve with pepper sauce, and garnish with fresh parsley.

California Strawberry Day

Thanks to California and its wonderful climate, we can enjoy strawberries year round. Though not necessarily local, sometimes one of the perks of living in an industrialized nation is we have the option of eating anything we want at any time of the year. And gosh-darn it, sometimes you just want some fresh strawberries. Why shouldn't you have them? When they're as delicious as those grown in Cali, no one can blame you.

CALIFORNIA STRAWBERRY CAKE

Serves 4–6

Perfect Chantilly Cream (Jan. 5)

Buttery Pound Cake (Mar. 4)

2 pints California strawberries

¼ cup powdered sugar (plus more for dusting)

1 lemon (juice and zest)

1. Prepare whipped cream. Prepare pound cake.

2. While cake is baking, wash strawberries thoroughly and slice thin. Place in bowl with powdered sugar and add juice of ½ lemon and zest. Toss until sugar has dissolved and chill in refrigerator for about 20 minutes.

3. When cake is finished cooking, cool slightly and slice into 3" x 3" squares about ½" thick.

4. Place one slice of cake on a plate, top with 2 tablespoons of strawberries (with juice, so cake absorbs it).

5. Top with 2 tablespoons of chilled cream.

6. Layer on another slice of cake, more strawberries, and more cream. Dust with powdered sugar and serve. Enjoy!

MAR. 22

Coq au Vin Day

Coq au vin is a classic French dish that has lasted the test of time. It is rustic and completely delicious peasant food! Coq au vin translates into "rooster with wine." The long braising softens the tough bird into succulent, tender poultry. Legend dates the dish back to the sixteenth century, but the earliest recorded version came from the Loire valley in France. This is one of those dishes that you can make one day and it will taste better reheated the next day. I've opted to use chicken instead of a rooster since it is more readily available and still produces a wonderful dish.

COQ AU VIN

Serves 4

1 3-pound chicken or 12 thighs

¼ pound bacon (have your butcher cut ¼" thick or use pancetta)

Salt and pepper

2 medium Spanish onions (cut into 12 chunks)

2 ribs celery (cut ½" thick)

2 medium carrots (peeled, ½" thick rounds)

2 bay leaves

4 garlic cloves (sliced in half)

2 tablespoons butter

10 fresh thyme sprigs

1 cup button mushrooms (cut in half, or quarters when too big)

2 tablespoons tomato paste

2 tablespoons cognac

1 bottle red wine (Beaujolais or pinot noir work well)

1 cup chicken stock

1. Rinse chicken and cut it into 12 pieces (2 wings, 2 thighs, 2 drumsticks, the back cut into 2, and both the breast cut in half for 4 pieces). Place on paper towels to dry.

2. In a large roasting pan over medium heat, cook bacon cubes (called *lardoons* in France) until lightly brown. Remove bacon from pan and put aside in a large bowl, leaving fat behind.

3. Season chicken liberally with salt and pepper on both sides. Place chicken pieces in roasting pan skin-side down, raise heat to high, and cook until chicken is golden, about 5 minutes. Flip chicken and cook for 3 more minutes on other side.

4. Lower heat to medium, remove chicken and add to bowl with bacon.

5. Add onions (reserving 2 tablespoons), celery, carrots, bay leaves, garlic, and a little salt and pepper to roasting pan. Cook for about 5 minutes over medium heat.

6. Empty vegetables into bowl with bacon and chicken.

7. Add butter to pan along with thyme and mushrooms and sauté for two minutes until mushrooms are almost cooked through. Add tomato paste and mix in well. Add cognac and cook for 30 seconds to allow the alcohol to evaporate, then add wine, chicken stock, and combine well.

8. Return chicken to roasting pan, placing skin-side up, and top with bacon-veggie mixture. Cover pan and cook for 1 hour at 350°F.

9. Remove roasting pan from oven and place on stovetop. Turn flame on high and reduce sauce for 15 minutes. Enjoy on top of pasta or rice.

Chip and Dip Day

MAR 23

Chips and dip are great for any occasion—from a birthday party to a game on TV or a late-night snack. Here I wanted to make something a little different. I once worked at a place called Milos, a Greek restaurant where they made awesome zucchini and eggplant chips then served them with a creamy yogurt dip called tzatziki. It's a great, healthy alternative to store-bought.

GREEK-INSPIRED CHIPS & DIP

Serves 4

Veggie Chips

1 medium eggplant

1 large zucchini

Salt

Vegetable oil for frying

All-purpose flour

Pepper

Dried oregano

Yogurt Dip

1 cup Greek yogurt

2 garlic cloves

1 tablespoon fresh dill

½ teaspoon fresh lemon juice

½ teaspoon salt

Black pepper to taste

1½" piece of cucumber

1. Slice veggies as thin as possible, preferably with a mandolin. Rinse and dry them, then lay in a single layer over paper towels and sprinkle salt (this will release some water from them, making for a crisper chip).

2. Bring about 3 cups of oil to 350°F.

3. Mix flour, pepper, and oregano, and toss veggie slices in the mixture. Press down, and dust off excess flour. Fry until golden and crisp. Remove from oil with basket or slotted spoon and drain on paper towels. Salt as soon as chips come out.

4. To prepare Yogurt Dip, combine yogurt, garlic, dill, lemon juice, salt, pepper, and cucumber in a food processor and purée until smooth.

Chocolate-Covered Raisins Day

It sounds so simple, right? Dark, bittersweet chocolate surrounding a morsel of a deep, sweet, sundried raisin. We mostly eat them while at the movies out of those boxes that are prominently displayed next to the Junior Mints, Milk Duds, Goobers, and Sno-Caps. The most popular brand is Raisinets, and they are made by tumbling raisins in a drum while chocolate is poured over them. The chocolate dries forming a nice shell, which is then polished with a little beeswax for shine.

CHOCOLATE-COVERED RAISINS

Makes 1 cup raisins

½ cup raisins

½ cup milk chocolate (melted)

---

1. Toss raisins in a metal bowl and drizzle a little chocolate at a time, coating each raisin.

2. Place the bowl inside fridge for a few minutes to solidify the chocolate.

Lobster Newberg Day

MAR 25

Foodie folklore traces this dish to the infamous Delmonico's restaurant in the heart of the Big Apple. Ben Wenberg, a wealthy sea captain in the fruit trade, introduced a new delicious way of cooking lobster to the restaurant's then-manager Charles Delmonico. After trying the dish, Mr. Delmonico and Chef Charles Ranhofer decided to put it on the menu. Not long after, a feud ensued between Mr. Delmonico and Mr. Wenberg, prompting the removal of the dish from the menu. But because there was demand for the dish, it was brought back with a clever switcharoo of letters— from Wenberg to Newberg. That simple change allowed Delmonico's to give the people what they wanted, and in this case we all reap the delicious rewards.

LOBSTER NEWBERG

Serves 2–3

2 1½-pound live lobsters

Olive oil

3 tablespoons butter

Pinch of saffron

1 medium Spanish onion (cubed small)

1 tablespoon tomato paste

2 tablespoons dry sherry

2 tablespoons cognac or brandy

1½ cups heavy cream

Salt

1 dash white pepper

1. In a pot or steamer, steam lobsters for 4 minutes. Remove from heat and using a nutcracker and scissors, remove claws from shells and split tail in two. Set lobster meat aside.

2. In a sauté pan add a little oil with butter and saffron and sweat onions until translucent (make sure not to color them). Add tomato paste and stir in, then add sherry, cognac, and heavy cream. Combine and season with salt and pepper to taste.

3. Add lobster meat and cook for 1–2 minutes while spooning sauce on top of lobster. Serve on top of basmati or jasmine rice with plenty of yummy sauce.

Spinach Day

Spinach was actually a favorite of Catherine de Medici, and when she left Florence to marry in France she brought it along with her. All dishes henceforth that were served on a bed of spinach are referred to "a la Florentine" here's to eggs Florentine! I wanted to tease out the nutty and earthy qualities, out so I combined it with a little onion and mushrooms and serve in little phyllo cups as hors d'oeuvres.

SPINACH AND MUSHROOM CUPS

Makes 2 dozen

5 phyllo sheets

¼ cup butter plus 2 tablespoons (for sautéing)

1 medium onion (sliced into small cubes)

1 large (8–10 ounce) bag fresh spinach

Salt and pepper

4 ounces button mushrooms (cleaned and sliced into small cubes)

1. Defrost phyllo and melt ¼ cup butter. Allow to cool to room temperature but still remain liquid.

2. Lay one phyllo sheet on a same-size cutting board, placing a towel or plastic wrap over remaining sheets. Brush with butter, and lay another sheet of phyllo on top. Repeat process until there are five layers.

3. Cut into little squares that fit inside mini cupcake molds. Place dough inside greased tin, press down, and bake at 350°F for 8–15 minutes until golden.

4. Gently remove phyllo cups from molds and allow to cool. Place a sauté pan over medium heat and melt part of remaining butter. Raise heat to high and wait until butter starts to smoke a little, then add onions, reserving 2 tablespoons. Cook for 30 seconds then add spinach and salt and pepper.

5. Cook spinach for 30 seconds, empty contents of pan into bowl and allow to cool.

6. Add remaining butter to pan and sauté remaining onions, adding mushrooms when onions are translucent. Cook mushrooms for 1 minute until tender, and add mixture to spinach bowl.

7. Fill phyllo cups with spinach-onion-mushroom mix, stuffing well to fit as much green goodness as you can without crushing them.

8. Return to oven and cook for another 5 minutes. Serve hot.

Spanish Paella Day

Paella is a wonderfully fragrant dish that originated in nineteenth-century Spain. The word itself is Catalan, derived from the Old French word paelle, *meaning pan. Its history can be traced back to Valencia on the eastern coast of Spain; home to the world's most popular paella. It's an impressive and flavorful dish that's not hard to make as long as you follow the directions, and like most things in life, the more you make it, the better you'll get at it! The largest paella made by Juan Carlos in Valencia on March 8, 1992, measured 65' 7" in diameter and was eaten by 100,000 people!*

SEAFOOD PAELLA

5 littleneck clams

5 mussels

5 jumbo shrimp

5 scallops

4 small calamari (bodies cut into ¼" thick rings)

1 cup chorizo (8 ounces, cut ½" thick)

Olive oil

Salt and black pepper

1 tablespoon paprika

1 tablespoon dried oregano

4 boneless chicken thighs (1" cubes)

1 medium Spanish onion (¼" cubes)

1 red pepper (thinly sliced)

4 garlic cloves (thinly sliced)

2 tablespoons fresh parsley (chopped)

1 large pinch of saffron

2 tablespoons cognac

2 tablespoons sherry

1½ cups medium grain or Arborio rice

2 cups crushed tomatoes

4 cups chicken stock

¼ cup peas

❶ To remove sand from the shellfish, place clams and mussels in a bowl filled with cold water and 2 tablespoons salt. After 10 minutes, change water and repeat process.

❷ Slice along backs of shrimp to devein, remove rubbery part of the scallops, and slice calamari.

❸ Chop chorizo and sauté in a dry roasting or paella pan over medium heat until it is golden, about 2 minutes on each side. Place chorizo in bowl and set aside.

❹ Drizzle olive oil in pan, season seafood with salt, pepper, paprika, and oregano, and sauté for about 1 minute on high heat, then put aside with chorizo.

❺ Add more olive oil to pan, season chicken with salt, pepper, paprika, and oregano, then sauté until golden. Place chicken in bowl with chorizo and seafood.

❻ Next, add more olive oil to the pan and sauté the onions, peppers, garlic, 1 tablespoon parsley, saffron, cognac, sherry, salt and pepper to make the base flavor of the paella—the sofrito. Sauté over medium heat until onions have wilted and are translucent.

❼ Add rice and sauté for 1 minute, then add tomatoes and stir, scraping bottom of pan to get good flavor into the sauce. Add chicken stock, chorizo, and chicken. Bring to a simmer. Continue to simmer for 10 minutes, stirring well. Add seafood, arranging in pan, cover and simmer for 15 minutes, undisturbed.

❽ Once 15 minutes have passed, remove lid and add peas. Close the pan until ready to serve. Sprinkle with fresh parsley and serve immediately.

Black Forest Cake Day

The mere mention of Black Forest cakes evokes an air of mystery and temptation that only the combination of intense chocolate cake with cherries and soft cream can deliver. This decadent cake, originally called Schwarzwälder Kirschtorte, gets its name from the Black Forest region in Germany where sour morello cherries are abundant and kirsch, a sour cherry brandy, is a town favorite. The name itself translates exactly into "Black Forest cherry liquor torte," and after only one bite you might just be packing your things and moving to this magical forest.

BLACK FOREST CAKE

Serves 6–8

1 cup water

1 cup Dutch processed cocoa powder

1 cup buttermilk

1½ cup plus 2 tablespoons all-purpose flour

2 teaspoons baking soda

½ teaspoon baking powder

Pinch of salt

1 cup butter (softened)

1¼ cups granulated sugar

4 large eggs

2 teaspoons vanilla extract

½ cup cherry brandy or liqueur

2 (14-ounce) jars cherry pie filling

Ganache

- 1½ cup heavy cream
- 1 tablespoon sugar
- 1 cup bittersweet chocolate (chopped)
- 2 tablespoons butter
- Perfect Chantilly Cream (Jan. 5)
- Bittersweet chocolate shavings for garnish

1 Bring water to a boil and whisk in cocoa powder. Let mixture cool, then add buttermilk.

2 Sift together flour, baking soda, baking powder, and salt; set aside.

3 In a large bowl, cream butter and sugar together until light and fluffy. Beat in eggs one at time, then stir in vanilla. Add flour mixture alternately with cocoa mixture. Spread batter evenly between 3 greased 9" round cake pans.

4 Bake 350°F for 25–30 minutes. Allow to cool.

5 While cake is baking prepare Ganache. Bring cream and sugar to a boil and add to chocolate. Let sit for 1 minute then whisk well. Add butter and whisk everything together until you have a smooth and glossy mixture.

6 To assemble, place first cake layer on serving plate, poke top with a fork, and drench with cherry brandy. Spread frosting on top of cake, then top with second layer. Repeat the process with all 3 layers.

7 Scoop some Ganache into a piping bag and make a border around circumference of top layer; frost sides with remaining Ganache. Top cake with cherry pie filling.

8 Garnish with whipped cream, and sprinkle chocolate shavings and press onto sides of cake.

Lemon Chiffon Cake Day

This magnificent, lemony cake was created by Harry Baker in 1972. Harry was an insurance salesman who had just turned caterer, which shows that, with enough desire, anybody can bake! Chiffon cakes are wonderful when making ice cream cakes or any cakes that you plan on refrigerating because the oil remains soft at lower temperatures as supposed to butter, which turns hard. Here's an easy cake that gets its fluff from whipped egg whites, and because of its lightness, it becomes a sponge when you drench it with syrups or cordials.

LEMON CHIFFON CAKE

Serves 5–6

- 2 cups all-purpose flour
- 1 tablespoon baking powder
- 1½ cups granulated sugar
- ½ teaspoon salt
- 8 eggs (separated)
- ½ cup fresh lemon juice
- ¼ cup water
- Zest of 2 lemons
- ½ cup vegetable oil
- ½ teaspoon cream of tartar

1. Sift flour and baking powder. Make a well in the middle of sifted ingredients and add sugar, salt, and egg yolks. Combine until it thickens up, then add lemon juice a little at a time to create a smooth paste. Continue to add lemon juice, then add water and continue whisking slowly until all ingredients are combined.

2. Add lemon zest, oil, and combine well.

3. In a clean bowl, mix egg whites on medium speed for about 1 minute until frothy. Add cream of tartar and mix on high until soft peaks form. With a spatula, gently fold about ½ of whites into batter. Add remaining whites and fold until batter is fluffy.

4. Coat a springform pan with nonstick spray and dust with a little flour. Pour batter in, place the pan on cookie sheet to prevent bottom from burning, and cover top with a piece of aluminum foil. Bake at 325°F for 40–50 minutes or until a knife inserted in the middle comes out clean.

5. When done baking, run a sharp knife around edges to release cake.

6. Cool until it's just warm and serve with a nice cup of tea.

Turkey Neck Soup Day

Sometimes called Shabbat soup, this dish is a Jewish staple. The tough neck calls for long cooking and adds a rich flavor to the soup Whenever we have chicken in my house, it is always my mom, dad, or I who battle it out for the chicken neck. The luscious little morsels that are entrapped between those neck bones full of collagen and packed full of flavor makes us dive and sometimes wrestle when apparently we should be at peace. Sometimes good food is worth fighting for even if it means snatching your favorite chicken part from your loved ones.

TURKEY NECK SOUP

Serves 3–4

2 turkey necks (found at the supermarket or your local butcher)

½ cup onion (chopped)

½ cup celery (chopped)

½ cup carrot (chopped)

½ cup fresh cranberries

Olive oil

4 cups chicken stock

1 cup water

4 cloves garlic (smashed)

1 bay leaf

Salt and pepper to taste

1. Chop necks into small pieces.

2. In a stockpot, sauté veggies with turkey and cranberries in olive oil until golden brown.

3. Add chicken stock, water, garlic, bay leaf, and salt and pepper.

4. Simmer on low until the meat is tender, about 1–1½ hours.

5. As soup simmers, remove foam that forms on top; those are impurities. Enjoy!

Tater Day

Every year in Benton, Kentucky, thousands of people get into costume and head out to the Tater Parade. The festival dates back to 1842 when the townspeople came out to trade sweet potatoes. The Tater Parade now features carnival rides, barbecue cook-offs—they even crown a Ms. Tater! I am a tater tot fanatic. In NYC, Trailer Park Lounge serves the best tots I've ever tasted, served with ranch dressing. . . . So, I decided to make a variation out of sweet potatoes in honor of the festival and serve them with ranch dressing as an ode to the Trailer Park Lounge.

KENTUCKY-TRAILER TATERS

Serves 2–3

2 sweet potatoes (peeled)

Vegetable oil

Salt and pepper

1. Grate sweet potatoes and soak in cold water.

2. Meanwhile, in a stockpot, heat oil to 325°F.

3. Blanch shoestring sweet potatoes for 3 minutes.

4. Remove with a slotted spoon, place in a flat, square container, and press down to 1" thickness.

5. Refrigerate until chilled, about 20 minutes.

6. Remove from fridge. The sweet potatoes should be soft and cooked without any color. Using a 1" cookie cutter or ring, cut as many tater tots as possible.

7. Raise oil temperature to 350°F and fry taters until lightly browned and crisp.

8. Remove from oil, drain on paper towels, and season with salt and pepper. Serve right away with ranch dressing on the side.

APRIL

Sourdough Bread Day

Sourdough bread begins with the creation of a starter, also referred to as the "mother" or "chef." By combining warm water and unbleached four, which contains spores and yeasts, you create a live culture. In time, after feeding the "mother" with fresh water and flour, it starts to create lactic acid, giving the bread its sour taste—hence the name sourdough. This live yeast not only gives the bread a wonderful lift, but it provides your palate with an undeniably tangy kick!

SERENDIPITY SOURDOUGH ROLLS

Makes 12

"Mother" or Sponge

- 1 cup unbromated, unbleached, organic flour
- 1 cup warm water
- 1 teaspoon fresh yeast

1. Make the "mother" by combining flour with yeast and water. Mix well and place inside a container with a lid and leave it at room temperature for 2 days.

2. On the second day, throw out half the mixture and replace with equal amounts of water with flour. At the end of the second day, refrigerate mixture.

Rolls

- 2 cups sponge
- 3 tablespoons olive oil
- 3 cups unbromated, unbleached, organic flour
- 3 teaspoons sugar
- 2 teaspoons salt

1. Combine all ingredients and knead for 1 minute. Cover with plastic wrap and let rise for 2 hours.

2. Roll into 2–3" balls, spray with oil, cover with plastic wrap, and let rise for another 30 minutes.

3. Bake on a greased cookie sheet at 350°F for 30–45 minutes or until golden.

Peanut Butter and Jelly Day

Peanut butter jelly time! Peanut butter jelly time! Peanut butter jelly, peanut butter jelly! I love that Family Guy *song so much sometimes I'll call people just to sing it to them. I don't know if it's the song itself or the fact that I'm singing about peanut butter and jelly that just cracks people up. Doesn't really matter, does it? They're laughing and that's all that's important.*

PEANUT BUTTER AND JELLY MUFFINS

Makes 1 dozen

- ½ cup butter (soft)
- 1 cup granulated sugar
- 2 eggs
- Zest of 1 lemon
- 2 teaspoons vanilla
- ½ teaspoon salt
- 1 tablespoon baking powder
- 2 cups flour
- ¼ teaspoon nutmeg
- ½ cup whole milk
- ½ cup blueberries

Frosting

1 cup heavy cream (very cold!)

1 cup powdered sugar

1 (8-ounce) package of cream cheese (soft, at room temp)

1 cup peanut butter

Honey peanuts and chopped peanut butter cups for topping

❶ Cream butter and sugar for about 10 minutes until fluffy and pale. Add eggs one at a time, then add lemon zest and vanilla.

❷ Sift dry ingredients together and mix ½ into butter mixture. Add milk, then dry, then milk, then dry intermittently until all incorporated. Gently fold in blueberries.

❸ With an ice cream scoop, portion batter into greased and floured (or lined) muffin tins, sprinkle with raw sugar for a crunchy top, and bake at 375°F for 15–20 minutes until golden.

❹ While muffins bake, prepare frosting. Whip heavy cream until stiff, adding sugar a little at a time, and set aside. Whip cream cheese until fluffy, add peanut butter, and whip again until smooth.

❺ Fold half whipped cream mixture into peanut butter-cream cheese mixture. Then repeat with remaining cream.

❻ Frost cooled muffins and garnish with honey peanuts and chopped peanut butter cups.

Chocolate Mousse Day

APR. 3

When you want chocolate you want chocolate. Normally, you have just a few options: chocolate ice cream, chocolate cookies, chocolate cake, or, of course, brownies. However, a French addition that is now fairly common in the States is delicious, smooth, and light-as-air chocolate mousse. Simple and überdecadent, this recipe will become your best friend—when frozen, it turns into a parfait; when baked it becomes the infamous flourless molten lava cake!

LAVA MOUSSE

¾ cup plus 2 tablespoons unsalted butter

1¾ cups bittersweet chocolate (roughly chopped)

10 large eggs

½ cup granulated sugar (plus 2 tablespoons)

⅛ teaspoon cream of tartar

Pinch of salt

❶ Melt butter in microwave or on stove until hot and completely liquid. Place chocolate in a bowl, add hot butter, let sit for 2 minutes, then whisk until smooth.

❷ Separate eggs. In a clean bowl, combine yolks with 2 tablespoons sugar and beat on high for 5 minutes until light and fluffy. Transfer whipped yolks into a large bowl (this is where you'll make the whole mousse).

❸ Clean out bowl and beaters and dry both thoroughly so no trace of yolks remain (otherwise, whites won't fluff up). Beat egg whites on medium until just frothy.

4 Add cream of tartar and beat for 20 seconds on medium. Add ⅓ of sugar and continue to beat on medium for 1 minute, add ⅓ more and beat for another minute, add remaining sugar and beat on high until semistiff peaks form.

5 To assemble, get your trusty spatula and whisk. Add molten chocolate-butter mixture to the whipped yolks, add pinch of salt, and whisk until you see ribbons but the mixture is not completely smooth.

6 Add half of egg white mixture and fold together until almost homogeneous. Add remaining egg white mixture and fold in until smooth.

7 At this point, your mousse is done. You can either scoop into little molds and freeze, simply eat after setting in the refrigerator for at least 2 hours, or bake in 4–5 ounce ramekins at 350–400°F until the top is set (about 3–4 minutes).

APR. 4

Cordon Bleu Day

The history of Chicken Cordon Bleu goes back as far as the early 1600s. The term "Cordon Bleu" refers to a high-ranking order of French knights. Around the late 1950s in America, Chicken Kiev began to gain popularity. The dish consisted of thinly pounded chicken that was breaded and fried, and evolved into Veal Cordon Bleu, which consisted of thinly pounded veal that was breaded and fried. The first account of Chicken Cordon Bleu appeared as part of an advertisement for United Airlines in the New York Times.

CHICKEN CORDON BLEU

Serves 4

12 spears green asparagus

4 boneless and skinless chicken breasts

4 slices good smoked Virginia ham

8 slices Swiss cheese

8 slices roasted red pepper

Salt and black pepper

2 eggs

1 cup all-purpose flour

1 cup bread crumbs

1 cup vegetable oil

1 Start by peeling about 3" off bottom of the asparagus stem (the outer skin is really tough and doing this will leave stem tender).

2 Bring a quart of water to a boil, add a little salt then cook asparagus for 1 minute in boiling water. Prepare a bowl with ice and cold water, drop in asparagus, and shock to keep bright green.

3 Slice each chicken breast in half without cutting all the way through. Stuff middle with a slice of ham, cheese, 2 pieces of roasted red pepper, and 3 asparagus pieces.

4 Roll chicken breast, season with salt and pepper, then set up 3-bowl dredging station. In one bowl whisk eggs, set up flour in another, and bread crumbs in the third. Dip chicken roulades in flour, followed by the eggs and finishing with the bread crumbs.

5 In a deep skillet, heat oil to 350–375°F and fry roulades until golden and crispy. Finish with a slice of cheese on top as soon as it comes out of oil so it melts. Serve right away with a nice green salad.

Caramel Day

Caramel is the base for thousands of desserts, sauces, and liqueurs. Its dark, complex hue, accompanied by its deep sweetness and bitter zing, makes it the perfect accompaniment to most sweet foods. Creating perfect caramel is a high-wire act as you try to transform simple syrup without creating a burning cloud of disgusting smoke. It takes patience, speed, caution, and experience—but most of all it takes guts! The process is very similar to the process of making glass. Solid sugar crystals are exposed to high heat, which creates caramelization at around 340°F. I was taught to make caramel by keeping a bowl of ice water nearby so you can periodically dip a spoon into the caramel, then into the water to monitor the progression of the sugar from soft and clear to soft ball, hard candy, and finally caramel. You'll know you're done when the caramel is dark reddish brown, the color of a worn penny.

SALTED CARAMEL FLAN

Serves 4–5

1 cup sugar

Pinch of salt

1 14-ounce can condensed milk

1½ cups evaporated milk

6 egg yolks

1 egg white

1 teaspoon vanilla

❶ In a heavy pot, melt sugar over medium heat until it is a caramel. Pour into shallow oven-proof pan that is large enough to hold all liquid, leaving about ½" from the top. Sprinkle caramel with salt and allow to cool.

❷ Bring milks to a boil.

❸ Whisk eggs with vanilla. Temper eggs by adding a little milk at a time while whisking. This warms eggs up slowly and prevents them from turning into scrambled eggs.

❹ Pour mixture into pan with cooled caramel. Place this pan inside another pan that's deep enough to hold it. Fill outer pan with hot water so it reaches halfway up the custard pan.

❺ Cook at 350°F for 40 minutes until set.

❻ Remove from oven and let flan cool inside water bath. Remove and chill for at least 2 hours or, even better, overnight. Serve with a dollop of whipped cream.

Caramel Popcorn Day

When you think of popcorn lots of things come to mind, but the first thing that I think of is popcorn balls. I first saw them on a Christmas tree as ornaments, and it struck me that they could make really cool little presents! The best thing about them? You can basically make them with anything you want and then wrap 'em up in colorful paper. I mean, who doesn't love an edible gift?

CARAMEL POPCORN BALLS

Makes 1 dozen

½ cup popcorn kernels

Oil for popping

5 cups mini marshmallows

5 tablespoons unsalted butter (soft)

1 cup M&Ms

Salt

1. Pop popcorn in 5-quart pot by heating a little oil over medium heat then dropping the kernels inside, placing the lid on and shaking pan until they start to pop.

2. Cook for about 1 minute until popping subsides.

3. Remove from heat and set aside in a large bowl until cool.

4. Melt marshmallows in microwave, heating 30 seconds at a time until completely molten, then add butter and mix well.

5. Add marshmallows to popcorn and coat thoroughly. Add M&Ms and a large pinch of salt. Oil hands and form 3" balls with popcorn mixture.

6. Allow to cool for at least 20 minutes, then eat or wrap in colorful cellophane to gift!

Coffee Cake Day

Scandinavians are perhaps most responsible for the adaptation of modern coffee cake in America. Germans made a large imprint in early New York, New Jersey, and Delaware with their sweet and buttery baked breads and pastries, but it wasn't until the late eighteenth century that the term "Coffee Cake" really came into play. Before coffee cakes? There were tea cakes, of course, but as we all know, Europeans drink tea; Americans drink coffee!

CAPPUCCINO CAKE

Serves 6

1 pound butter (soft)

3 cups granulated sugar

1½ cups heavy cream (room temperature)

2 tablespoons instant coffee

1½ tablespoons baking powder

4½ cups all-purpose flour

½ teaspoon salt

6 eggs (room temperature)

1 tablespoon vanilla

Crumble Topping

½ cup butter (melted)

1½ cups all-purpose flour

½ cup light brown sugar

½ teaspoon salt

¼ teaspoon cinnamon

1. For cake, cream butter with sugar for at least 10 minutes until pale and fluffy.

2. Heat cream on the stove until warm and dissolve coffee into it. Cool to room temperature.

3. Sift dry ingredients.

4. Add eggs and flour intermittently to butter and sugar mixture, mixing to form a smooth batter. Add cream-coffee mixture, vanilla, and combine.

5. For crumble, melt butter, sift flour, and combine with remaining ingredients in a food processor. Mix well.

6. Pour cake batter into a 10–12" springform pan, top with crumble, and bake at 350°F for 40 minutes or until a toothpick comes out clean when inserted in the middle. Cool, then unmold from Springform pan. Serve with coffee, of course!

Empanada Day

Empanadas can be made in many different ways, but the basic categories are white flour or corn based, fried or baked. My favorites, of course, are fried ones since they produce a crisp crust and wonderfully moist center. When working with a wet filling, I find that corn-based empanadas, when fried, insulate better, which keeps the crust crunchy. The term comes from the Spanish verb empanar *loosely translated as "to coat in bread." Any way you translate it, it's* delicioso! *Here, I combine an American and Spanish classic to put a unique spin on a great little snack.*

MAC 'N' CHEESE EMPANADAS

Serves 8–10

2 cups chorizo (optional; cut into small chunks)

Large pot of water

Olive oil

2 teaspoons salt

1 stick butter

½ cup all-purpose flour

5 cups whole milk

½ pound American cheese (shredded)

½ pound Cheddar (shredded)

½ pound mozzarella cheese (shredded)

Salt and fresh ground pepper

1 pound macaroni

Empanada Dough

2½ cups masa arepa (corn flour)

2 cups warm water

Pinch of salt

Canola oil for frying

1. Cook chorizo in a pan over medium heat.

2. Bring large pot of water with salt and olive oil to a rapid boil for pasta.

3. Once chorizo is crispy, add butter and allow to melt, then add flour and cook while stirring for 1 minute. Add milk slowly while whisking continually until incorporated and you have a smooth, thick cream.

4. Add cheeses, salt, and pepper, and turn off heat. Mix everything together for cheese sauce.

5. Cook macaroni 5 minutes less than package instructions. (Or just bite a piece; if there's a speck of white, it's done.)

6. Drain pasta well and add to cheese sauce. Stir and chill for at least 30 minutes until completely cold.

7. To make empanadas, add flour to salted water slowly and work with your hands until dough is smooth. Cover and let rest for 5 minutes.

8. Roll out dough between two pieces of wax paper. Remove the top paper and place a scoop of chilled mac 'n' cheese in the middle, fold over, and seal using edge of a round plate that's about the same size as the circumference of empanada. Repeat process with remaining dough and pasta mixture.

9. In a deep skillet, heat about 2" of oil to 375°F and fry 2–3 empanadas until golden. Drain on paper towels and serve with lots of hot sauce.

Chinese Almond Cookie Day

APR. 9

Pichet Ong is a wonderfully gifted pastry chef who owns Spot in NYC, consults for many restaurants, and is the author of The Sweet Spot. *Here's an adaptation of his recipe for yummy almond treats.*

PICHET'S ALMOND COOKIES

Makes 2 dozen

1 cup unsalted butter (soft)

1 cup plus 2 tablespoons granulated sugar

1¾ cups all-purpose flour

½ teaspoon baking soda

1¼ cups almond flour

½ teaspoon salt

1 egg

1 egg white (beaten)

1 teaspoon almond extract

½ cup blanched sliced almonds

1. Cream butter with sugar until light and fluffy.

2. Sift dry ingredients, except for the almonds, and add to butter-sugar mixture.

3. Add eggs and remaining ingredients, thoroughly combine.

4. Spoon small dollops of batter onto a cookie sheet lined with parchment paper, top with a sprinkling of sliced almonds, and bake at 225°F for 15 minutes or until golden brown. Cool and enjoy!

Cinnamon Crescent Day

You know the cartoons in which the main character is sleeping in the middle of the night, and nearby there's a bakery that's making fresh bread, and the plume of sweet smells swirl into the characters bed right under their nose and lifts them out of bed? That's how I feel when I smell these puppies. It's like culinary fantasia. . . .

1. Combine lard (or shortening), ¼ cup sugar, milk, and butter in pot and cook over medium heat until sugar is dissolved. Pour into plastic container and chill in fridge until room temperature.

2. Combine water, 1 tablespoon sugar, and yeast in stand mixer bowl. Cover with plastic wrap and let foam for 5 minutes.

3. Add butter mixture to yeast and combine well. Slowly add eggs, followed by sifted flour and salt. Change to dough hook and increase speed to high. Knead for about 10 minutes until dough is a bit elastic and separates from bowl.

4. Spray bowl with oil, cover with plastic wrap, and allow dough to rise until it doubles in volume (about 1–2 hours in a room temp-warm place; normally, I'll rest in a turned-off oven or on the stovetop).

5. Once dough has risen, roll out on clean, lightly floured surface to size of a baking sheet. Using a sharp knife, cut dough in half horizontally, then cut both pieces in 10–12 triangles about 3" at wide end.

6. Sprinkle triangles with brown sugar, cinnamon, and salt. Starting from wide end, roll into crescent shape. Place on baking sheet lined with parchment paper or aluminum foil, leaving at least 1½" all around each.

7. Spray heavily with nonstick spray, cover rolls with plastic wrap, and let rise another hour. Sprinkle rolls with more sugar and cinnamon and bake at 350°F for 15–20 minutes until golden.

CINNAMON-SUGAR CRESCENT ROLLS

Makes 1 dozen rolls

¼ cup lard or vegetable shortening

¼ cup sugar plus 1 tablespoon (for yeast mixture)

1¼ cups whole milk

¾ cup unsalted butter

¼ cup water (warm, but no hotter than 110°F)

1 envelope active dry yeast

2 large eggs

5½ cups all-purpose flour

2 teaspoons salt

1 cup brown sugar

Cinnamon

Salt

Cheese Fondue Day

Fondue—fondu—literally means melted. This big pot of melty goodness is traditionally served in a large pot over a wick or candle to keep it warm. Forks that are teeny little yet überlong are used for dipping items in cheese or chocolate. Cheese fondues as we know them today originated in Neuchâtel, Switzerland, in the eighteenth century. However, melted pots of cheese are not exclusive to the Alps; there are similar dishes in Mexico (queso fundido) *and France* (raclette).

BEER CHEESE FONDUE

Serves 2–4

1 large shallot (2 tablespoons, finely chopped)

Olive oil

2 cups button mushrooms (½" cubes)

1 pound Swiss cheese

1 tablespoon cornstarch

1 cup Belgian beer (such as Hoegaarden)

1 teaspoon salt

Pinch of nutmeg

½ teaspoon white pepper

2 teaspoons dry sherry

2 tablespoons brandy (optional)

1 teaspoon fresh lemon juice

❶ In a stockpot, sauté shallots in olive oil with mushrooms over medium heat.

❷ Chop cheese into small cubes, then toss in bowl with cornstarch.

❸ Once mushrooms are soft, add beer, and cheese mixture. Whisk continually until everything is melted.

❹ Turn off heat, and add salt, nutmeg, pepper, sherry, brandy, and lemon juice. Whisk fast until it is a homogenous, sticky, and shiny pot of incredibly amazing fondue. (If you have a handheld electric beater, use it here).

❺ Serve with toast points, strawberries, crostini, pita chips, or any kind of fruit or bread.

Grilled Cheese Sandwich Day

I'm not going to attempt to trace the history of grilled cheese, because man has been eating bread and cheese in some form or another for millennia. Instead, let's keep things simple by making a grilled cheese sandwich with a runny yolk inside. Enjoy!

ONE-EYED JACK

Serves 1

2 slices white bread

Butter (soft)

2 slices American cheese (or jack cheese for an authentic One-Eyed Jack!)

1 egg

Salt and pepper

❶ Coat bread with butter, then make sandwich with cheese. Using a 1½–2" ring, cut a hole in middle of sandwich.

Cheese Fondue Day, April 11

② Add pat of butter to skillet over medium-high heat. Let butter melt and place sandwich in skillet with mini sandwich aside it so both cook at same time.

③ Break an egg so yolk falls in the hole.

④ Season with salt and pepper and cook on each side for about 2 minutes or until golden, flip and cook until golden on other side. Serve immediately!

① Melt butter in microwave then add milk, cream, and vanilla.

② In another bowl, sift flour and baking powder. Make a well in the middle of flour and add the sugar, salt, and milk mixture. Mix slowly until a batter forms.

③ Rub a 9" loaf pan with butter and dust with flour. Pour in batter and plop sliced peaches all around. Sprinkle with a little more sugar and bake for 40–50 minutes at 350°F.

④ Serve warm with vanilla ice cream.

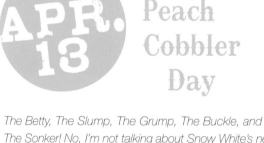

APR. 13 — Peach Cobbler Day

The Betty, The Slump, The Grump, The Buckle, and The Sonker! No, I'm not talking about Snow White's new dwarfs, I'm talking about the varieties of cobblers in the States. They range from stovetop styles to cakelike, but they are always more akin to a biscuit than a crisp. Characterized by a layer of batter that rises around the fruit, you can spot a beautiful cobbler by its golden crust.

PEACH COBBLER

Serves 4–6

8 tablespoons butter

1 cup milk

½ cup heavy cream

1 teaspoon vanilla

1½ cups all-purpose flour

½ teaspoon baking powder

1¼ cups sugar

Pinch of salt

3 cups canned sliced peaches

Pecan Day — APR. 14

The sweet representative of the South and the national tree of Texas, the pecan is the delicious fruit of the pecan tree. Stemming from the Algonquin word for "requiring a stone to crack," the nut is a sibling to the hickory. The love for this native son is so strong that Mississippi, Alabama, Illinois, Arizona, and Texas are some of the many states that have a pecan festival every year!

PECAN FUDGE

Serves 4–5

2–3 quart pot of water

1 (14-ounce) can condensed milk

1½ cups bittersweet chocolate (chopped)

4 tablespoons butter

2 cups chopped pecans

Coarse salt

Cook's Note

Be extra careful not to pierce or open the can after you've cooked it for that long. Pressure builds up inside, and when opened, it will splatter hot liquid all over the place!

1. Fill a 2–3 quart pot with water, remove peel from milk can, and cook in boiling water for 1½ hours. Remove from heat, and chill in cold water for 30 minutes.

2. After can has cooled, open, and empty into microwave-safe bowl. Heat in the microwave slowly until hot, add chocolate, and stir until it dissolves. Add butter and 1½ cups chopped pecans.

3. Line a 12" x 12" pan with plastic wrap and pour the fudge inside. Sprinkle remaining pecans on top and sprinkle liberally with salt. Refrigerate until hard, about half an hour. Chop into 1" pieces and serve. Keep chilled.

1. Blend 1 cup maple syrup with garlic and Dijon. Coat entire ham with mixture, getting inside all those little slices.

2. Cover every inch of ham with bacon. Use toothpicks if there are unsecured slices.

3. Bake in roasting pan at 300°F for 1 hour, then glaze with the remaining maple syrup. Cover with pineapple slices and cherries using toothpicks to hold in place. Turn heat up to 350°F and cook until golden, about 10–15 minutes.

4. Serve with juices on the side in a gravy boat.

Glazed– Spiral Ham Day

Ham is much celebrated for its versatility, buttery flavor, and salty decadence. Spiral ham—either salt-cured or smoked—makes a perfect holiday dish. Traditionally roasted, we did it up big-time with this one, covering the entire thing with bacon. Yes, I said bacon. A whole package of bacon. Go on, you know you want to make it.

HAWAIIAN SPIRAL HAM

Serves 1 big, happy family of 4–5

1½ cups maple syrup

¼ cup garlic (chopped)

½ cup Dijon mustard

1 8-pound spiral ham

1 package bacon

1 (20-ounce) can pineapple rings

10–12 maraschino cherries

Eggs Benedict Day

APR. 16

As far as I'm concerned, brunch is the one meal where you are always allowed to go nuts. It's the only time where a drink before noon is not only the custom—it's encouraged! Let's set the scene: You just woke up, haven't eaten in 8 hours, and probably regretting that last drink from the night before. Your body if famished and in dire need of food. Enter eggs Benedict, a sweet combo of buttered English muffin, topped with ham and poached, runny eggs, and then smothered with a warm, whipped, tangy, heaven-sent sauce . . . hollandaise.

EGGS BENEDICT SLIDERS

Serves 4–6

1 Simple Burgers recipe (Dec. 21), divide into 8 portions

2 teaspoons white vinegar

8 eggs

4 English muffins

8 slices Canadian bacon

Fresh parsley (finely chopped)

Secret Hollandaise

4 egg yolks

1 tablespoon fresh lemon juice

½ cup unsalted butter (melted)

⅛ teaspoon cayenne

3 tablespoons ketchup

Pinch of salt and pepper

1½ tablespoons pickle relish

❶ To make hollandaise, whisk egg yolks with lemon juice in a metal bowl on high until doubled in volume and fluffy, about 5 minutes.

❷ Bring pot of water to a slight simmer and place bowl with fluffy yolks on top. Whisk continuously for 30 seconds, then drizzle in melted butter. Continue to whisk until sauce is thick. Remove from heat; mix in cayenne, ketchup, salt and pepper, and relish to taste.

❸ Cover and set aside in a warm place.

❹ Prepare Simple Burgers, then eggs. Fill skillet with at least 2" of water, add white vinegar, and bring to a slight simmer over medium heat.

❺ Gently break eggs into separate small cups or bowls and season with salt and pepper. Slowly and gently drop eggs into water and cook for 3½ minutes. Using a slotted spoon, remove eggs and drain on paper towels.

❻ To assemble, split English muffins and toast. Heat ham slices in a skillet or in the microwave. Place 1 burger on top of English muffin half, top with 2 eggs, 1 slice of ham, and finish with a good tablespoon of the hollandaise. Assemble remaining sliders, garnish with parsley, and serve immediately.

Cheeseball Day

If you're wondering whether I'm talking about addictive, crispy little orange fluorescent balls of cheesy fun or those Cracker Barrel balls of creamy spreadable cheese, know that these fall into a different category altogether. I created my Cheeseballs back when I was looking to pair a martini with something really cool, and came across Bocconcini. Bocconcini are little balls of fresh mozzarella. I know, exactly! Cheeseballs! Here I marinate them, toss them in bread crumbs, and fry 'em up crispy on the outside, melted on the inside.

BOCCO BALLS

Serves 4

1 pound bocconcini

2 cups flour

4 eggs (beaten)

3 cups bread crumbs

❶ Toss bocconcini in flour, then toss in eggs, then bread crumbs.

❷ Fry until golden and drain on paper towels.

❸ Serve nice and hot! (Don't forget the hot marinara sauce on the side.)

Animal Crackers Birthday

It wasn't until 1902—when they took the name of "Barnum's Animals" and got those cool little circus boxes—that Animal Crackers achieved their awesome status. But are they crackers or cookies? Well, in the States, cookies are normally sweet and crackers are salty. So the whole animal crackers thing is a misnomer—a sweet, delicious, and fun misnomer. But don't take my word for it. According to Merriam-Webster, an Animal Cracker is "a small cookie in the shape of an animal." Read it and weep.

GINORMOUS ANIMAL CRACKERS POPS

Makes about 2 dozen

1 cup unsalted butter (soft)

1 cup sugar

3 cups all-purpose flour

1 teaspoon baking soda

2 large eggs

1 teaspoon pure vanilla extract

Zest of 1 lemon

2 dozen Popsicle sticks

Royal Icing

2 egg whites

3 cups powdered sugar (sifted)

1 teaspoon lemon juice

① Cream butter and sugar until fluffy.

② Sift dry ingredients and add to butter mixture along with eggs. Mix in vanilla and lemon zest and form into dough.

③ Wrap dough into a block and refrigerate for at least 2 hours.

④ Roll dough to ¼" thickness on a clean, well-floured surface and cut into animal shapes of various sizes.

⑤ Position cookies with plenty of space between them on cookie sheet lined with parchment paper, then stick one popsicle stick halfway into each cookie.

⑥ Bake at 350°F for about 8 minutes. Allow to cool and decorate with icing.

7. To make Royal Icing, combine all the ingredients and mix well until it forms a smooth paste. Make icing as thick as batter.

8. Frost cookies, dry, and finish with the black icing (which you want a little thicker) for the eyes and mouth. This is easy when you pipe it from a little cone made with parchment paper.

1. Combine all ingredients except bread and olive oil in food processor and blend.

2. Slather loaf with garlic-butter mixture.

3. Roast in an oven at 350°F for 6–10 minutes until golden brown.

4. Drizzle with olive oil and serve warm.

APR. 19 — Garlic Day

From its amazing health properties (it kills more than 23 types of bacteria) to its mystical aura and ethereal flavor, Garlic is truly the food of the Gods! So awesome is this little Alliaceae that archeologists even found garlic sculptures in a tomb dating back to 3200 B.C. In America, garlic wasn't as loved as it is today because people were turned off by the halitosis it created. It wasn't until the nineteenth century with the huge influx of immigrants that garlic really gained its rightful place in America's kitchen. And the rest, as they say, is glorious history!

GARLIC BREAD

Serves 3–4

10 garlic cloves

Handful fresh parsley

1 cup Parmesan cheese

1 cup butter (softened)

1 long Italian or French loaf (sliced lengthwise)

Olive oil for drizzling

Pineapple Upside-Down Cake Day — APR. 20

What came first? Canned pineapple rings and maraschino cherries, or the Pineapple Upside-Down Cake? Rewind to 1493, when Christopher Columbus visits the Caribbean, finds pineapples, and brings them back to England, describing them as having the exterior of a pine cone and the flesh of an apple. Pineapple is imported to the States, mostly shipped dried or in syrup. Around 1925, recipes start popping up for in newspapers across America, but as to who first decided to line the bottom of a pan with luscious tangy fruit, we may never know. . . .

PINEAPPLE-MANGO UPSIDE-DOWN CAKE

4 tablespoons unsalted butter

¾ cup light brown sugar

1 fresh pineapple (peeled, cored, and sliced into ¼" rings)

1 mango (peeled, sliced ¼" thick)

Pinch of salt

Cake Batter

½ cup butter (soft)

1 cup granulated sugar

¼ teaspoon salt

1 teaspoon vanilla extract

2 large eggs (separated)

1½ cups all purpose flour

2 teaspoons baking powder

½ cup buttermilk

¼ teaspoon cream of tartar

1. Combine butter and sugar in a sauté pan and cook over medium heat until caramel starts to form. Swirl pan slowly. Using a wooden spoon, mix caramel until thick and smooth. Turn off heat and pour caramel into a greased 10–12" round cake pan.

2. Arrange fruit in caramel so it's overlapping, sprinkle with salt, and set aside.

3. To make cake, cream butter with sugar and salt and add vanilla and yolks, setting whites aside.

4. Sift dry ingredients. Add flour along with buttermilk to butter-sugar mixture, alternating between the two until you have a smooth batter and stopping halfway to scrape the bowl to incorporate any stuck bits.

5. Set batter aside and whip whites with cream of tartar in a clean bowl with clean beaters. Whip the whites to stiff peaks, then fold into cake batter in two batches.

6. Pour batter atop pineapple and mango and bake at 350°F for 30–45 minutes until a knife inserted in middle comes out clean. Carefully invert pan on top of nice plate and serve.

Chocolate-Covered Cashew Truffle Day

APR. 21

This is one holiday I wasn't quite sure what to do with. It's pretty straightforward, it just wasn't clicking for me— until it totally did. I simply combined shredded coconut with softened cashews before adding a touch of honey to create a paste. Pop in the fridge, and voilà, my truffle filling. Add chocolate and it's done. Simple!

CASHEW TRUFFLES

Makes 2 dozen

- 1 cup toasted cashews (finely chopped)
- 1 cup toasted cashews (soaked in water for 1 hour)
- 1 cup shredded unsweetened coconut
- 3 tablespoons honey (you may need a little more or less depending on if the coconut is sweetened or not)
- 1 cup dark chocolate (melted)

❶ In food processor, pulse unsoaked cashews until coarse, place in bowl and set aside.

❷ Drain nuts that have been soaking and combine in food processor with coconut until you have a cornmeal-thick paste. Add honey little by little until a smooth paste forms. Remove from processor, form into ball, cover with plastic wrap and refrigerate for 30 minutes.

❸ When hard, break into small balls and refrigerate again until hard.

❹ Coat balls with the melted chocolate one at a time then toss in nut mixture. Refrigerate until hard about 20 minutes. Serve cold.

Earth Day

APR. 22

Mother Earth has been taking a beating. Over-farming, over-fishing, and lack of respect are the main culprits. The scary thing is that dead earth = no more food, and no more food = no more us. So what can you do? Be conscious, plant a tree, plant an herb garden. Plant something that you can eat. I know eating healthily can get expensive, but by growing your own veggies you not only help clean the air, but you can decrease your shopping bill by up to 20 percent! Or, simply bake this sweet cake as a reminder of the beautiful planet we live on.

MOTHER EARTH CAKE

Serves 6–8

- Buttery Pound Cake (Mar. 4)

Sweet Dream Butter Cream

- 10 egg whites
- 15 ounces granulated sugar
- 2½ pounds butter (unsalted and soft)
- Green food coloring
- Blue food coloring

Cook's Note

Take two Ziploc bags or piping bags with small tips and use these to frost the cake.

❶ In a clean, dry bowl whip egg whites. Once foamy, add sugar gradually. Whip on high speed for about 10 minutes.

❷ Add butter one stick at a time then whip on high again. Whip for another 10 minutes until you have beautiful butter cream.

3. Scoop half butter cream into another bowl. Add blue to one bowl and green to another. Now you have the earth and the water to frost cake.

4. Prepare pound cake, but bake it in a metal bowl to resemble the earth. When cool and ready to frost, print an image of the globe. Cut out land parts and place on cake with tooth-picks. Trace using green piping bag, then remove template and fill everything in. Do the same with the water part, but fill in with blue. Enjoy your half-globe cake with a big glass of organic milk.

Cherry Cheesecake Day

Doesn't this sound incredible? Sweet and tart cherries crowning a timbale of light, creamy, semisalty cheese-cake, all swirled around with a viscous and vibrant red glaze. It makes me want to go to the nearest bakery, buy one, ask for a fork, and eat straight out of the box. I've been known to find creative ways of covering up the gaping hole I leave when I can't wait and dig into that night's dessert. (But if they didn't want me to taste until I got home, why didn't they wrap it a little better?)

CHERRYLICIOUS CHEESECAKE

Serves 6–8

Italian-American Cheesecake (July 30)

1 cup cherry juice or cranberry juice

½ lemon (juiced)

1 cup granulated sugar

1 tablespoon cornstarch

2 cups fresh or frozen cherries (pitted)

1. Prepare cheesecake.

2. Mix and bring all remaining ingredients to a boil. Cook until thickened, about 3 minutes, then chill. Top cake with cherry topping and serve.

Pigs-in-a-Blanket Day

All-American favorites require time and preparation. They require plan-ning and dedication. And then there are hot dogs. What's easier than boiling hot dogs and putting them in a steamed bun? Why not wrap the dog—that way, they're ready to go as soon as they come out of the oven? I decided to change them up a bit here with Bears in a Blanket since I love Chicago-style dogs, and their football team, of course, is Da Bears! These have all the Chicago fixings inside the warm snuggly blanket.

BEARS IN A BLANKET

Makes about 2 dozen bears

Cinnamon-Sugar Crescent Dough, sans cinnamon, (or use Pillsbury, that stuff's great!) (Apr. 10)

24 cocktail wieners

½ cup mustard

6 small pickles (gherkins or cornishons, quartered)

4 small red peppers (sliced into thin rings)

1 cup (8 ounces) mozzarella (cut into small, thick sticks)

Poppy seeds

❶ Roll out dough, fill with cocktail wiener, a little mustard, pickle, a slice of red pepper, and cheese.

❷ Roll up Bear, sprinkle with poppy seeds, set out on a lightly greased cookie sheet, and bake at 375°F until golden. Serve with mustard.

Zucchini Bread Day

This is one of those recipes that turned out amazing by complete accident. I made a carrot cake but subbed out the carrots and forgot the sugar. When deciding what else to add I came across Parmesan cheese and eureka! It turned out great! I also forgot the rest of the egg whites, which led me to make a denser bread but one that's extremely flavorful with a wonderful crumbly texture. Bright green and full of olive oil, it tastes even better the next day.

ZUCCHINI BREAD

Serves 6–8

3½ cups all-purpose flour

1½ teaspoons baking soda

1½ teaspoons baking powder

2½ cups grated zucchini

3 eggs, separated

1½ teaspoon salt

¼ cup granulated sugar

1½ cups grated Parmesan

1 teaspoon dried oregano

1 tablespoon olive oil

❶ Sift flour, baking soda, and baking powder.

❷ Combine zucchini and yolks. Whip egg whites until soft peaks form and put aside.

❸ Add zucchini mixture to flour mixture, then add salt, sugar, Parmesan, and oregano.

❹ Mix everything slowly with your hands until it starts to turn thick, then add oil little by little until all incorporated.

❺ Add egg whites to dough and mix in well.

❻ Bake in 12" cake pan so dough is only 1" thick.

❼ Bake at 350°F until golden, for about 30 minutes. Invert onto wire rack and cool. This bread tastes better the next day!

Pretzel Day

American pretzels came to be around the eighteenth century with the arrival of a large German immigrant population (the German name "brezel" comes from the Latin "bracchiola" meaning little arms). When they landed in Philadelphia, the Pennsylvania Dutch set up shop selling these salty marvels from street carts and later, in 1861, established America's first commercial pretzel bakery. In 1993, the pretzel museum officially opened in the City of Brotherly Love to honor the humble pretzel's delicious contribution to food history.

EVERYTHING PRETZELS

Makes 1 dozen

2 teaspoons dried yeast

1½ cups warm water

1 tablespoon sugar

4½ cups all-purpose flour

1½ tablespoon salt

2½ tablespoons butter (melted)

Nonstick spray

4 quarts water

½ cup baking soda

2 eggs (beaten)

½ cup "Everything Mix" (poppy seeds, salt, sesame seeds, and dried coarse garlic)

1 Mix yeast with warm water and sugar in a bowl. Cover with plastic wrap and allow yeast to hydrate and rise for 10 minutes.

2 Sift flour and add to yeast mixture along with salt and melted butter. Mix with dough hook for 5 minutes. Cover with plastic and let rise for 1 hour in warm place.

3 After dough has risen, roll into a 3" thick log. Cut dough into 1½" pieces. Spray two baking sheets with nonstick spray. Roll dough pieces out and shape into pretzels.

4 Bring water and baking soda to a boil. Drop one pretzel at a time and cook for 15 seconds on each side. After blanched (partially cooked in boiling liquid), brush pretzels with eggs and sprinkle with "Everything Mix."

5 Cook at 400°F until golden brown.

Prime Rib Day

Steak is the reason my Mom doesn't let me cook in her house anymore. As a matter of fact, I can't think of any place I've ever lived where I haven't set off the smoke alarm when attempting to get a thick, black crust on my steak. See, in my steak book, there are rules. Super-high heat creates smoke and a beautiful scar; short time yields a nice rare and juicy steak. Of course, this depends on the cut of meat, but in this case it's just perfect.

PRIME RIB CHIMICHURRI

Serves 4–6

⅛ cup minced shallots

6 garlic cloves

2 tablespoons Dijon mustard

½ tablespoon salt

3 tablespoons mixed whole peppercorns (coarsely crushed)

⅛ cup fresh parsley

1 9-pound prime rib beef roast (about 4 ribs)

Chimichurri Sauce

1 cup fresh parsley (packed)

4 whole garlic cloves

½ cup olive oil

⅛ cup white vinegar

½ lemon squeezed

¾ teaspoon dried crushed red pepper

½ teaspoon ground cumin

½ teaspoon salt

Pinch of pepper

❶ In a blender, combine shallots, garlic, mustard, salt, pepper, and parsley. Coat prime rib all around and set in a roasting pan, fat-side up.

❷ Roast at 450°F for 15 minutes, then lower heat to 350°F, cover pan in foil and cook for 2 hours. Remove roast when it reaches an internal temperature of 125°F.

❸ Let roast rest for 10 minutes.

❹ Prepare Chimichurri Sauce by blending all ingredients together until smooth.

❺ To serve, cut prime rib and top with sauce.

Blueberry Pie Day

Nothing says American like blueberry pie. Well, maybe apple pie, but not really, because apples trees originated in Asia (brought to the United States by colonists in the 1600s) and blueberries are native to the States. When I think of blueberry pie, I think of the '50s, when the perfect-picture American home had a white picket fence and an open window with a pie cooling on the sill. Creating a great blueberry pie comes down to two things: a lot of great blueberries and a nice flaky crust. That's it! Well, maybe a dollop of vanilla ice cream for kicks. . . .

VINTAGE BLUEBERRY PIE

Serves 5–6

Pie Dough

1 cup and 2 tablespoons all-purpose flour

½ cup great-quality imported salted butter (like Lescure or Plugra)

2 tablespoons cold water

Filling

5 cups fresh blueberries

1 tablespoon cornstarch

2 tablespoons powdered sugar

❶ In a large bowl, sift flour and add butter in small chunks.

❷ Break up butter and rub it into flour with your fingertips. When you have a crumbly texture (about 2 minutes) add cold water and knead until a nice dough forms.

3 Dust your clean counter and rolling pin with a little flour and roll out dough about ¼" thick and 1" thicker than your pie shell.

4 Roll dough onto rolling pin and place on top of pie pan. Press dough into the sides so all walls of pan are covered. Place pan in fridge for 5 minutes.

5 Using a serrated knife, slice along top edge, using lip of pan as your guide until neat and smooth all around.

6 In another bowl, toss blueberries with cornstarch and sugar and fill pie shell.

7 Bake at 350°F for 45 minutes, or until pie is bubbling and crust is golden brown. Cool slightly and serve with Homemade Vanilla Ice Cream (July 23).

APR.
29
Shrimp
Scampi Day

According to the Merriam-Webster Dictionary, Scampi, comes "from the Italian word Scampo, a small European lobster, also known as Langoustine or Dublin prawn." Traditionally served fresh with a garlic-butter-white wine sauce, this dish is a simple classic that has now evolved to mean the style in which the dish is prepared, as supposed to the ingredient itself. Here, "Shrimp Scampi" is normally found on Italian-American menus and traditionally served with pasta. However, keep in mind that scampi is now mostly the style in which the dish is prepared as the Italian word for shrimp is actually gamberi *or* gamberetti.

SHRIMP SCAMPI

Serves 4

1 pound linguine (1 pound = 16 ounces)

3 tablespoons olive oil

4 tablespoons butter

1 pound large shrimp (peeled and deveined)

Salt and pepper

Garlic powder

5 cloves garlic (minced)

⅛ teaspoon hot red pepper flakes

½ tablespoon dried oregano

Juice of 2 lemons plus zest of ½ lemon

Splash of white wine

¼ cup fresh parsley (chopped)

1 Boil pasta in salted water with a little olive oil. Meanwhile, prepare sauce.

2 In skillet big enough to hold cooked pasta and shrimp, add olive oil and 2 tablespoons butter. Heat on medium-high heat and melt until sizzling.

3 Season shrimp with salt, pepper, and garlic powder.

4 Add garlic to butter and cook for 30 seconds (don't allow to brown). Add shrimp and sauté 30 seconds on each side.

5 Add hot pepper flakes, oregano, lemon juice and zest, and white wine, and crank heat to high. Cook for 1 minute, then turn off heat and add parsley (save some for garnish).

6 Keep an eye on pasta and cook until just al dente. Transfer pasta into skillet, making sure to include some pasta water. Return to stove and crank heat to high. Cook for 30 seconds to a minute until sauce is thick and pasta is cooked al dente.

7 Remove from heat and add remaining butter. Stir until sauce is smooth, serve immediately, and garnish with remaining parsley and lemon wedges.

Cook's Note

I usually try to make sure there's enough shrimp to go around, so figure 4–5 shrimp per person.

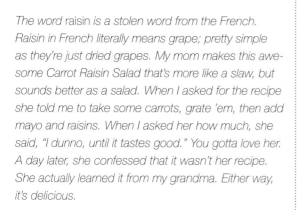

Raisin Day

The word raisin is a stolen word from the French. Raisin in French literally means grape; pretty simple as they're just dried grapes. My mom makes this awesome Carrot Raisin Salad that's more like a slaw, but sounds better as a salad. When I asked for the recipe she told me to take some carrots, grate 'em, then add mayo and raisins. When I asked her how much, she said, "I dunno, until it tastes good." You gotta love her. A day later, she confessed that it wasn't her recipe. She actually learned it from my grandma. Either way, it's delicious.

MOM'S (OR GRANDMA'S) CARROT RAISIN SALAD

Serves 3

3 cups freshly grated carrots

½ cup mayonnaise

½ teaspoon salt

3 teaspoons white vinegar

1 cup golden raisins

1 Combine ingredients and allow to marinate at least 2 hours, or overnight if you can.

2 I like eating between two pieces of toasted rye bread.

MAY

Chocolate Parfait Day

This dessert is just perfect—Parfait means "perfect" in French. But while we borrow the word from the French, American parfait couldn't be further from theirs. Ours consists of a tall glass filled with ice cream or pudding and whipped cream with the addition of any other ingredients you want to add for texture or plain-old fun. Growing up, I remember snack time at my neighbor's house where my friend's mom would serve warm chocolate pudding. I love pudding warm, probably because I can't wait for it to chill, but this gave me an idea for a warm parfait. Enjoy!

CHOCOLATE PUDDING

Serves 4

3 cups whole milk

½ cup granulated sugar

4 tablespoons cornstarch

4 ounces bittersweet chocolate

½ teaspoon vanilla extract

Pinch of salt

❶ Bring 2½ cups milk and sugar to a boil stirring constantly to avoid burning to bottom of pan.

❷ Combine remaining ½ cup milk with cornstarch and whisk together.

❸ Once milk has boiled, add cornstarch slurry while whisking continually. Keep whisking over medium-high heat for 3 minutes.

❹ Turn off heat and add chocolate. Whisk until chocolate has been incorporated, add vanilla and salt and serve immediately topped with a dollop of Perfect Chantilly Cream (Jan. 5) and chocolate shavings.

Truffles Day

Truffles are little magical tubers that grow in fairyland. They're actually what you find at the end of the rainbow instead of a pot of gold. I'm kidding, of course, but they are so rare that eighteenth-century French gourmet Brillat Savarin called them "The Diamonds of the Kitchen." They come in two varieties: white are summer truffles; black are winter truffles. You may also be familiar with the "chocolate" variety—the candy was named for its resemblance to the tuber! I love truffles on pizza, and my favorite time to chow down on pizza? The morning.

BREAKFAST PIZZA

Serves 2–3

Pizza dough recipe (Sep. 5; or buy from your local pizzeria)

1 cup robiola, taleggio, or another soft creamy cheese like Camembert

1 small truffle

1 cup mozzarella cheese (shredded)

1 medium portabella mushroom (thinly sliced)

2 eggs

Dried oregano for sprinkling

Olive oil (or truffle oil) for drizzling

❶ This pizza, like most pizza, is super simple. Warm your oven to 450°F for at least 15–20 minutes. Stretch your dough and set it on your lightly floured paddle. Top with the sliced taleggio or robiola cheese, followed by thin slices of truffle and top with mozzarella.

❷ Sprinkle portabella slices all around the top. Then to the oven. Place tip of paddle at the far end of the pizza stone. Lightly tap the paddle on the stone, then in one swift motion, slide the pizza onto stone.

❸ Bake for about 12–15 minutes, but at the 11-minute mark, crack oven door and break eggs in the middle of the pizza. Cook until eggs are set, about 3–4 minutes.

❹ Remove pizza from the oven, sprinkle with oregano, and drizzle with olive oil. Serve immediately.

Raspberry Tart Day

Eating a fresh, wild raspberry that is slightly warm from the morning sun is something of an epiphany. Delicate, tart, a bit jammy, and slightly toothsome from the petite seeds that are left on your tongue after you have pressed them against the roof of your mouth and crushed them. Your brain is telling you to chew but your mouth knows better. Wild varieties are available in different colors during summer months because of advance farming methods, and with wonderful transportation they can be now be enjoyed year-round. But I still prefer them under the summer sun.

RASPBERRY LEMON TART

Serves 4

½ 17-ounce package puff pastry (1 sheet)

Pastry Cream (Feb. 20)

Zest of 1 lemon and juice of ½ lemon

½ cup raspberry jam

2–3 pints fresh raspberries

Powdered sugar and fresh mint for garnish

❶ Cook puff pastry inside tart shell according to package instructions and cool.

❷ In the meantime, make Pastry Cream, cool, then add lemon zest and lemon juice and mix to combine.

❸ Spread bottom of tart with raspberry jam, then layer pastry cream. Smooth and top with fresh raspberries (little hole facing down). Dust with powdered sugar and garnish with mint sprig. Serve with fresh whipped cream or whipped Devonshire cream.

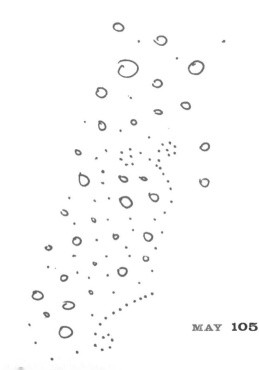

Homebrew Day

Every man has two things he wants to do in life: Ride a bull and brew his own beer. So I recently ordered a Brooklyn Brew Shop kit (Brooklynbrewshop.com) which had everything I needed to make beer. Then I realized I had no idea what I was doing! So I booked a class to see Erica Shea and Stephen Valand in action. What I learned was awesome! It's not hard, but it is a lengthy process. I suggest checking out the website, ordering one of their beer kits, and then sitting back and watching their video. In the meantime, to hold you over, here's Grammy's Beer Sauce that's great on everything from chicken to steaks and so much more!

GRAMMY'S BEER SAUCE

2 cups

1 12-ounce bottle homebrewed beer (flat)

½ cup honey

½ cup brown sugar (tightly packed)

¾ cup chili sauce (Heinz)

Juice of 1 lemon

1–2 tablespoons Worcestershire sauce

❶ In a medium saucepan, combine all ingredients and stir over medium heat for several minutes until mixture thickens a bit.

❷ Taste and add more chili sauce or Worcestershire if too sweet; if not sweet enough, add more honey or sugar and stir for a minute longer.

❸ Cool slightly and use as a marinade for chicken or beef. Reserve ½ for dipping and drizzling!

Cinco de Mayo

That means fifth of May in Spanish, so happy May 5 to you! But what is Cinco de Mayo? Contrary to popular belief, Cinco de Mayo is not Mexican independence day; it actually commemorates the David and Goliath story of a small Mexican army defeating the large French army at the battle of Puebla on May 5, 1862. It is a beautiful tale that brings us lots of tacos, margaritas, and piñatas!

SKIRT STEAK QUESADILLAS

Serves 4

1 pound skirt steak

2–3 tablespoons cumin

Salt and pepper

1 red pepper (sliced)

1 medium Spanish onion (sliced)

1 pound (16 ounces) Oaxaca or mozzarella cheese (shredded)

Flour tortillas (burrito-size wraps are perfect)

Salsa Verde

½ cup sour cream

⅛ cup fresh parsley or cilantro

2 garlic cloves

Monkey Sauce

½ cup sour cream

2 chipotles in adobo (from a can, found in Spanish section of supermarket)

❶ Season steak with cumin, salt, and pepper. Over the grill or in a grill pan, sear steak for 2–3 minutes on each side, remove from pan and set aside.

Cinco de Mayo, May 5

2 In sauté pan or in same grill pan, cook peppers and onions over high heat until caramelized and slightly charred, then set aside with steak.

3 Slice steak into thin strips and return to pepper and onion mixture with and juices leftover from rested meat, then toss all together.

4 Heat grill pan to high. Fill one tortilla at a time with some pepper-steak mixture and top with shredded cheese. Fold quesadilla so cheese rests on top of meat.

5 Cook on meat side first for 1–2 minutes (this will give cheese ample time to melt from the heat of the meat, but you're really looking for those little grill marks). Flip and cook on cheese side until you hear sizzling from cheese seeping onto the grill pan.

6 Make sauces by simply blending the ingredients together. Rinse the blender and blend the second sauce till smooth. Serve right away or keep warm in oven until ready to serve.

Crepes Suzette Day

The crepe is a Breton invention, but Crepes Suzette have a royal origin. Apparently, a fourteen-year-old assistant was making dessert for the Prince of Wales, and accidentally ignited it with Grand Marnier liqueur. When he tasted it, he declared it a magical combination—the kiss of flames was exactly what the dish needed. When served to the prince, they boy presented it as Crepes Princesse in honor of his lady companion. The prince asked the boy if he would

change it to Crepes Suzette, as his lady companion was named. The boy baptized his creation as such, and an incredible dish was born.

Cook's Note

If you don't have a gas burner, just ignite with any sort of lighter. But make sure your face is not right on top of the pan unless you're holding a grudge against your eyebrows and have been plotting to get them back somehow.

CREPES SUZETTE

Serves 4–5

Crepes (Feb. 6; omit banana and Nutella)

Pastry Cream (Feb. 20) chilled or Vanilla Pudding (May 22)

3 oranges (peeled and segmented)

½ cup granulated sugar

½ cup butter (soft)

½ cup Grand Marnier

1 tablespoon orange juice

1 Prepare Crepe batter and let rest, overnight if possible, but for at least 1 hour. Make Crepes. Make Pastry Cream and chill well.

2 Heat nonstick sauté pan over medium-high heat. In the meantime, fill as many crepes as possible each with 2 tablespoons Pastry Cream and a few orange segments, then fold twice into quarter circles.

3 Fill a bowl with the granulated sugar and place crepes in one at a time to coat completely.

4 Once pan is hot and starts smoking, add 1 tablespoon butter. Add a few crepes so you fill pan, but don't overcrowd. Sauté while moving pan back and forth until sugar starts to caramelize. Once caramelized on one side, flip crepes and repeat on other side, adding a little more butter to pan.

5. Once second side is caramelized (take a spoon and lift one side of crepe to check), add 3 tablespoons Grand Marnier to pan.

6. Carefully tilt pan away from you until outer lip almost touches the flame and liqueur ignites. While the crepes are still in the pan, add 1 tablespoon orange juice, ½ tablespoon butter, and a few more orange segments to pan. Swirl pan to make a sauce.

7. Serve crepes immediately with sauce and cold whipped cream. Repeat entire process with remaining crepes, making sure to clean out pan in between batches. If you want to serve hot, simply keep warm in a 225°F oven until you have all the crepes you need.

Roast Leg of Lamb Day

MAY 7

Lamb is one of the most aromatic and gamey meats in the world, prized for its exotic aroma and hearty taste. Lamb refers to a young, domesticated sheep; older sheep are referred to as hogget or mutton. Records show that the first batch of domesticated sheep arrived with Christopher Columbus during his second voyage in 1493. Though always delicious, lamb is a more popular meat in Mediterranean cultures, Ireland, and around the Persian Gulf. Lucky for us, it is now raised here and easily available in any United States supermarket or from your local butcher.

WHISKEY-ROASTED LEG OF LAMB

Serves 6

5 garlic cloves

1 large fresh rosemary sprig (leaves only)

1 good bunch fresh oregano

Salt and pepper

½ cup mustard

1 leg of lamb

3 tablespoons olive oil

6–7 fresh rosemary sprigs

1 cup whiskey

❶ Purée garlic with rosemary leaves, spices, and mustard then rub on leg.

❷ Wrap in plastic wrap and refrigerate overnight.

❸ In a roasting pan, drizzle 3 tablespoons olive oil then line the bottom with the rosemary.

❹ Place leg on top of the rosemary and add the whiskey to the bottom.

❺ Roast leg for 40–60 minutes at 400°F, or until it reaches an internal temperature of 125°F for rare, and 135°F for medium rare. Baste every 20 minutes.

❻ Remove leg and place on cutting board. Allow to sit for 15 minutes.

Empanada Day

MAY 8

Growing up in Venezuela, I'd wake up and go play with my friends in the plaza in front of our building. The plaza was our universe with a broken waterfall that we'd climb and pretend was our castle. We'd run around playing with marbles and skateboarding. At lunchtime, we'd head to the bakery for empanadas and a large bottle of Coke to share—that's all we could afford. But they wouldn't sell it to us until we turned in an empty bottle of Coke, so we'd also spend the morning looking for bottles. Thankfully, now things are easier and I can have as many empanadas as I want.

PIZZA EMPANADAS

Makes 1 dozen

Warm water (enough to form a workable dough)

Pinch of salt

1 cup masa harina (fine corn flour)

1 pound mozzarella cheese (shredded)

1 cup pepperoni

1 cup marinara

3–4 cups vegetable oil frying

❶ Work water and salt into masa harina slowly until soft dough forms. Cover and let sit at room temperature for 10 minutes.

❷ Make a little ball from dough, wet hands, and roll out dough between two pieces of wax paper or plastic wrap.

③ Fill middle with about 1 tablespoon of cheese, a few slices of pepperoni, and a little marinara. Close empanada and press lightly on corners. Use a bowl to trim excess dough.

④ Fry at 350–375°F until golden. Serve immediately with a side of marinara and a nice, cold Coke.

Butterscotch Brownie Day

Butterscotch is quite deceiving because there is no scotch in butterscotch! The concoction is more akin to a caramel or toffee and was first on record as being made by Samuel Parkinson in 1817 in Yorkshire, England. Comprised of brown sugar and butter (with the addition of lemon at times), it's a pretty simple concoction, but it seems unfair to be so misleading, so I added some scotch to my recipe!

BLONDIES HAVE MORE FUN

Makes 1 dozen

Blondies (Jan. 22)

½ cup scotch

❶ Prepare Blondies recipe, but add scotch to mixture, stirring to fully incorporate before placing mixture into pan.

❷ Finish baking following Blondies recipe.

Shrimp Day

Eating shrimp goes back as far as the 1600s in Louisiana. Whenever I think of shrimp, I'm reminded of Forrest Gump, when Bubba says, "Shrimp is the fruit of the sea. You can barbecue it, boil it, broil it, bake it, sauté it. Dey's uh, shrimp kabobs, shrimp creole, shrimp gumbo, pan-fried, deep-fried, stir-fried. There's pineapple shrimp, lemon shrimp, coconut shrimp. . . ." It goes on forever. Once I made coconut shrimp for my friend Melissa. Ever since she's been begging me to make them again, so this is for her.

MELISSA'S COCONUT SHRIMP

Serves 2

½ pound jumbo shrimp (peeled and deveined)

Salt and pepper

½ cup all-purpose flour and more for dusting

¾ cup beer

2–3 cups vegetable oil

3 cups sweetened shredded coconut

Sauce

½ cup duck sauce

1 tablespoon orange juice

½ teaspoon vinegar

½ scallion, sliced thin

A little grated ginger (optional)

❶ Butterfly shrimp, then rinse and dry. Season with salt and pepper then dredge really well in flour.

❷ Add beer slowly to flour while whisking until a smooth batter forms.

❸ In a deep, 2–3 quart pot, heat oil to 350°F.

4 Dip shrimp into batter, making sure it's completely open and covered completely in batter, then press coconut into shrimp. You should have a flat shrimp covered in coconut.

5 Fry in oil until golden brown, about 2 minutes. Remove from oil and drain on paper towels.

6 Make sauce by combining all ingredients and garnishing with scallions and ginger.

7 Serve shrimp hot, with a cool sauce.

Eat What You Want Day

When you think of cooking as a craft, what comes to mind? The art of butchery? Farming the perfect carrot? Cake decorating, perhaps? Personally, I think of pasta. It's amazing what can be done when you mix a little flour and water with a little egg. So when it came time to pick a recipe for Eat What You Want Day, I decided on gnudi. Filled with creamy ricotta cheese, drizzled with olive oil, and sprinkled with Parmesan, this stuff's awesome and the true definition of cooking as a craft.

FRESH RICOTTA GNUDI

Serves 2

⅛ teaspoon salt plus more for seasoning later

Dash of white pepper

1 cup ricotta cheese

¼ cup mozzarella cheese (shredded)

1 tablespoon fresh parsley (finely chopped)

2–3 cups semolina flour

Olive oil

Cook's Note

If you can find fresh ricotta and mozzarella at an Italian market, I recommend making the trip—it's worth it! But the recipe also tastes great with grocery store cheese.

1 Combine salt, pepper, ricotta, mozzarella, and parsley in a bowl.

2 Pour semolina onto cookie sheet or large plate. With two teaspoons, scoop ricotta mix onto semolina one teaspoon at a time using both spoons to keep them roundish. Dust tops of little balls with more semolina.

3 Fill medium-sized bowl with cold water.

4 Keeping one hand in wet ingredients and one in dry, take one little ball at a time and gently roll it between your hands. Dip one hand into the water while holding gnudi with the other, then transfer gnudi to the wet hand. Roll in your wet hand so that the surface gets moistened. Drop it gently into semolina again and with the dry hand roll it around until flour adheres to wet surface. (You are making a pasta around the cheese ball.) Do this four times, and the last time drop ball gently into water for a millisecond, then remove it, shake it off a little, and drop it into semolina for a final time. Roll it until the final coating of semolina forms the pasta around the gnudi. Leave it in the flour, as the semolina will cushion and support the little ball shape. Refrigerate for at least 1 hour.

5 Bring pot of water with salt and olive oil to a rapid boil. Drop gnudi a few pieces at a time and boil for 2 minutes. Remove with slotted spoon and place onto plate drizzled with olive oil and sprinkled with salt.

6 Toss gnudi around in oil to coat and serve immediately with a little tomato sauce and Parmesan cheese.

Nutty Fudge Day

MAY 12

Fudge is the predecessor to the American candy bar—super-simple and incredibly decadent. What I like about this fudge is that it's super caramely and complemented by the saltiness of the nuts.

NUTTY DULCE DE LECHE FUDGE

Serves 3–4

1 can condensed milk

⅛ cup white chocolate

2 tablespoon butter (soft)

Mixed salted nuts

❶ Peel label and boil can of condensed milk for 3 hours. Chill can. *Do not try and open it! The contents are under pressure and will explode!* Chill for at least ½ hour.

❷ While chilling, melt chocolate and set aside.

❸ Open condensed milk can that has now turned into dulce de leche and spoon into a microwave-safe bowl.

❹ Nuke the dulce de leche 20 seconds at a time until it's warm. Add melted chocolate and whisk together until smooth. Add butter and nuts and stir well, reserving some nuts to decorate top of fudge.

❺ Place plastic wrap in square container that will make the fudge 1" thick and scoop in mixture. Press fudge in well until you have a thick sheet and sprinkle on remaining nuts.

❻ Refrigerate until firm, about 1 hour. Cut with sharp knife and serve.

Fruit Cocktail Day

MAY 13

It would be wrong to try and credit anyone with the "invention" of the fruit cocktail. I mean it's merely a mélange of fruit often sweetened with syrup. I'm sure it sounds familiar! Over the years this has become a staple of cafeterias across the country and for many years the easiest way to get your fruit fill while out of your house, on the job, or in school. What always got to me was the fact that there was never a variation with alcohol. Well, my friends, I'm about to fix that. Meet my fruit cocktail—for adults only!

SPIKED FRUIT COCKTAIL

Makes about 8–10 drinks

2 cups fresh peaches (½" cubes)

2 cups fresh watermelon (½" cubes)

1 cup grapes (frozen)

1 cup fresh pineapple (½" cubes)

1 cup fresh blueberries

1 bottle of chilled bubbly (Champagne, prosecco, or sparkling wine)

1 cup orange liqueur (such as Grand Marnier, Cointreau, or Combier)

❶ Make sure all ingredients are chilled in advance.

❷ Combine them all in a large bowl and serve immediately, really cold. Cheers!

Buttermilk Biscuit Day

Here's the kind of shortdough crust you want and expect, lightly amber, and just giving way when you reach for one. The pressure of your hand makes them crumble slightly under your thumb and forefingers. As you tear into it, a wonderful plume of butter, milk, and fresh-baked aromas flood your senses. You see all the nooks and crannies just steaming and fluffy. You spread a dab of butter, and then as you place that first hot piece into your mouth and close your eyes, you are forced to chew with your mouth open while you blow the steam out. And for that second, life is good.

HEAVENLY BISCUITS

Makes 1 dozen

4 cups all-purpose flour

1 tablespoon baking powder

2 teaspoons baking soda

1 tablespoon salt

¼ cup cold butter

¾ cup cold lard or vegetable shortening (cut into small little cubes)

1½–2 cups buttermilk, plus a little more for brushing (cold)

❶ Sift dry ingredients in a large bowl or onto a clean surface with ample room to work.

❷ Add salt and butter with lard to dry mixture, and crumble between fingers until coarse.

❸ Add buttermilk while mixing with hands until you have a shaggy mess. Fold dough over a few times to create layers in biscuits. Press dough so it's 1" thick, and cut with round cookie cutter.

❹ Place on buttered cookie sheet, brush with buttermilk, and bake at 375°F for 20–25 minutes until golden.

Chocolate Chip Day

When you think of a fair, what comes to mind? The rides? The games? Maybe, but there's also cotton candy, and curly fries covered in cheese, and pop-corn—and funnel cakes! What's better than hot fried dough covered with an avalanche of powdered sugar? How about hot fried dough covered with an avalanche of powdered sugar and filled with gooey chocolate chips? Make this for the kids and I guarantee the dishes will get done, the rooms will get cleaned, and who knows? Maybe they'll even stop drinking milk directly out of the carton. . . .

CHOCOLATE CHIP FUNNEL CAKES

Serves 6

1 cup water

1 tablespoon sugar

Pinch of salt

6 tablespoons butter

5¾ ounces all-purpose flour (sifted)

4 large eggs and 1 egg white

½ cup mini chocolate chips

Oil for frying

❶ Combine water, sugar, salt, and butter in pot and bring to boil.

❷ When butter has melted, add sifted flour and stir with wooden spoon until dough forms. Cook over medium heat for 1 minute, stirring constantly. Remove pot from heat, pour into stand mixer, and let sit until warm.

③ Mix on medium high adding one egg at a time until you have a smooth mixture. Make sure batter is cold by putting it in the fridge if you need to, then add chocolate chips, and spoon mixture into pastry bag. Cut tip large enough so chips fit though and form funnel cakes by drizzling the dough on top of the oil.

④ Fry in pan with clean oil at 350°F. Cook until golden on one side, flip, and cook on other side until golden. Remove from the oil and drain on paper towels. Some chocolate chips will naturally melt into oil, but don't sweat it; they will cook and just float up where you can sift them out.

⑤ Dust with a lot—and I mean *a lot*—of powdered sugar and serve right away.

MAY 16
Coquilles St. Jacques Day

So Franch, oui? From the French, coquilles *means "shell" and has been come to be known as the iconic ridged shell that protects scallops, those delicious little white nuggets from the sea. Scallops can be eaten raw when really fresh or cooked at high temperatures to create a nice caramel sear. With this recipe, they're paired with a little cheese and cream.*

COQUILLES ST. JACQUES

Serves 2

10 medium scallops

1 cup water

⅔ cup heavy cream

3 tablespoons medium tapioca pearls

Salt and white pepper

1 tablespoon olive oil

5 tablespoons butter (2 melted)

½ cup oyster mushrooms (you can use button, chanterelles, or anything you like)

¼ cup white wine

½ teaspoon fresh tarragon (finely chopped) plus more for garnish

½ cup Swiss cheese (shredded)

½ cup bread crumbs

Cook's Note

Open a window and set the fan above your stove on high. You will be creating a lot of smoke with this recipe. If you don't, you're not doing it right!

① Rinse off scallops, removing tough little muscle on the side, and set aside to dry on paper towels.

② Combine water, cream, and tapioca in a little pot with pinch of salt and pinch of white pepper, and bring to boil over high heat. Once boiling, reduce to barely a simmer and cook for about 15 minutes, stirring every couple of minutes to prevent tapioca from sticking to bottom.

③ Set a sauté pan over superduper high heat.

④ Season scallops liberally with salt and white pepper. Cover bottom of pan with olive oil, then add 1 more tablespoon (scallops will suck up some of the oil).

5. Drop scallops into pan, flat side down, one by one. Allow to cook for about 2 minutes without moving that dial on the heat. (I told you it was going to smoke a lot!)

6. With tongs, lift one side of scallops one by one to allow some oil to come between them and pan. Continue to cook until they have a nice crust, about another minute. Flip and add 1 tablespoon butter. Cook for 1 minute and transfer into shallow casserole dish. Add 1 tablespoon butter, and drizzle of olive oil.

7. In the same pan, cook mushrooms for 1 minute, adding salt and pepper to taste. Drizzle white wine and deglaze, which will remove all the yummy bits from the bottom of pan and make a wonderful sauce. Allow to reduce until there's 1 tablespoon of liquid left.

8. At this point, tapioca should be almost done. You can check by taking one of the pearls and looking at it; if it still has a little white center, it needs a little more time. Tapioca turns clear while it cooks. White means raw.

9. Combine mushrooms with tapioca mixture and finish with 1 tablespoon butter and tarragon. If it looks thick, add cream until smooth and creamy.

10. Spoon mixture over scallops and top with shredded cheese. Combine melted butter with the bread crumbs and layer on top of cheese. Broil until golden about 20 seconds.

Cherry Cobbler Day

MAY 17

Cobblers can be either sweet or savory depending what side of the pond you're on. In England, they are more like savory meat pies topped with a biscuitlike crust, but in America, my friends, cobbler means one thing: buttery biscuit dough encased in syrupy warm filling. Cherry cobbler is the sweet-tart sister to the peach cobbler and can be made with fresh cherries, frozen, or even canned! I love making it in the height of summer with a ton of fresh cherries and serving with a big scoop of vanilla ice cream.

CHERRY COBBLER

Serves 4–6

8 tablespoons butter

1 cup milk

½ cup heavy cream

1 teaspoon vanilla extract

1½ cups all-purpose flour

½ teaspoon baking powder

1¼ cup sugar

Pinch of salt

3 cups fresh cherries (pitted)

1. Melt butter in microwave then add milk, cream, and vanilla.

2. In another bowl, sift flour with baking powder. Make a well in the middle of flour and add sugar, salt, and milk mixture. Mix slowly until a batter forms.

❸ Butter a loaf pan and dust with flour. Pour in batter and plop cherries all around.

❹ Sprinkle with more sugar and bake for 40–50 minutes at 350°F. Serve warm with vanilla ice cream.

Cheese Soufflé Day

When I started cooking I was an apprentice at a restaurant called La Caravelle in Manhattan. My teacher, Pastry Chef Laurent Richard, is a genius with sweets. Trained in classic French pastry, this guy is exactly the person you want to learn from. He's extremely knowledgeable and his work is precise, clean, and delicious. This is where I learned how to make the classic soufflé—we cranked out dozens of air-light baked-to-order gems every day. It's actually a simple dish, albeit extremely temperamental. It also needs to be served right away, but it makes a spectacular entrance every time!

BLUE CHEESE SOUFFLÉ

Serves 4

1 cup milk

4 eggs (separated)

4 tablespoons flour

Butter

Sugar

⅔ cups blue cheese

¼ cup Parmesan cheese

⅛ teaspoon cream of tartar

¼ cup bread crumbs

2 scallions (thinly chopped)

Hot sauce

❶ Bring milk to a boil. In the meantime, combine yolks with flour, mix well, and set aside.

❷ Butter and sugar 4 ramekin molds. Set aside.

❸ When milk has boiled, add to yolk mixture a little at a time while whisking constantly.

❹ Return to pot and cook for 3 minutes on medium-high heat while whisking rapidly and scraping bottom.

❺ Add cheeses and mix well. Make a skin with plastic wrap touching the mixture directly and chill completely, about 30 minutes.

❻ In the meantime, whip whites in clean bowl. When fluffy, add cream of tartar and whip whites to form soft peaks. Add half of whites to chilled cheese mixture and fold in well, then fold in remaining whites.

❼ Pour into ramekins and bake at 400°F for 10–15 minutes until golden.

❽ Top with chopped scallions and a dash of hot sauce.

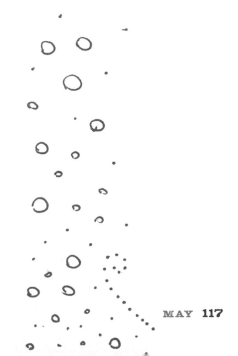

Devil's Food Cake Day

This is the cake of all cakes. When you think of choco-late cake, this is what you will remember for the rest of your days. It's so good, eating it should be a sin. So sinful, it seems evil—or devilish! Recipes for Devil's Food Cake started popping up around the turn of the twentieth century. No one really knows where the "Devil's Food" moniker came from, but common sense points to the Angel Food Cake, which is a light, airy vanilla cake. The Devil's Food Cake is rich and intense, and the complete opposite, therefore creating a per-fect harmony for cake eaters.

DEVIL'S FOOD CAKE

Serves 6–8

½ cup butter (soft)

1 cup sugar

½ cup light brown sugar

½ cup and 2 tablespoons cocoa powder

1¼ and 2 tablespoons all-purpose flour

⅛ teaspoon salt

¼ teaspoon baking powder

1 teaspoon baking soda

2 eggs

1 cup lowfat milk

½ cup chocolate chips

1 teaspoon vanilla extract

Frosting

1¼ cups bittersweet chocolate (melted)

½ cup evaporated milk (warm)

¾ cup butter

⅛ teaspoon salt

❶ Cream butter and sugars in an electric mixer for about 5 minutes until fluffy.

❷ Sift dry ingredients and set aside. Once butter is fluffy, add eggs one at a time and mix until incorporated.

❸ Alternate between adding liquid and dry ingredients until a smooth batter forms, then add the chocolate chips and vanilla and mix in well.

❹ Bake in two buttered and floured 9" round pans at 350°F for 25 minutes or until a knife inserted in middle comes out clean.

❺ Prepare frosting by combining chocolate with evaporated milk until smooth. Allow mixture to cool until slightly warm, then add butter in chunks and salt and mix until frosting is smooth.

❻ When cake has cooled, frost and serve at room temperature with a big glass of cold milk.

Quiche Lorraine Day

Real men do eat quiche. So do woman, children, farmers, bankers, and even some animals! Although a French staple that came to the States in the 1950s, quiche actually has German origin, from the word kuchen, *which means "cake." It can be made with bread, puff pastry, or short crust but is always served open-faced with a creamy egg-custard base. What you add to that is up to you. This quintessential quiche is made with bacon, eggs, and heavy cream, and it gets its name from the Lorraine region of France. But in America we like cheese, so I added lots of it!*

NOT-SO-QUINTESSENTIAL QUICHE LORRAINE

Serves 4–6

Crust

2 cups all-purpose flour

1 teaspoon salt

1 cup plus 2 tablespoons butter (cold and cubed)

¼ cup ice cold water

¼ cup Parmesan

1 teaspoon fresh rosemary (finely chopped)

1 egg (for wash)

Filling

1 pound bacon (cut into ½" chunks)

1 cup heavy cream

1 cup milk

5 eggs

2 sprigs fresh thyme

¼ teaspoon salt

Pinch of nutmeg

¼ teaspoon white pepper

1 cup Gruyère or Swiss cheese

½ onion (thinly sliced)

Fresh parsley for garnish

1. Prepare shell by sifting dry ingredients then mixing quickly with butter, until you can see streaks of butter in dough. Add Parmesan, rosemary, and cold water and mix a little more until dough forms and chill for at least 1 hour.

2. Roll out dough and cover a 2" deep fluted pan with a removable bottom, allowing edges of dough to hang over the pan. Don't trim excess; simply press dough gently into the pan (make sure there are no holes, if you see one, seal with a little dough).

3. Cover with a little paper and fill with dry beans to weigh down, then bake at 375°F for 15–20 minutes. Remove paper and beans, and glaze with egg wash (this will create a leakproof shell). Cook for another 2 minutes, then remove from oven and allow to cool.

4. Prepare filling by cooking bacon on baking sheet at 350°F for about 12 minutes until soft but cooked.

5. In the meantime, bring cream and milk to a boil, then add that to eggs a little at a time while whisking, then mix in the fresh thyme, salt, nutmeg, and white pepper. Allow to cool for 10 minutes until room temperature.

6. Line cooled shell with half of cheese, ⅔ of bacon, and top with egg mixture. Cook at 375°F for 1 hour, add remaining cheese and sprinkle sliced onions on top. Cook for another ½ hour until cheese is melted and bubbling and onions are browned.

7. Remove from oven and allow to cool on the counter. Finish by trimming shell edges with a serrated knife (if you want) and sprinkle with parsley. Serve chilled or reheated.

MAY 21

Strawberries and Cream Day

On Strawberry Ice Cream Day (January 15) I spoke about my Queen of Strawberries, Franca. She owns Berried Treasures and grows the most delicious strawberries. I mention it again because when you have a simple recipe such as Strawberries and Cream, the quality of your ingredients is imperative. So forget Reddi-wip, Cool Whip, and frozen berries. There's a mountainous part of Venezuela called Merida. Every time we went there we would get fresh strawberries and cream and sit by the mountain in our ponchos just gobbling up this simple treat. Here's a simple treat in the form of a napoleon.

STRAWBERRIES AND CREAM NAPOLEON

Serves 3–4

1 sheet puff pastry

3 cups fresh strawberries

Perfect Chantilly Cream (Jan. 5)

Powdered sugar

Fresh mint for garnish

❶ Defrost puff pastry into 3 even, long pieces. Bake according to box instructions until golden, then cool.

❷ Layer Perfect Chantilly Cream with strawberries in between layers of puff pastry. (Taste berries. If they need a little more oomph, cut them up and toss with a little powdered sugar and a little lemon juice.)

❸ Dust napoleon with powdered sugar and garnish with mint leaves.

Vanilla Pudding Day

MAY 22

Vanilla pudding is a great staple to know how to make since it can be the base for many desserts. Once you master making pudding, you can make pastry cream, frozen custard, crème bavarois, soufflés, and many other classic desserts. It is also the same base as making many cream sauces and can be used to make fruit creams for pies. The process of making pudding merely involves cooking cornstarch with milk and eggs, then flavoring with vanilla and spices, nuts, or pastes. The difference between puddings and custards is the addition of cornstarch.

VANILLA PUDDING

Serves 3–4

3½ cups whole milk

1 vanilla bean (scraped) or 2 teaspoons vanilla extract

2 whole eggs

2 yolks

4 tablespoons cornstarch

4 tablespoons sugar

Pinch of salt

2 tablespoons butter (unsalted and soft)

❶ Heat milk with vanilla, turn off heat, cover, and allow flavor to infuse milk for 15 minutes. (If using vanilla extract, don't add until the end.)

2. Combine eggs with cornstarch and sugar and whisk well.

3. Drizzle milk into egg mixture slowly while whisking, then return to pot.

4. Cook on medium heat for 3 minutes while whisking constantly and scraping bottom.

5. Remove from heat (if you are using vanilla extract, add it now), add salt, pour pudding into a bowl, press a piece of plastic wrap on top so a skin doesn't form on pudding, and refrigerate until cold, about 1 hour.

6. Finish by whipping soft butter into cold pudding.

7. Spoon into individual cups and top with a dollop of whipped cream. Serve with Shorties (Jan. 6).

MAY 23
Taffy Day

When you think of taffy, the first thing that probably comes to mind is Saltwater Taffy. Invented in Atlantic City, New Jersey, it probably got its name from the saltwater used to make the taffy since it was readily available. But legend goes that one day the tide was super high and seeped into a candy store that sold taffy. Some of the saltwater got onto the taffy, and the shopkeepers, not wanting to discard it, simply sold it as "Saltwater Taffy." Taffy is made from the combination of corn syrup, butter, and glycerin boiled and then pulled and stretched until fluffy and chewy.

SALTWATER TAFFY

Makes about 2 dozen small candies

1 cup water

1 cup light corn syrup

2 cups sugar

1 teaspoon salt

2 tablespoons butter

Extract for flavoring (cherry, banana, grape, or any other flavor you like)

Food coloring

1. Butter sides of a heavy bottomed pot, then add water, corn syrup, sugar, and salt, and stir once. Cook until a thermometer reads 275°F.

2. Turn off heat and add butter as well as flavoring and coloring. (At this point you can separate into different greased bowls to add different colors and flavors.)

3. Allow to cool until just able to handle.

4. If you have gloves, put them on and grease slightly; if not, grease hands with butter, vegetable shortening, or oil.

5. Work taffy, pulling and stretching until it starts to harden slightly.

6. Pull into a long rope about ½" thick and cut into bite-size pieces with a greased scissor.

7. Eat right away or wrap in wax paper and keep at room temperature.

Escargot Day

Escargot is French for land snail. Weird as it might sound, they're delicious, and with more than 15 percent protein, they're also nutritious! Escargots are normally removed from their shells, cleaned, cooked in garlic butter, then returned to their shells. And you get tongs to hold them and little forks to pry them out and eat them. The texture is similar to clams and they're wonderful fried and in spaghetti. Here, I create hush puppies and serve them with pesto mayo. Don't look away—ancient archeological sites indicate that snails were an elite food for the Romans. So pucker up, buckaroo, because escargots are good eats!

ESCARGOT HUSH PUPPIES

Serves 3

1½ cups cornmeal

½ cup self-rising flour

½ teaspoon baking soda

½ teaspoon salt

1 cup buttermilk

1 egg

1 cup snails, cleaned (you can find these online or in some specialty supermarkets)

2 tablespoons fresh parsley (chopped)

Oil for frying

Pesto Mayo

3 garlic cloves

2 tablespoons olive oil

1 large handful fresh basil (washed and dried)

1 cup mayonnaise

Pinch of pepper

¼ cup Parmesan cheese

① Sift dry ingredients, then add wet ingredients, escargot, and parsley.

② Drop batter one tablespoon at a time into 350°F oil and fry until golden. Remove with slotted spoon and drain on paper towels. Salt puppies as soon as they come out of oil.

③ To prepare mayo, in a food processor, blend garlic with olive oil and basil. Add mayo and blend well. Finish by blending in pepper and cheese.

④ Serve mayo with hot puppies garnished with the chopped parsley.

Wine Day

I heard someone once say "Wine is a living thing," which is sometimes hard to wrap your head around. It's a fascinating thought considering that wine is simply fermented grape juice. But what I think is most fascinating about wine is what the French call terroir. *The Romans called it* genius loci, *or spirit of place, and it is the same idea as* terroir. *The flavors of the wine are reflected by the land, the air, the water, the rock or soil on which the vines struggle and get the minerals and nutrients needed to produce the grapes used to make wine—all these are enwrapped around the idea of terroir. We always drink wine in family gatherings, and since we all have an uncle who drinks too much wine, here's to you (lifting a glass) cheers!*

DRUNKEN UNCLE PASTA

Serves 4

1 bottle red wine plus 1 cup

1 tablespoon salt

2 tablespoons olive oil plus more for sautéing

1 Spanish onion sliced thinly

1 cup sundried tomatoes (sliced)

¼ teaspoon red pepper flakes

6 garlic cloves (minced)

3 tablespoons tomato paste

1 cup tomato crushed tomatoes

10 ounces spaghetti

1 tablespoon butter

3 tablespoons fresh parsley (chopped)

8 ounces soft fresh goat cheese

❶ Fill large stockpot with water and add bottle of red wine, salt, and olive oil. Cover and bring to a rapid boil.

❷ In the meantime, in a large sauté pan, cook onions, sundried tomatoes, and dried pepper flakes in olive oil over medium heat until onions are translucent. Add more olive oil and garlic, and cook until tender (about 1 minute).

❸ Add tomato paste and mix everything together followed by 1 cup red wine and crushed tomatoes. Cook for 1 minute.

❹ Cook spaghetti according to package instructions and drain, adding a little pasta water to sauce.

❺ Toss pasta with sauce. Mix in butter and serve. Garnish with fresh parsley and big disks of fresh goat cheese. Top with a drizzle of olive oil and a bit of cracked pepper.

Blueberry Cheesecake Day

I think cheesecake is so much better when served with fresh blueberries. I have a proven and tested cheesecake recipe I always use, which I modified here. I add a handful of berries into the batter before I bake it, then top it with fresh whipped cream and toss a mountainfull of berries with a little lemon juice and powdered sugar and fresh mint on top. That's what you call a farm-fresh cheesecake.

FARM-FRESH BLUEBERRY CHEESECAKE

Serves 6–8

Crust

¼ cup butter (melted)

1½ cups oatmeal cookie crumbs

1 tablespoon granulated sugar

⅛ teaspoon salt

Filling

1 pound (two 8-ounce packages) cream cheese (at room temp)

⅔ cup granulated sugar

3 eggs

2 cups Greek yogurt or sour cream

1 cup fresh blueberries

1 teaspoon vanilla extract

½ teaspoon salt

Topping

5 cups fresh blueberries

1 teaspoon fresh lemon juice

A few mint leaves (thinly sliced)

2 tablespoons powdered sugar

1 cup Perfect Chantilly Cream (Jan. 5)

1 To make crust, melt butter in a small pan over medium heat while whisking until it browns slightly. Add to cookie crumbs, along with sugar and salt. Using your hands, incorporate butter into crumbs.

2 Wrap a 9" springform pan with heavy-duty aluminum foil, butter inside, and press crust into bottom, leaving no gaps. Set aside.

3 Whip cream cheese with sugar and eggs, adding one egg at a time. Whisk well. Add yogurt, incorporate well, then add blueberries. Whisk in vanilla and salt.

4 Pour cream cheese mixture atop crust in springform pan.

5 Bake at 325°F for 45 minutes in a water bath, remove from oven, and rest in water until cool. Refrigerate overnight or at least 5 hours.

6 To finish cake, unmold and set on a platter. Toss berries with lemon juice, mint, and powdered sugar.

7 Top cake with whipped cream then berry mixture. Serve right away.

Grape Popsicle Day

MAY 27

You're sitting on the couch watching TV when all of a sudden a giant human pitcher of Kool-Aid rams through the wall like a deranged maniac, screaming, "Oh, yeah!" Who was the ad guy who came up with this kooky campaign? Kool-Aid, known as Nebraska's official soft drink, is what we all grew up drinking, so here's a throwback—mixed with booze.

PURPLE RAIN POPS

Makes 6 pops

2 cups seedless red grapes

1 6-ounce packet grape Kool-Aid

½ cup sugar

1 cup water

3 ounces vodka

Popsicle sticks

1 In a blender, blend all ingredients together Pour into popsicle molds and place sticks.

2 Put in freezer and enjoy several hours later.

Brisket Day

Brisket is a magical cut of meat. While all animals have it, we normally refer to beef when speaking of brisket. It is a large cut located in the chest of the steer and is part of the primal cuts. Brisket is traditionally a tough and therefore inexpensive cut of meat, which is why I say its magic. When meat is tough, the best way to enjoy it is to smoke it or simply cook it low and very slow. When I say slow, I mean upwards of 10 hours to truly allow the fibers to break down and give you soft meat. Brisket is popularly used to make Corned Beef (Mar. 17), but my absolutely fave is barbecue brisket, which is the barbecue of choice in Texas.

SIMPLE OVEN BRISKET

Serves 6–8

1 5–6 pound beef brisket with a thick layer of fat (ask your butcher)

A few drops of liquid smoke (try Deep South Natural Hickory or Mesquite)

2 teaspoons brown sugar

1½ teaspoons fresh ground black pepper

1 teaspoon ground cumin

1 tablespoon kosher salt

1 tablespoon chili powder

1 tablespoon paprika

❶ Rinse brisket in cold water and pat dry. In the meantime, preheat oven to 225°F.

❷ Rub brisket with liquid smoke. Mix spices together in a bowl and rub onto meat.

❸ Roast brisket wrapped in aluminum foil, fat-side up, for 6–8 hours until tender. (It usually takes 1½ hours per pound of meat.)

❹ When done, remove brisket from oven and let sit for at least 15 minutes. Slice and serve. I like it with a splash of apple cider vinegar and a little hot sauce!

Coq au Vin Day

Translated from the French as "rooster with wine," this dish is a classic one-pot wonder akin to our crock-pot braises. When I think of Coq au Vin, I always run to my copy of It Must Have Been Something I Ate, by Jeffrey Steingarten. He devotes sixteen pages to the dish in the chapter "Red Wine and Old Roosters." With the most detailed multipage recipe at the end, it is probably the best I have ever tasted. Steingarten was on to something . . . Coq au Vin is such a renowned rustic dish, there are actually two days dedicated to it! See March 22 for the recipe. For a truly authentic take on it, try to get your hands on an old rooster—the distinct taste makes it worth the extra effort!

Mint Julep Day

And they're off! Mint juleps have been the official drink of the Kentucky Derby since 1938, and more than 120,000 of the drinks are served at the event each year. This refreshing yet potent elixir is considered a Southern drink, and since Kentucky is the home of bourbon, it seems natural that it would be the spirit of choice. The first Mint Julep recipe, penned by John Davis in 1803, reads, "a dram of spirituous liquor that has steeped mint in it, taken by Virginians of a morning." It doesn't specify what spirituous liquor was used, which might be why Americans have enjoyed them with vodka and gin. But we all know it's most delicious with bourbon.

GRASS-BOURBON MINT JULEP

Makes 1 drink

1 bottle bourbon

½ cup wheatgrass (plus more for garnish)

3 large mint stems plus 4 mint leaves

2 teaspoons simple syrup

Crushed ice

❶ Infuse bourbon with wheatgrass and 3 large mint stems. Place in a cool, dark place for at least a few days.

❷ Place mint at bottom of a chilled silver glass (a regular glass will also do, but only if you must) and muddle—just bruise a little to release flavor, you don't want to break up mint.

❸ Add 3 ounces of grass-infused bourbon and stir, then add simple syrup and stir again.

❹ Fill glass with crushed ice and stir until glass gets frosty. Top with more crushed ice and enjoy!

Cook's Note

To make this drink extra fun, take some wheatgrass and tie the bottom with string, then stick the string's knotted side into the crushed ice. The whole point is to have a handful of grass right at your nose when you sip, so you feel as if you're sitting on the grass at the Aqueduct!

Macaroon Day

Florian Bellanger owns a company called MadMac (madmacnyc .com) and is the crowning embassador of two wonderful cookies—the queen of cookies (the Madeleine) and the king of cookies (the Macaroon)— hence the name MadMac. He makes the most divine and creative macaroons I've ever had the pleasure of eating. Delightful little cookies, Macaroons were created by Italian monks and come in two basic forms: coconut and classic. I personally prefer the latter.

EASY MACAROONIES

Makes 2 dozen

3 extra-large eggs (whites only)

¼ cup granulated sugar

1 cup sliced, blanched almonds (finely ground)

1¼ cups plus 2 teaspoons powdered sugar

Pinch of salt

Cook's Note

When grinding the almonds, do it slowly and make sure everything stays cold. Grinding creates friction which releases oils from the nuts and they'll want to turn into a paste! If this starts happening, add powdered sugar and pulse again until finely ground.

1. In a clean bowl, whip egg whites slowly then a little faster, adding the granulated sugar in 3 parts and beating on medium high until a meringue forms.

2. Combine the ground almonds with powdered sugar and add almond-sugar mixture with salt and fold in until smooth.

3. Fill a piping bag with a large round tip or a clean plastic bottle with a wide mouth. Pipe batter onto baking sheets lined with parchment paper, making sure to leave space in between each one because batter will spread as it bakes. Leave tray out so macaroons dry a bit, about 20 minutes.

4. Bake in 350°F oven with door slightly ajar (I put a wooden spoon to keep my oven door open) for 10–15 minutes. Allow to cool at room temperature.

5. Once cool, fill with Nutella, jam, or buttercream. I fill with ice cream, wrap them up, and freeze them. The cookies absorb a little moisture in the freezer—they're super tender and go great with creamy ice cream!

JUNE

Hazelnut Cake Day

One of the first cakes I ever made was a nut cake with smoked almonds. The batter didn't seem right so I kept adding things—an extra egg here, soft butter, melted butter, a banana, a sock, an umbrella—whatever made sense at the time. I was lost, with no idea of all that I'd added, but decided to bake it for fun. It ended up being one of the most flavorful cakes I ever tasted! And it was even better the next day. Here, I use a basic pound cake recipe with hazelnuts and add hazelnut oil to enhance it.

HAZELNUT CAKE

Serves 6

1 pound unsalted butter (soft)

3 cups granulated sugar

6 large eggs

1½ tablespoons baking powder

4½ cups all-purpose flour

½ teaspoon salt

1½ cups heavy cream

1 tablespoon vanilla extract

1 teaspoon hazelnut extract or 2 tablespoons Frangelico liqueur

2 cups hazelnuts (finely chopped)

❶ Cream butter and sugar with mixer for about 10 minutes. Add one egg at a time, incorporating well in between additions.

❷ Sift dry ingredients. Add dry ingredients and heavy cream, alternating between one and the other while mixing on medium. Finish by adding extracts and hazelnuts. Pour batter into greased and floured Springform pan.

❸ Bake at 325°F for 45–50 minutes or until a knife inserted in the middle comes out clean.

❹ Remove from pan and cool until it's just warm and serve.

Rocky Road Ice Cream Day

Rocky Road Ice Cream was just named America's tenth-favorite flavor. Which leads to an obvious question: "Who the hell is running these surveys?!!" We're talking about chocolate ice cream with marshmallow, chocolate chunks, and nuts. Now, that's just some good stuff right there. Rocky Road was created by William Dryer, who used his wife's scissors to slice up the marshmallows and add to his ice cream. After the market crash of 1929, the company dubbed the creation "Rocky Road" to give folks something to smile about. Hopefully, this will make you smile.

ROCKY ROAD ICE CREAM CAKE

Serves 6–8

Devil's Food Cake (May 19)

1–2 pints dark chocolate ice cream

1 cup mini marshmallows

1 cup chocolate chips

1 cup slivered or sliced almonds (toasted and chilled)

Chocolate Frosting (Dec. 15)

❶ Bake cake in 9" Springform pan. Once done, slice in half lengthwise (getting a separate top and bottom) and place in fridge until completely cold.

❷ Place a large bowl in freezer for at least 30 minutes.

❸ Let ice cream soften in fridge for about 10 minutes, then empty it into bowl and combine with marshmallows, chocolate chips, and almonds. Using a wooden spoon or a spatula, mix everything roughly.

❹ Take bottom of cake and place back in springform pan. Top cake bottom with ice cream mixture, flatten as much as you can, and top with top of cake and flatten. Freeze for 2 hours.

❺ Make frosting, unmold cake, and coat with frosting.

❼ Decorate the cake with marshmallows, chocolate chips, and almonds on top.

JUNE 3 Egg Day

Eggs have been an integral part of our diet for as long as humans have been eating. Eggs are great because they are inexpensive, super nutritious, and delicious at any meal. They are indispensable to pastry and are great at the forefront or playing a supporting role to a dish. I came up with this one day when I was imagining the ultimate Bloody Mary for a brunch menu. I was thinking bacon and eggs in a cocktail, Yes, you heard me right! I ended up making a Bloody Mary with this fried egg and served it with two crispy bacon strips—a.k.a. The Red Eye. These are marvels to behold, perfect as late-night snacks.

GOLDEN EGGS

Serves 3–6

6 eggs plus 2 for the breading

1 cup all-purpose flour

1 cup seasoned bread crumbs

3–4 cups oil for frying

Smoked paprika for sprinkling

Salt and pepper to taste

❶ Bring a quart of water to a boil.

❷ Prick your eggs with a tack and drop 3 of them gently into the water. Cook eggs for 3 minutes then remove them and place them in an ice bath. Repeat the process with the other 3 eggs.

❸ Once the eggs have cooled, about 5 minutes, peel them carefully and place them on paper towels so that they dry out a little.

❹ In the meantime, set up 3 bowls: one with the flour, one with the two raw eggs whisked slightly, and the third one with the bread crumbs.

❺ In another pot heat the oil to 350°F.

❻ Bread the eggs by dipping them in the flour followed by the eggs and finishing with the bread crumbs.

❼ Fry the eggs in the oil until golden, about 2–3 minutes. Remove the eggs from the oil with a slotted spoon and allow them to drain on paper towels.

❽ Sprinkle with salt and smoked paprika then serve.

Cognac Day

Cognac is a double distillation of white wine, specifically produced in the Cognac region in France. Cognac is traditionally made from the Ugni Blanc grape, which is perfect for distilling because of its high acidity and low sugar content. In order for it to be called Cognac it must also be distilled in copper pot stills and aged in French oak barrels. The Sidecar is the most popular cocktail made with the spirit, and I love making them! I add orange juice and make a really long twist using the peel from half an orange.

SIDECAR

Makes 1 drink

¼ cup sugar in the raw

Honey or agave syrup

¾ ounce orange liqueur (Cointreau or Grand Marnier)

1½ ounces cognac

¾ ounce fresh lemon juice

¼ ounce fresh orange juice

1 whole orange

❶ Chill a martini glass by chilling it. Sprinkle sugar on a plate.

❷ When glass is cold, rim top with honey or agave by putting two drops on fingertip and running it all along the edge, then dip glass in sugar.

❸ Shake remaining ingredients (except orange) vigorously in shaker with lots of ice and pour into the prepped glass. Garnish by making one peel from the whole orange with a peeler.

❹ Squeeze the twist on top of drink then drop in. Cheers!

Gingerbread Day

Making gingerbread is a celebrated tradition throughout America, and it's one that's been alive since Queen Elizabeth I reigned. The queen would impress her guests by having gingerbread cookies made to their likeness. But why bread? It doesn't taste like bread, it doesn't look like bread. . . . The name has no connection to bread whatsoever; it's actually an evolution of gingerbras, a word from the Old French meaning "preserved ginger." And the house? Well, credit for that goes to the Brothers Grimm and their tale of Hansel and Gretel.

GINGERBREAD ICE CREAM SANDWICHES

Makes 6–8 sandwiches

11 tablespoons butter

⅔ cup brown sugar

4 cups all-purpose flour

¾ teaspoon baking soda

1 teaspoon salt

4 teaspoons ground ginger

1 teaspoon ground cloves

½ teaspoon ground nutmeg

1 tablespoon ground cinnamon

10 turns of fresh ground black pepper

3 eggs

⅔ cup molasses

2 pints vanilla ice cream

❶ Cream butter with sugar on high speed for 5 minutes. Sift all dry ingredients and combine. Add eggs and flour mixture little by little, mixing in between so dough emulsifies well. Finish with molasses and mix in well. Refrigerate dough overnight or at least for 2 hours.

2 Roll out, refrigerate until hard, then cut with cookie cutter. Bake on greased cookie sheet at 350°F for 7 minutes. (It's better to remove them early rather than late so that they don't dry out.) Cool.

3 To assemble sandwiches, spread ice cream in a cake pan lined with either parchment paper or aluminum foil. Freeze until hard again. about 15 minutes.

4 Remove from freezer and cut into shapes you've chosen (I like the old-school ginger-bread man shape). Carefully place cut-out ice cream in between the two cookies of the same shape, enclose in plastic wrap, and freeze again until hard.

JUNE 6 Applesauce Cake Day

When life gives you lemons, you make lemonade, but what to do when you go apple picking and have a ton of beautiful fresh apples? Well, you make apple pie! And with the leftovers? You make applesauce. Applesauce is delicious and when properly jarred can last indefinitely. It pairs incredibly well with pork chops, ham, and is used in strudels and cakes. I often add applesauce to my carrot cakes and puddings since it lends great texture and moisture.

ROSEMARY APPLESAUCE

3–4 cups applesauce

3 pounds of apples (peeled, cored, cut into ½" chunks)

½ cup of apple cider or apple juice

1 teaspoon cinnamon

1 tablespoon brown sugar

1 rosemary sprig

1 Combine all ingredients in pan or Dutch oven, stir.

2 Cover and bake at 250°F for 30–45 minutes or until nice and creamy.

ROSEMARY APPLESAUCE CAKE

Serves 6

2 cups light brown sugar

½ cup butter (unsalted and soft)

2 teaspoon baking soda

2 ¼ cups all-purpose flour

½ teaspoon salt

1½ teaspoon cinnamon

2 eggs

2 cups applesauce

½ teaspoon vanilla extract

½ cup dried cranberries

1 Cream sugar with butter on high speed until light and pale. Sift all dry ingredients.

2 Add eggs one at a time to butter mixture, combining well in between additions.

3 Add applesauce and dry ingredients, alternating until well incorporated.

4 Stir in vanilla and cranberries.

5 Bake at 350°F in an oiled and floured loaf pan for about 40–45 minutes or until a toothpick inserted in the middle comes out clean.

6 Remove from oven, cool slightly, flip and dust with powdered sugar and garnish with fresh cranberries and rosemary sprigs.

7 Dust with sugar again, and serve.

Chocolate Ice Cream Day

There are thousands of variations on simple chocolate ice cream. Finding a label that simply reads "chocolate" is hard since now there's rocky road, heavenly hash, chocolate swirl, milk chocolate, dark chocolate, Mayan chocolate with a little cinnamon . . . I'm not complaining, I'd rather buy plain ice cream and mix with my own stuff. That way I get to be a little more creative. Here's a simple chocolate ice cream that I make into cannolis that'll knock your socks off.

CHOCOLATE ICE CREAM CANNOLIS

Makes 1 dozen

4 cups half-and-half

½ cup unsweetened cocoa powder

1½ cups condensed milk

8 large egg yolks

2 teaspoons pure vanilla extract

1 dozen cannoli shells

½ cup bittersweet chocolate (melted)

❶ Bring half-and-half and cocoa powder to a boil. Combine condensed milk and egg yolks. Temper eggs by adding cream mixture a little at a time while whisking. Once you have combined 2 cups of cream mixture into eggs, return everything to the pot and cook on low while scraping bottom of pan until you reach 170°F. Remove from heat and strain through a fine mesh.

❷ Allow mixture to cool in refrigerator or in an ice bath, for about 30 minutes to an hour. When cool, add vanilla and freeze according to ice cream machine's instructions.

❸ Get cannoli shells from your local Italian bakery. Dip completely in chocolate and let cool so chocolate hardens.

❹ Fill cannolis with ice cream using a piping bag, and freeze until hard, about 1 hour. Sprinkle with powdered sugar before serving.

Jelly-Filled Doughnut Day

JUNE 8

There's this little children's book in which the character has a really pointy head, and to conceal it he wears a hat made out of doughnuts! I often wish I had the same problem so I could wear a snack-hat of colorful squishy doughnuts. I'm not talking about day-old doughnuts, either. I'm talking about soft, still-warm doughnuts that cost just pennies on the dollar. Make this recipe and fill them with your favorite jelly, or even peanut butter and jelly! Serve warm with an ice-cold glass of milk.

PB&J DOUGHNUTS

Makes 14–20 doughnuts

5 tablespoons warm water (about 90°F)

3½ tablespoons fresh yeast

2 cups powdered sugar

6 cups flour

3 eggs (at room temperature)

1½ cups whole milk (warm)

⅛ cup unsalted butter (soft)

1 teaspoon salt

Canola oil for deep-frying

2–3 cups jam, jelly, marmalade, or preserves

2 cups smooth peanut butter (optional)

Jelly-Filled Doughnut Day, June 8

1. In a bowl, combine water with yeast until dissolved, then add 1 tablespoon sugar and ½ cup flour. Cover with plastic wrap and set aside to allow yeast to rise for 10 minutes.

2. In a separate bowl, sift remaining flour and powdered sugar then combine with eggs, milk, butter, and salt. In an electric mixer with a paddle attachment, combine until it forms a dough.

3. Add yeast mixture and continue to combine. If dough is really sticky, add a little more flour until it hardly sticks to your hands.

4. Cover with plastic again and allow to rise for 1 hour, undisturbed.

5. When ready to make doughnuts, bring 5–6 cups of oil to 350°F in a large stockpot (use a thermometer to make sure it stays at this temperature).

6. On a floured work surface, pat down dough to 1" thickness. Use a 2–3" ring cutter to cut doughnuts (don't cut a ring in the middle— remember we're stuffing these).

7. Fry until golden, about 2 minutes on each side. Remove doughnuts from oil, drain on paper towels, and cool.

8. Using a chopstick (or something similar), prick a hole in doughnut for filling. Scoop the jam in a piping bag and fill each with as much jam as you want! Add peanut butter in the same way. Dust with powdered sugar on both sides before serving.

Cook's Note

It's easier to simply dust these with powdered sugar instead of the crafty "put-the-doughnuts-in-a-bag-with-powdered-sugar, close-bag-and-shake" method. Since they are filled with jelly you'll just end up with a big, gooey mess!

Strawberry-Rhubarb Pie Day

JUNE 9

Traditional Strawberry-Rhubarb Pie is made with strawberries and rhubarb cooked to a jammy consistency and poured into a tender and crisp shell. This is something I love and have come to expect. In the kitchen we have a saying that goes "what grows together, goes together," referring to fruits, veggies, and herbs grown in the same season. Rhubarb and strawberries to me are the quintessential telltale signs that winter is long gone, spring just whizzed past us, and we are headed into the heat of summer.

STRAWBERRY-RHUBARB CUSTARD PIE

Serves 6–8

Pie Dough (Apr. 28)

½ cup heavy cream

1½ cups rhubarb purée

2 tablespoons cornstarch

4 egg yolks

1 cup sugar

About 1 dozen medium fresh strawberries (sliced)

2 tablespoons powdered sugar

1 tablespoon chopped mint

1. Bake pie crust and allow to cool.

2. In the meantime prepare the rhubarb pastry cream by bringing the heavy cream and rhubarb purée to a boil in a 2-quart nonreactive pot.

3. In the meantime combine the cornstarch with the egg yolks and sugar and stir until smooth and homogeneous.

4. Once the cream mixture comes to a boil, temper the eggs by adding a little cream at a time while whisking. Once half the cream has been incorporated into the eggs, return the eggs to the remaining cream in the pot and cook over medium heat while whisking continuously until thickened, about 2 minutes.

5. Pour the rhubarb cream into a bowl or Tupperware container and place a plastic wrap skin directly on top of the cream to prevent a hard skin from forming on top and refrigerate until cold, or for about 1 hour.

6. While the cream cools, clean the strawberries and slice them in quarters. Place the strawberries in a container with a lid and sprinkle with powdered sugar and chopped mint.

7. Cover the container and place in the fridge to macerate.

8. Once the cream is cooled, compose the pie by spooning plenty of the rhubarb cream into the bottom of the pie shell, smooth it out, and top with the strawberries. When ready to serve sprinkle with powdered sugar and serve with a little whipped cream.

Iced Tea Day

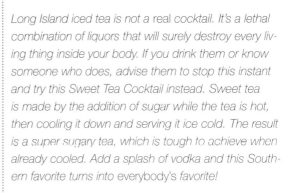

Long Island iced tea is not a real cocktail. It's a lethal combination of liquors that will surely destroy every living thing inside your body. If you drink them or know someone who does, advise them to stop this instant and try this Sweet Tea Cocktail instead. Sweet tea is made by the addition of sugar while the tea is hot, then cooling it down and serving it ice cold. The result is a super sugary tea, which is tough to achieve when already cooled. Add a splash of vodka and this Southern favorite turns into everybody's favorite!

SWEET TEA COCKTAIL

Serves 3–4

1 quart plus 2 cups water

1 cup sugar

8 tea bags (Lipton Iced Tea Brew works great but use any tea you like)

3 mint sprigs and more for garnish

1 cup lemon-flavored vodka (preferably by just adding a few lemon peels to a bottle of vodka and placing it in the fridge overnight)

Sliced lemon for garnish

1. In large stockpot, bring one quart water and sugar to a boil, stirring until dissolved.

2. Add tea bags and mint and infuse for about 6 minutes. Remove tea bags from mixture and add remaining 2 cups water and vodka.

3. Chill until ready to drink.

4. Serve on ice (if you can shake before serving it, that will give your ice tea a little froth, which I really like), garnish with fresh mint and slice of lemon.

German Chocolate Cake Day

Contrary to popular belief, German Chocolate Cake was not brought over to America by German immigrants. Instead, it was created by Sam German for the Baker Chocolate Company and named so in his honor. Sam German created the baking chocolate bar from which this delicious cake is made, and it is believed he is responsible for the cake's creation. However, he created the bar in 1852, and the first published recipe came from a Texas homemaker in 1957. What happened in those 100 years the world may never know.

GERMAN CHOCOLATE CAKE

Serves 8

1 cup salted butter

1½ cups sugar

3 ounces Baker's unsweetened chocolate

1 ounce Baker's bittersweet chocolate

2 cups all-purpose flour

1 teaspoon baking powder

1 teaspoon baking soda

4 eggs (separated)

4 tablespoons water (room temp)

2 tablespoons milk (room temp)

1 teaspoon vanilla extract

1 cup buttermilk (room temp)

Coconut rum (for soaking later)

Preparing the Cake

❶ Cream butter with 1 cup sugar and beat until pale and fluffy, about 5–10 minutes.

❷ Melt chocolates in microwave monitoring closely until smooth. Sift dry ingredients and set aside.

❸ Once butter is fluffy, add egg yolks one at a time. Add remaining ingredients, except egg whites and remaining sugar, alternating between dry ingredients and liquids until combined well.

❹ In another bowl, whip egg whites. Once fluffy, add sugar and beat on high until they hold soft peaks. (Do not over whip; keep a close eye on them and slow whipping if necessary).

❺ Add half of whites to chocolate batter and fold gently until there are no streaks, then fold in remaining whites.

❻ Spread into two 9" cake molds that have been oiled and dusted with flour.

❼ Bake for 40–45 minutes at 350°F until a toothpick inserted in middle comes out. Remove from oven and cool completely.

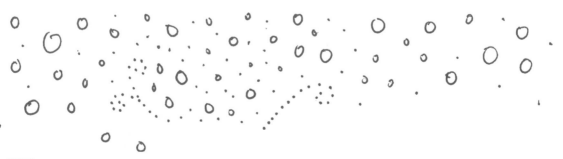

Preparing the Filling

1. In a heavy bottomed pot, bring milk to a boil. In another bowl, cream butter with chocolate, pecans, and coconut. In yet another bowl, combine sugar and egg yolks.

2. Once milk is boiling, temper eggs by adding hot mixture a little at a time while whisking.

3. After adding half of hot milk, return entire mixture to pot and cook on medium heat until it reaches 165°F.

4. Remove from heat and add to butter mixture. Let sit for 4 minutes, then whisk everything together, adding vanilla and salt last.

Preparing the Whipped Cream

1. Melt chocolate in microwave. In meantime, bring cream to a rapid boil.

2. Add sugar to cream until dissolved. Once chocolate completely melts add cream to chocolate in a slow, steady stream while whisking. *Do not add chocolate to cream, this does not melt chocolate evenly and you will have a grainy cream.*

3. Once cream is incorporated into chocolate, place in clean container and refrigerate overnight or at least 4 hours, until superduper cold.

4. When ready to whip cream, do so by hand over a bowl with ice water. If using an electric beater, keep slow and still over ice bath. Whip slowly for 3 minutes until a beautiful whipped cream forms.

5. Refrigerate until ready to use.

Assembling the Cake

1. Cut both in half with serrated knife, so each has a top and bottom.

2. Soak 4 layers with a little coconut rum, then top each with Coconut-Pecan Filling.

3. On a large plate, layer one on top of another. Frost with Whipped Chocolate Cream.

4. Garnish with maraschino cherries for a festive flair.

Coconut-Pecan Filling

1 cup evaporated milk

3 tablespoons butter

4 tablespoons bittersweet chocolate (chopped)

1 cup pecans (toasted and chopped)

1½ cups sweetened shredded coconut

½ cup brown sugar

3 egg yolks

½ teaspoon vanilla extract

Pinch of salt

Whipped Chocolate Cream

3 ounces bittersweet chocolate

2 cups heavy cream

2 tablespoons sugar

Peanut Butter Cookie Day

Peanut butter cookies are a great snack to have around the house for those moments when you need a sweet treat. Not only is peanut butter super nutritious and full of protein, vitamins B3 and E, magnesium, folate, dietary fiber, arginine, and lots of antioxidants, it's also delicious and helps render moist and buttery cookies. I bake big batches of these puppies and freeze them. They also make great presents and a wonderful addition to the kids' bagged lunch.

PEANUT BUTTER COOKIES

Makes 2 dozen

¼ cup butter (soft)

1 cup brown sugar

½ teaspoon salt

¾ cup all-purpose flour

½ teaspoon baking soda

1 egg

1 teaspoon vanilla extract

1 cup chunky peanut butter

1 tablespoon honey

❶ Cream butter with sugar until creamy and fluffy. Sift dry ingredients and add them a little at a time along with the egg until well combined. Mix in vanilla, peanut butter, and honey.

❷ Scoop 2 tablespoon-sized balls onto a baking sheet lined with parchment paper or aluminum foil. Press dough down until cookies are ½" thick.

❸ Bake at 350°F for 10 minutes. Allow cookies to cool and serve warm.

Kitchen Klutzes of America Day

I tend to be a bit of a klutz at times, I think we all are when we're distracted by a million pressing things and find ourselves dropping stuff, cutting ourselves, burning our fingers, burning food. And at times, everybody feels like throwing in the towel. But don't fear! When you feel overwhelmed, ready to throw the pot out the window, just walk away. Walk away from it all and take a breather. Here's a foolproof recipe that appeals to us klutzes, always satisfies, and feeds an army.

MA! THE MEATLOAF!

Serves 4–5

3 slices soft white bread (without crusts, torn into chunks)

¼ cup whole milk

1 pound ground beef

1 pound ground pork

½ pound ground veal

2 eggs

3–4 dashes of liquid smoke (look for it next to the Worcestershire sauce)

Leaves from 2 fresh thyme sprigs or 1 tablespoon dried oregano

½ tablespoon red pepper flakes

1 cup mozzarella cheese (shredded)

Salt and freshly ground black pepper

1 cup ketchup

1 cup ricotta cheese

Tomato sauce

Parmesan cheese

1. Begin by soaking bread in milk.

2. In a clean bowl, mix remaining ingredients except ketchup, ricotta, tomato sauce, and Parmesan (OK, you can add a little ketchup to the mix if you like).

3. On cookie sheet lined with aluminum foil and covered with nonstick spray, form a log 10" long.

4. Glaze with ketchup and bake at 350°F for 1–1½ hours, or until internal temperature reads 125–130°F.

5. To serve, blend ricotta cheese in food processor until smooth. Serve cheese with slice of meatloaf atop. Spoon on a little tomato sauce and douse with lots of Parmesan.

JUNE 14
Strawberry Shortcake Day

This cake is super simple and really yummy. The trick is to get really good-quality berries, toss them together with a little mint and sugar, and let them marinate for a few minutes. Technically this dessert is made with a short dough, a biscuitlike cake that soaks up the juice of the berries perfectly. However, I've made this with sponge cake, pound cake, and even puff pastry—all with yummy results!

STRAWBERRY SHORTCAKE

Serves 6

2 ½ cups all-purpose flour

1 tablespoon plus 1 teaspoon baking powder

4 tablespoons butter (cubed and cold)

½ teaspoon salt

⅛ cup granulated sugar

1 cup plus 2 tablespoons heavy cream (cold)

1 egg (beaten for wash)

Oatmeal

Coarse sugar

½ pound of the freshest most beautiful strawberries you can find

Lemon juice

Powdered sugar

Perfect Chantilly Cream (Jan. 5)

1. To make shortcake, sift flour with baking powder.

2. Combine butter with sifted flour, salt, and sugar until small crumbs form. Add cream and mix with your hands until you have a shaggy mess. Pat down with hands and make into rounds with cookie cutter.

3. Place on a cookie sheet lined with parchment paper, brush with egg, sprinkle with oatmeal and coarse sugar, and bake for 15 minutes at 350°F until lightly golden.

4. Allow shortcakes to cool, split, then slice strawberries and toss with lemon juice and powdered sugar.

5. Stuff shortcakes with strawberry mixture and top with a huge dollop of whipped cream, top with shortcake, sprinkle with powdered sugar, and serve.

Lobster Day

It was December 30 and we were in Los Cabos, Mexico. We were catering a wedding at a ritzy hotel and decided to stay through New Year's. After working we needed a night of dancing so we went into town. Several drinks later, we ended up at an abandoned fishing boat on the beach. We were haphazardly climbing all over it when out of the darkness we spotted a figure emerging from the water walking toward us. I squinted, thinking this is nuts, when it becomes clear the guy has a dozen huge still-moving lobsters in hand. Turns out, he free dives at night to catch the crustaceans to sell to area hotels. You gotta love Mexico! My favorite way to eat lobster is in a roll; the addition of green apple puts it over the top.

LOBSTER CLUB

Serves 2

1 cup water

1 2-pound lobster

6 garlic cloves

2 teaspoon fresh lemon juice

A good handful of fresh dill (just eyeball it, clean it and dry it)

¾ teaspoon salt

Pinch of white pepper

½ cup Greek yogurt

1 fresh, crusty baguette

Soft butter

Iceberg lettuce

1 green apple (peeled and thinly sliced)

1 ripe avocado (thinly sliced)

1 seedless cucumber (peeled and thinly sliced)

❶ In a large stockpot, bring 1 cup water to a boil.

❷ Crumple a large piece of aluminum foil into a flat ball that covers the bottom of the pot—now you have a steamer. The aluminum when crumpled creates a barrier between the bottom of the pot and allows the steam to come up and around to cook the lobster. Place lobster inside pot and cover, cook for 8 minutes making sure there is always water in bottom of pot. (If you don't see steam coming out of the seam between pot and lid, add some more *hot* water).

❸ Remove pot from stove and place it in sink. Remove lid and run cold water directly on lobster for about 2 minutes. Let lobster sit another 10–15 minutes in cold water.

❹ Combine garlic, lemon juice, dill, salt, pepper, and yogurt in a blender until smooth and green (about 1 minute).

❺ When cool enough to handle, remove lobster meat.

❻ Coarsely chop lobster, place in bowl, add about 4 tablespoons of dill yogurt, toss, and let sit.

❼ Slice open baguette and brush with butter all around and inside. Place bread open on a cookie sheet inside a 400°F oven until crispy (about 5 minutes).

❽ Open baguette, layer lettuce, lobster mixture (trying not to grab too much liquid), apple, avocado, and cucumber slices. Drizzle with remaining dill yogurt and garnish with fresh dill sprigs. Close sandwich and enjoy!

JUNE 16

Fudge Day

We've encountered a few fudge recipes in this book already, and they're all amazing, really yummy, but the most common fudge I use is hot fudge, on sundaes. Hot fudge on cold ice cream. 'Nuff said.

HOT FUDGE

Makes 4–5 servings

1 can condensed milk

½ cup heavy cream

½ cup dark chocolate

2 tablespoons butter

Pinch of salt

❶ Peel label from can condensed milk and boil for 2 hours.

❷ *Once it has cooled*, scoop into pot, add heavy cream, and whisk together over medium heat.

❸ Once hot, add chocolate and continue to whisk until completely dissolved, then add butter and salt. Now you have hot fudge, so that's that.

❹ Go get some ice cream to drench in hot fudge. (I hope you remembered to buy ice cream!)

Apple Strudel Day

JUNE 17

Being the official pastry of Texas is no easy job. But strudel has been standing tall since it was officially declared as such in 2003. Strudel is a layered pastry similar to puff pastry or baklava. Apple Strudel is the most popular type of strudel in the world and it comes to us by way of Germany where they refer to it as apfelstrudel, loosely meaning "whirlpool with apple." Here we make it with phyllo dough, which produces wonderful results and is a lot easier.

APPLE STRUDEL

Serves 6–8

¼ cup sugar

1 cup melted butter plus 3 tablespoons solid

3 Granny Smith apples (peeled, cored, and cut into small chunks)

½ cup applejack, rum, or bourbon

1 teaspoon cinnamon

1 cup golden raisins

½ lemon (juiced)

6 sheets of phyllo dough

½ cup pecans or walnuts (toasted and chopped)

½ cup brown sugar

Honey (for drizzling)

❶ Heat sugar with the 3 tablespoons butter in a sauté pan until it starts to turn to caramel, add apples followed by applejack, cinnamon, raisins, and lemon juice.

2. Cook for 2 minutes on high heat. Remove from heat and pour contents of pan into a bowl to cool.

3. Brush phyllo one sheet at a time with melted butter, stacking one sheet on top of another until all sheets have been used. Position phyllo horizontally, scoop apple filling into a straight line at bottom side closest to you.

4. Sprinkle with nuts then gently and gingerly roll strudel away from you into a log. Make sure seam is below log; this will prevent strudel from unrolling.

5. Sprinkle with brown sugar and bake at 350°F for 20–25 minutes until golden brown.

6. Drizzle with honey and a little more cinnamon as soon as ready. Eat right away!

Picnic Day

Picnics are often forgotten in today's hectic and overbooked world. Their beautiful simplicity is often trumped by going out to eat, which is faster but not necessarily better. I don't understand why picnics aren't more popular. I personally own three baskets! Picnics are leisurely—an invitation to lay in the sun reading and eating until the sun comes down. Here is my packing list for a perfect picnic. Whether with your husband, wife, girlfriend, or family, it's got the makings of a wonderful memory.

THE PERFECT PICNIC BASKET

A picnic for 2

1 sandwich (your preference, maybe Oct. 9)

Potato Chips (July 18)

Éclair Cream Puffs (June 22)

1 bottle of wine

Corkscrew (unless you've got screw-top wine)

Blanket big enough to hold everything—and everyone

A copy of Hemingway's *A Movable Feast*

Dry
Martini Day

The Martini is by far the most iconic cocktail in America. Seemingly born around 1862 in California, it consisted of 1 part Old Tom gin (a superduper junipery gin) with 4 parts sweet vermouth, bitters, and a cherry. Over time, the recipe evolved from sweet to dry vermouth, and from bitters to orange bitters. Fast-forward to today and it's basically anything served in a Martini glass! Remember: "Shaken, not stirred"—shake with good clean ice (you know what I mean, no ice with crusty ice-fungus growing on top). This awakens the spirit and chills the heck out of your drink. (In my opinion, the worst martini is a warm martini.) Bottoms up!

CLASSIC DRY MARTINI

Makes 1 martini

2½ ounces great-quality gin

½ ounce Dolin dry vermouth

Large, clean ice cubes

Olives

Fresh lemon twist

❶ Combine all ingredients in a glass shaker. Add a lot of fresh ice and shake like crazy for 10 seconds.

❷ Strain into a chilled martini glass.

❸ Garnish with olive and fresh lemon twist made with a peeler.

Vanilla
Milkshake
Day

Milkshakes are the quintessential summertime treat. Usually accompanied by a burger and some fries, they're a glassful of nostalgia and a breeze to make. Try them with any flavor and watch your kids' faces light up.

VANILLA MILKSHAKE

Makes 1

2 cups really good-quality vanilla ice cream

1 teaspoon vanilla extract

2 tablespoon sugar

½ cup milk

Perfect Chantilly Cream (Jan. 5) and maraschino cherries for topping

It's a milkshake. You shouldn't need instructions. But just in case:

❶ Blend all ingredients until smooth.

❷ Pour into your favorite glass and top with whipped cream and a cherry.

❸ Serve with straws.

Peaches and Cream Day

Soft, lightly sweetened vanilla whipped cream is a wonderful addition to any dessert, but there's something about the marriage of succulent peaches with the velvety comfort of the cream that makes this pairing extraordinary. I like to simply serve this with a Latin Tres Leches cake. Tres Leches translates from Spanish into "three milks." That's because you use three kinds of milks to make the cake: evaporated, condensed, and heavy cream. This makes all the flavors explode in your mouth when you bite into it.

PEACHES AND CREAM TRES LECHES

Serves 6

5 eggs (at room temperature)

1 cup sugar

1 cup flour

1 teaspoon baking powder

1 cup canned peaches (chopped)

1 teaspoon vanilla extract

2 tablespoons plus ¼ teaspoon water

Soaking Milk

1 can condensed milk

1 can evaporated milk

1½ cups heavy cream

½ cup peach schnapps or peach syrup

½ teaspoon vanilla extract

❶ Whip eggs with sugar for 15 minutes on high until tripled in volume.

❷ Sift flour and baking power.

❸ Once eggs are ready add flour mixture and fold with rubber spatula, then add peaches, vanilla, and water.

❹ Fold until mixed well. Oil and flour a 12" x 12" pan (or any pan you have, just make sure batter is no more than 1" deep).

❺ Bake at 400°F for 10–15 minutes until cake is set and toothpick inserted in middle comes out clean.

❻ Remove from oven, poke little holes in cake using toothpick, and let cool.

❼ To prepare soaking milk, boil all ingredients together for 1 minute and pour on cake.

❽ Top with any remaining peaches (thinly sliced) and whipped cream. Serve cold.

Chocolate Éclair Day

Eclairs are the elongated versions of cream puffs, otherwise called profiteroles. It all starts with a dough that you cook on the stovetop that then gets baked into light and hollow Twinkie-shaped logs. Éclairs are filled with a myriad of creams then glazed—the most popular being vanilla cream-filled and chocolate-glazed. Noted chef Antoine Carême is credited to have invented these in France around the 1860s.

ÉCLAIR CREAM PUFFS

Makes about 1 dozen

1 cup water

1 tablespoon sugar

Pinch of salt

6 tablespoons butter

5¾ ounces all-purpose flour (sifted)

4 large eggs and 1 white plus 1 for wash

1 Combine water, sugar, salt, and butter in a pot and bring to a boil. When butter has melted, add sifted flour and stir with wooden spoon until dough forms. Cook on medium heat for 1 minute, stirring constantly.

2 Remove pot from heat, pour dough into stand mixer, and let sit until warm. Mix on medium-high, adding one egg at a time until you have a smooth mixture.

3 Pipe mixture onto a greased baking sheet in oblong shapes 3–4" long. Bake for 10 minutes at 400°F then lower the temperature to 325°F. Glaze with egg wash (1 egg and 2 teaspoons water) and return to oven until dry and golden, about 10 minutes.

4 Remove from oven and let cool (do not refrigerate). Fill a pastry bag with pastry cream and fill the puffs. Make the chocolate glaze, then dip the éclairs in the glaze so that you only glaze the top a bit. Flip the puff so that its glaze side up on a rack and place in a cool place. Allow to cool so that the glaze sets for about 20–30 minutes and eat them all!

Chocolate Glaze

4 ounces bittersweet chocolate

4 tablespoons unsalted butter, softened

1 To make glaze simply melt the chocolate in a microwave 1 minute at a time until smooth.

2 Add the butter and whisk until smooth.

Pecan Sandy Day

Sandies are named because of the cookie's sandy texture. It's merely a combo of eggs, sugar, and flour with a little baking powder. Here, we pack them with buttery pecans and bake 'til crisp.

PECAN SANDIES

Makes 2 dozen

1 cup butter (soft)

1 cup light brown sugar

2⅛ cups all-purpose flour

1 tablespoon baking powder

½ teaspoon salt

5 yolks

1 cup chopped pecans (cool)

1 teaspoon vanilla extract

Coarse salt and sugar for topping

1. Cream butter with sugar for at least 10 minutes until white and fluffy. Sift flour and baking powder.

2. Add dry ingredients and mix well, then add remaining ingredients, making sure to scrape down sides and thoroughly combine.

3. Stretch piece of plastic wrap and scoop out half of dough, then roll into a log. Tie ends tightly with string or another piece of plastic wrap. Repeat with remaining dough.

4. Preheat oven to 325°F, cut log into ½" disks, remove plastic wrap, and place disks inside muffin baking cups, sprinkle with coarse salt and sugar, and bake for 10–15 minutes until golden.

5. Chill and enjoy.

JUNE 24 Pralines Day

Pralines are a New Orleans favorite! Brought over by the French who initially made them with almonds, they switched to pecan after settling in the bayou. Backtrack 200 years earlier to the seventeenth century when a count by the name of Cesar de Plessis created these confections as his own personal calling card while courting beautiful and famous women in France. The French candies were simply nuts and sugar, but by the time the Creoles got a hold of them a little butter and cream made these a household name.

N'AWLINS PRALINES

Makes 1 dozen

2 tablespoons butter

1 cup light brown sugar

1 cup sugar

½ cup heavy cream

1 teaspoon salt

2 cups pecans (toasted and chopped)

1. In a heavy-bottomed pot, carefully combine all ingredients except pecans, making sure not to get sugar on the sides of the pot (if you do, clean it up with a wet napkin. This is important because if there is sugar on the sides as the pot heats up, the sugar will crystallize and not caramelize, ruining the whole batch). Bring to boil.

2. Line cookie sheet with wax paper and place on top of cutting board (the cutting board acts as an insulator and protects your counter).

3. Lower heat and cook until a candy thermometer reads 239°F. Remove from heat and add pecans.

4. Stir with wooden spoon until mixture thickens and turns a little pale, then quickly scoop (using an ice cream scooper is easiest) onto wax paper, leaving room between each one to account for spreading.

5. Allow to cool on a counter for about 1 hour then eat 'em up!

Strawberry Parfait Day

Ever meet someone who doesn't like parfait? Of course not. That's because parfait's gotta be the tastiest thing on the whole damn planet! There are two kinds: the French kind, which are light airy mousses that are frozen and then served; or the layered kind, which are visually appealing concoctions served in a parfait glass (basically, a tall fluted glass). Quick to make and delicious, they can be assembled with almost anything you want. (Nacho parfait, anyone?) As long as it's in the right kind of glass, you have the green light to call it a parfait.

STRAWBERRY PARFAIT

Serves 6

Homemade Vanilla Ice Cream (July 23)

Buttery Pound Cake (Mar. 4)

Perfect Chantilly Cream (Jan. 5)

2 cups beautiful, ripe strawberries (sliced and dusted with powdered sugar)

❶ Cut cake into small pieces.

❷ Layer all ingredients in a parfait glass and serve with a long spoon.

❸ Enjoy! (That's it. See? I told you they were simple.)

Chocolate Pudding Day

In today's age of food blogs, it's not uncommon to see hundreds of plates of food a day just surfing the web. One of my faves is my friend Allison Hagendorf's; she's a lifestyle artist, host on Fuse TV, and a voracious eater. One day I posted a picture of a milkshake on Facebook and she commented "I want to shove my face into this!" That's exactly what I think when I make pudding—forget utensils! It resembles a banana split but its with pudding! This pudding goes out to Allison.

"SHOVE YOUR FACE INTO IT" CHOCOLATE PUDDING SUNDAE

Serves 3

1 Chocolate Pudding recipe (May 1), poured into wide sundae bowls and chilled

3 bananas (split in half)

1 Perfect Chantilly Cream recipe (Jan. 5)

1 Hot Fudge recipe (June 16)

¼ cup chopped peanuts

9 maraschino cherries

❶ Once pudding is chilled, slice bananas and place slices on either side of glass.

❷ Top with whipped cream, drizzle with chocolate, sprinkle with peanuts, and garnish with cherries.

❸ Serve without utensils. And maybe a bib. Camera suggested.

JUNE 27

Orange Blossom Day

Orange Blossom water is the distillation of orange flowers from orange trees. It's widely used in Middle Eastern cooking and often added to bad drinking water to make it more palatable. This fragrant water is also used in confections but mostly known to grace cocktails, specifically the Ramos Gin Fizz. Originally the New Orleans Fizz, this drink was created by Henry C. Ramos in 1888 at his restaurant Meyer's in the Big Easy. It uses raw egg whites, but don't worry—the citrus and alcohol practically pasteurize the egg so it's safe to drink. You can also just use pasteurized egg whites from the start. No harm, no foul. Now, let's drink!

RAMOS GIN FIZ

Makes 1 drink

2 ounces gin

6 drops of good-quality orange blossom water

1 egg white

½ ounce heavy cream (lightly beaten)

½ ounce lemon juice

½ ounce lime juice

1 tablespoon superfine sugar or 1 ounce simple syrup

Club soda

Ice

❶ Combine all ingredients in shaker, close and shake for 20 seconds (even though all you have is liquids, this is called a dry shake because you haven't added ice yet); hold the container tight because the foaming whites will create a little pressure and the glasses will want to come apart.

❷ Carefully open shaker, fill with ice, and shake again; this time for 30 seconds. Strain into Collins class and top with club soda while stirring lightly. Garnish with a orange twist and serve with a straw.

Cook's Note

Orange Blossom water is a must for this. You can find it at your local Mediterranean market or online for about $7. Orange blossom water is wonderful in lemonades or to rub on your ears to smell light and fresh.

Tapioca Day

JUNE 28

Tapioca is made from the root of the cassava plant, which is cultivated and native to South America. Tapioca is sometimes considered the South American equivalent to our American corn since its uses are as varied and integral to the diet of our neighbors to the south. The most traditional use of Tapioca is in pudding, but in Asia, it's all about bubble tea—sweet, delicious tea with milk and lots of Tapioca pearls served with a colorful straw. Don't you love it already?

Cook's Note

You can find Thai tea online or in your ethnic market. If not, don't worry. Use your favorite tea and feel free to add flavorings (Torani makes great tasting syrups)!

THAI BUBBLE TEA

Serves 1

¼ cup large tapioca pearls (cooked and cooled)

1 cup strongly brewed Thai tea (regular black tea is okay, too, but doesn't look as cool)

Lots of ice

¼ cup condensed milk

Straws

1. Combine tapioca with cooled tea.

2. Pour over ice and top with the condensed milk, don't stir to create the layers of colors, then serve. Serve with a straw.

JUNE 29
Almond Butter Crunch Day

The best info I can gather on Almond Butter Crunch is it's uncanny similarity to Almond Roca, which in my book is basically the same thing, so we'll go with that. Almond Roca was created by Brown & Haley in 1923. This confection gets its name from the word "rock" in Spanish and has since then been used in pies, ice cream, and even candy bars!

ALMOND BUTTER CRUNCH

Serves 4–6

1 cup granulated sugar

1 cup white chocolate (melted)

2 cups chopped almonds (toasted and cooled)

1 tablespoon butter

½ teaspoon salt

½ cup sliced almonds (toasted and cooled)

1. In a heavy-bottomed pot, melt sugar over high heat while stirring slowly. Once caramel starts to form, don't walk away, stay with it, stirring slowly.

2. When sugar has completely melted, add white chocolate and remove from heat. Stir until mixture is smooth, then add chopped almonds, butter, and salt and combine thoroughly.

3. Spoon onto Silpat or wax paper and immediately top with sliced almonds.

1. Carefully press almonds into the caramel using a spatula and flatten until you have a thin layer. Let cool for at least 1 hour on the counter at room temperature.

2. Store covered in a cool, dry place or eat everything immediately without sharing a single morsel.

Ice Cream Soda Day
JUNE 30

Back in the day, there weren't stores that carried the rainbow-colored corn-syrup concoctions that are ubiquitous today. Sodas were made by baristas who served up drink after customized drink for thirsty Americans. What's more is that they were traditionally doled out in pharmacies! Which brings us to today. Here I make an espresso coffee soda—my go-to drink during the hot days of summer.

CAPPUCCINO ICE CREAM SODA

Makes 1 drink

10 ounces Manhattan Special espresso soda (chilled)

1 pint vanilla ice cream

Cinnamon for topping

1. Pour soda in tall, frosty glass leaving at least 1" at top.

2. Top with scoop of ice cream, sprinkle with cinnamon, and enjoy!

Cook's Note

If you can't find espresso soda, mix about 2 tablespoons of instant coffee with 2 tablespoons of sugar and a little hot water to make a syrup, then mix that into soda water, and top with ice cream and cinnamon.

JULY

Creative Ice Cream Flavor Day

So it's July 1 (my birthday, by the way!), it's hot, and you're craving ice cream. There are a million flavors out there, but why not think of something new? This holiday is meant to let your imagination run wild so you can you create your very own flavor. Need inspiration? I turned to Google and I found lox ice cream, bacon ice cream, barbecue ice cream, octopus ice cream, spaghetti Bolognaise ice cream, and fish ice cream, tons of fish ice cream. I like this one a whole lot better than any of those options. I hope you do, too!

OVALTINE ICE CREAM

Serves 5–6

2 cups whole milk

1 cup sugar

1 vanilla bean

9 large egg yolks

2 cups heavy cream

Pinch of salt

1½ teaspoon pure vanilla extract

1 cup Ovaltine (feel free to add more if you want it stronger and richer)

① In a heavy-bottomed pot, combine milk and sugar. Split vanilla bean in half and scrape insides into milk mixture and bring to simmer. Turn off heat and infuse for 30 minutes.

② Separate eggs and give yolks a good whisk.

③ Fill bowl with ice water, put another metal bowl on top and fill with heavy cream, salt, and vanilla extract.

④ Bring milk mixture to boil again and temper yolks by drizzling milk into them slowly while whisking constantly. After adding half of milk to yolks, return mixture to pot with remaining milk.

⑤ Cook on low-medium heat while scraping bottom of pot with a heatproof spatula until coated with custard.

⑥ Remove from the heat, whisk in the Ovaltine, then pour into cool, heavy cream mixture and refrigerate for at least 2 hours.

⑦ Remove vanilla bean, rinse it off and pat it dry, then plop into a bottle of wine for vanilla wine, into oil, or into sugar for vanilla sugar.

⑧ Freeze ice cream according to your ice cream maker's instructions. (If you want, when ice cream is done, add crushed malted milk balls for crunch and freeze until hard.)

JULY 2 Anisette Day

Anise—the main ingredient in the liqueur Anisette—is a flowering plant native to the Mediterranean and southwest Asia whose flavor resembles fennel, tarragon, and licorice. When you think of anise the first thing that probably comes to mind is star anise, but they are not the same. Anise is widely used worldwide in the production of local spirits—from the Bulgarian Mastika, the Greek Ouzo, the French Pastis, Colombian Aguardiente, Arab Arak, German Jägermeister, Italian Sambuca, and Turkish Raki. It is also used to make root beer in the United States. For my family, it's all about the cookies.

ANISETTE COOKIES

Makes 2 dozen cookies

1 cup powdered sugar

1 cup granulated sugar

4 cups all-purpose flour

6 tablespoons baking powder

¾ cup oil

½ cup milk

2 eggs

2 tablespoons hot water

1 teaspoon anise extract

1 cup pine nuts

❶ Sift dry ingredients. Make a well in middle of flour mixture and add wet ingredients. Combine slowly until completely incorporated and dough forms.

❷ Oil hands and make 1–2 tablespoon-sized balls of dough. Place about 2" apart on a lightly oiled cookie sheet lined with parchment paper or a Silpat.

❸ Press cookies lightly so they flatten but are still ½" thick. Add about ½ teaspoon of the nuts on top and press in gently using your hand. Bake at 375°F for 7 minutes.

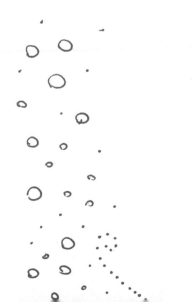

Eat Beans Day

Beans are a fantastic source of protein, a great crop that, when dried, lasts indefinitely in the pantry, extremely inexpensive, and totally satisfying. Here, I bring you a savory bean pie with a little sprinkle of sugar on top.

BLACK BEAN PIE

Serves 6

2 slices good-quality smoked bacon (chopped small)

¼ onion (chopped small)

1 (15.5-ounce) can black beans

½ teaspoon salt

¼ teaspoon white pepper

¼ teaspoon granulated sugar and more for dusting

2 teaspoons cornstarch

Quiche crust (cooled to room temp; May 20)

❶ Cook bacon and onions in a 2-quart pot over medium heat until translucent, about 5 minutes.

❷ Add beans (reserving 1 tablespoon of liquid), salt, pepper, and sugar. Combine cornstarch with reserved liquid and mix well.

❸ Once beans come to a boil, add cornstarch slurry while stirring and cook for 1 minute. Pour into cooled quiche crust and let chill at room temperature, about 10 minutes.

❹ Sprinkle with ½ tablespoon sugar and cover edge of pie with aluminum foil to prevent it from burning.

❺ Cook for 6 minutes at 350°F, remove from oven, and allow to cool until just warm, about 6 minutes. Cut and serve.

JULY 4

Barbecued Spareribs Day

Ribs, ribs, ribs . . . I could say it all day. There are few words that sound as beautiful in the English language. Spareribs are the most inexpensive kind of rib, which is crazy, because they taste great. They are the long ribs cut from the bottom of either the hog or cattle right behind the shoulder. My little brother Johnny is the biggest rib fan I know. He reminds me of his love of ribs about 2 times a week, so I know we'll celebrate America's independence with a fat stack glazed in smoky barbecue sauce!

RIDICULOUSLY DELICIOUS RIBS

Serves 2–4

  1 rack of pork spareribs

Garlic Rub-a-Dub

  10 garlic cloves

  2–3 rosemary sprigs

  ½ onion

  Olive oil

Smoke Dust

  ¾ cup brown sugar

  2 tablespoons freshly ground white or black pepper

  ¼ cups smoked paprika

  ⅛ cup kosher salt

  1 tablespoon ground cumin

  1 tablespoon chili powder

  1 teaspoon cayenne pepper

  ½ cup dry rice (if using a shaker to keep the ingredients dry)

  Smoking chips

  ½ cup apple juice

  ½ cup apple cider vinegar

  Your favorite barbecue sauce

1. Rinse ribs and pat dry. With a knife, remove skin on back side. (The easiest way is to stick knife in between skin and meat, make a little flap, then with paper towel or hand towel, pull skin off.)

2. To prepare Garlic Rub-a-Dub, blend garlic, rosemary, onion, and enough olive oil to make a paste. To prepare Smoke Dust, mix dry ingredients.

3. Rub ribs thoroughly with garlic paste then sprinkle Smoke Dust generously and pat in. Wrap with plastic wrap and let marinate overnight or for at least 2 hours.

4. Sprinkle ribs with more Smoke Dust and set aside.

5. To prepare for smoking, line roasting pan with aluminum foil, add ½ cup of smoking chips, and set on stovetop. Position a grill inside pot, so there's at least 2–3" between bottom of pot and grill. Heat pan over high heat, or if you have a torch, light the chips until they start smoking. Place a metal cup with hot water inside pot right next to the rack or next to the ribs. Cover the roasting pan and place inside oven and cook at 225°F for 3 hours.

6. Fold piece of aluminum foil twice as big as rack of ribs in half. Remove ribs from on top of the rack and place in the middle of a large piece of aluminum foil that is big enough to wrap around the ribs and lift the sides up making a pouch. Mix the apple juice and vinegar together then add ¼ cup of apple juice/vinegar mixture over the ribs and seal pouch, and return to pot, then return to oven. Cook for another hour.

7. To finish ribs, cook on top of grill with open fire. Cook for 5–10 minutes, basting with the remaining apple juice/vinegar mix.

8. Remove from heat, let sit for 2 minutes, and slice. Finish with a sprinkle of Smoke Dust and more barbecue sauce on side.

Apple Turnover Day

JULY 5

Apple Turnovers are just apple pie, the to-go version. Which rocks, because pie is delicious and we're always on the go. Don't get me wrong: I think we should find time to enjoy fresh-baked pie with a velvety scoop of ice cream, but sometimes you gotta go! This is what makes apple turnovers perfect. Bake a bunch and you'll have snacks for the week.

APPLE TURNOVERS

Makes 6–8 turnovers

3 cups Granny Smith apples

2 tablespoons unsalted butter

5 tablespoons sugar

½ teaspoon vanilla extract

½ teaspoon cinnamon

½ tablespoon cornstarch

6 tablespoons apple juice (or water)

Zest of 1 lemon

½ 17-ounce box frozen puff pastry

1 egg

1. In a heavy-bottomed pot, combine apples with butter, sugar, vanilla, and cinnamon and cook over medium heat, cooking for 2–3 minutes.

2. Combine cornstarch with apple juice and add to pot. Cook on low heat while stirring for 1 minute, then add lemon zest, stir and cool.

3. Lay the puff pastry out and cut the pastry into 4 square pieces. Whisk the egg with a little water and use a pastry brush to wet the edges of the puff pastry squares. Spoon 1 tablespoon of apple mixture. Close squares to make turnovers and press firmly to close edges. With a knife trim the edges to make them straight and clean, or press them with a fork to create ridges.

4. Place turnovers on wax paper or sprayed aluminum and a cookie sheet. With a sharp knife, make 3 slits across top of pastries and bake in a 400°F for 10 minutes until golden.

5. Remove from oven, brush with remaining egg wash, and return to the oven. Bake for another 5–10 minutes until golden and glossy. Allow to cool until warm and enjoy. Yes! I said allow them to cool a little; puff pastry is better when it cools a little since it becomes super crunchy.

JULY 6

Fried Chicken Day

Fried chicken—you like it the way you like it, and I'm guessing the best chicken is the one your mom made (of course, she probably got the recipe from your grandmother, who got it from her mother, and so on). This dish has been around for thousands of years, being fried up in China, Mexico, and all over Europe. But it wasn't until it was introduced to the South, and lard became a staple, that chicken carved a place in American culinary history. There are three things to remember when it comes to fried chicken: the soak, for flavor and tenderizing; the dredge-fry, for crispiness; and temperature control for a juicy bird.

CRISPITY FRIED CHICKEN (A.K.A. CFC)

Serves 3–4

5 garlic cloves

1 cup buttermilk

2 teaspoons salt

2 teaspoons pepper

1 tablespoon fresh rosemary plus 2 fresh rosemary sprigs

½ lemon juiced

1 chicken (about 3 pounds) cut into 8 pieces (drums, thighs, and breasts cut in half)

2 quarts vegetable oil

1 egg

1 cup all-purpose flour

1 teaspoon ground oregano

1 teaspoon chili powder

1 teaspoon dried sage

1 teaspoon dried basil

1 teaspoon dried marjoram

2 tablespoon paprika

1 tablespoon onion powder

1 teaspoon garlic powder

¼ teaspoon cayenne

1 teaspoon cumin

4 garlic cloves

1. Blend 2 garlic cloves with buttermilk, 1 teaspoon salt, 1 teaspoon pepper, rosemary, and lemon juice until smooth. Pour brine into large Ziploc and add chicken. Close bag and toss chicken to coat, then refrigerate overnight or at least 3 hours.

2. In a pressure fryer, or in a heavy metal pot with a lid, heat oil to 365°F over medium-high heat.

❸ Open bag with chicken and pour extra buttermilk into a bowl. Mix buttermilk with the egg and whisk well.

❹ In another larger bowl, mix flour and spices and whisk together. Dip chicken piece by piece into buttermilk-egg mixture then bread on both sides with seasoned flour (for extra crispy chicken, double coat). Lay the chicken down on top of a rack and allow to dry for at least 15 minutes while your oil comes up to temperature. Place 4 chicken pieces carefully into oil and cover and fry undisturbed for 8 minutes.

❺ Strip rosemary sprigs from stem and slice the 3 garlic cloves thinly, like chips. After 8 minutes, carefully open fryer (following the manufacturer's instructions) and drop in half of garlic chips and rosemary. Toss chicken with the garlic chips and rosemary using a fine wire skimmer and fry until golden (about 30 seconds to 1 minute).

❻ Remove everything from oil and drain on paper towels (make sure to strain out all bits of rosemary and garlic; if they burn it will make the next batch taste burned). Repeat process with the remaining chicken. Serve with lots and lots of hot sauce on the side.

Strawberry Sundae Day

The creation of the sundae is widely disputed, but the adoration is easily understood. Simple desserts always do the trick in my house. Just get decorative glassware and those cool, long spoons and voila! Think about it, sundaes, banana splits, parfaits . . . they're all simple desserts composed of simple ingredients, but what elevates them to legends are the fanfare with which they are presented. So next time you're making dessert, remember to serve with a little panache to make the history books.

STRAWBERRY SUNDAE

Serves 2

5 tablespoons sugar

2 cups strawberries (puréed)

1 tablespoons cornstarch

1 lemon

Homemade Vanilla Ice Cream (July 23)

2 cups strawberries (chopped into large pieces)

Perfect Chantilly Cream (Jan. 5)

❶ In small saucepan, combine sugar with puréed strawberries. Cook over low heat for 5 minutes until mixture is hot.

❷ Combine cornstarch with 1 tablespoon water then add to strawberries and cook until thick, about 1–2 minutes. Remove from heat and add 1 teaspoon of fresh lemon juice and zest of half the lemon into strawberries mixture and allow to cool until just warm.

❸ Fill sundae glass with vanilla ice cream, top with strawberry syrup, fresh strawberries, and whipped cream. Serve with a long spoon.

Chocolate with Almonds Day

JULY 8

A classic combination and by far one of the most popular in the world, but have you ever seen it in the form of a hedgehog? Yep, I'm talking about that cute little spiky mammal. Cast your eyes on these babies. They can be made individually in cups, served on plates, or even in a large bowl as a mousse-hedgehog cake!

CHOCOLATE ALMOND HEDGEHOGS

Makes 4–5

Chocolate Mousse (Jan. 10)

German Chocolate Cake (June 11)

Sliced or slivered almonds

Cocoa powder

Powdered sugar

❶ Make cake and cool it, then cut out circles with a cup. Pipe or scoop Chocolate Mousse with an ice cream scoop dipped in warm water to make scooping easier on top, and chill in fridge for at least 30 minutes.

❷ Once hard, decorate with almonds in a shingled formation resembling scales. Decorate by dusting with cocoa powder then powdered sugar. Enjoy!

Sugar Cookie Day

Remember those colorful candy necklaces you loved as a kid? Remember when the candy would melt and form a temporary rainbow tattoo around your neck? Well why not try something different for your kids and make a cookie necklace? It's just as fun, and perhaps a little better than only sugar. I bet your kids won't be able to keep it on long enough to create any real damage, so say goodbye to sticky rainbow tattoos.

SUGAR COOKIE NECKLACES

Makes 6 necklaces

1 cup butter (unsalted and soft)

1 cup sugar (brown or white)

3 cups all-purpose flour

1 teaspoon baking soda

2 large eggs

1 teaspoon pure vanilla extract

1 lemon, zested

Royal Icing (Apr. 18)

1. Cream butter and sugar until fluffy. Sift dry ingredients and add to butter mixture, along with eggs, then finish with vanilla and the lemon zest.

2. Wrap dough into a block and refrigerate for at least 2 hours.

3. Roll out dough on clean, well-floured surface to ¼" thick and cut into small rounds using a ring or bottle cap. Either cut a small hole in cookie so you can string them up later, or, with piece of butcher string and big needle or long wooden stick, run string through cookies, making a necklace.

4. Lay on baking sheet lined with parchment paper and bake at 350°F for 8 minutes. After they cool, decorate with Royal Icing and wear, er, eat!

Piña Colada Day

You know the song—sing it with me! It's the only way to do this right. Piña Coladas are the quintessential vacation drink. Piña = pineapple; colada = blended. Folklore credits the drink to a pirate in the 1800s, but Puerto Rican history cites a man by the name of Ramon "Monchito" Marrero who invented it for the Caribe Hilton's Beachcomber bar back in 1954.

Either way, it should be served in a coconut or large pineapple with lots of fun straws, umbrellas, and enjoyed while wearing a swimsuit. If that means you have to buy a kiddie pool, set it out in your living room, fill it with water, and enjoy while watching TV, so be it.

PIRATED PIÑA COLADAS

Makes 2 drinks

1 fresh pineapple (about 22 ounces, peeled and cored)

1 can Coco Lopez

1 cup rum

3 cups ice

❶ Combine all ingredients in blender and process until smooth.

❷ Pour into a tall glass or hurricane glass. Or, if you're really feeling adventurous, hollow a pineapple with an ice cream scoop or melon baller and serve drink inside.

❸ Serve with fun, colorful straws and a little cocktail umbrella.

JULY 11 — Blueberry Muffin Day

I grew up on muffins. I think we all did, right? Blueberry muffins, cranberry muffins, banana muffins, and corn muffins were the most popular at the bakery near my school. The baker would take the muffin, cut it in half, butter it up, and throw it on the griddle. The muffin would toast and create this warm buttery crust that is unmatched. Did you know that the Blueberry Muffin is the official muffin of Minnesota? Yeah, they're that good!

BLUEBERRY MUFFINS

Makes 1 dozen muffins

½ cup butter (soft)

1 cup sugar

2 eggs

1 lemon, zested

2 teaspoons vanilla extract

½ teaspoon salt

1 tablespoon baking powder

2 cups flour

¼ teaspoon nutmeg

½ cup whole milk

1 cup fresh blueberries

❶ Cream butter and sugar for 10 minutes until fluffy. Add eggs in one at a time then add lemon zest and vanilla.

❷ Sift dry ingredients and add ½ to butter mixture. Add milk, then dry, then milk, then dry intermittently until all has been incorporated. Gently fold in blueberries.

❸ With an ice cream scoop, portion batter into greased and floured muffin tins, sprinkle with raw sugar for crunchy top, and bake at 375°F for 15–20 minutes until golden.

JULY 12 — Pecan Pie Day

The history of pecan pie is like a story that's been passed down for years without ever really knowing where it came from. The pecan got its name from the Native American word pecane, *which means "nut to be cracked with a stone." For this pie, you just need a spoon.*

PECAN CRANBERRY PIE

Serves 6–8

Pie Dough (Apr. 28)

3 large eggs

1 cup light brown sugar

¾ cup light corn syrup

3 tablespoons butter (melted)

1 tablespoon vanilla extract

¼ teaspoon salt

1 cup dried cranberries

1½ cups pecan halves (toasted and cooled)

Ripe pears (sliced; optional)

Crumbled goat cheese (optional)

❶ Line pie tin with dough.

❷ Combine eggs with remaining ingredients except optional items, and mix well until a smooth batter forms.

❸ Pour filling into crust and bake at 350°F for 55 minutes or until set. Allow pie to cool.

❹ Now for the optional part. If you're familiar with that delicious salad of spinach, fresh pears, creamy cheese, pecans, and cranberries, this was my inspiration. Once pie has cooled, top with pears drizzled with olive oil and goat cheese. (Blue cheese works wonderfully, too.) If you're really adventurous, make the salad and top pie with salad! Trust me, it's really yummy.

French Fries Day

JULY 13

They are so simple, yet so many people manage to mess up the humble French Fry. I think the worse thing you can do to a French Fry is serve it cold and/ or soggy. Imagine you're a potato, and you're about to become a Fry; it's your destiny, so to speak. And someone doesn't take the time to wash you, or cut you properly, and you're fried in old, dirty, or not-so-hot grease so you soak up gobs of oil and are served cold, oily, and limp. What a sad tater you'd be. There's a better way—it's about karma, man!

GOOD KARMA FRIES

Serves 2

2 quarts peanut oil

3 fresh rosemary stems (1 whole, 2 in sprigs only)

2 lemons (2 thin slices plus zest)

1 pound medium Idaho potatoes (washed and peeled)

Salt

Parmigiano-Reggiano cheese (optional; grated)

❶ In a large stockpot, heat oil with 1 rosemary stem and 2 lemon slices to 350°F (use a thermometer, that's the trick to perfect fries).

❷ Cut potatoes into ⅜" strips, rinse in cold water, and in separate pot, cook in salted water just shy of boiling for 12–13 minutes or until tender.

❸ Strain potatoes, shaking off excess water and leaving them at room temperature for at least 15 minutes so they dry out a bit. Drop half into oil and stir with wooden spoon so potatoes don't stick, keeping an eye on oil temperature so it stays constantly at 350°F. Cook for 3–4 minutes until the fries form a crust but have no color.

4. If oil gets too hot, add ½ cup of room temperature oil and turn heat down. Remove fries and drain on paper towels.

5. Repeat with second half of potatoes.

6. Remove rosemary stem and lemon slices (save lemon slices for decoration). Raise oil temperature to 375°F and drop fries into oil again.

7. Fry for 2½ minutes, while moving them around, then add half of rosemary sprigs and continue to fry until golden. Remove fries from oil and drain on paper towels. Salt lightly right away, and sprinkle with lemon zest and cheese.

8. Repeat with second batch of fries. Garnish with more cheese and two slices of fried lemon on top.

Grand Marnier Day (Bastille Day)

Celebrated on this day every year, Bastille Day (or La Fête Nationale, as it's known regionally) is a French holiday that commemorates the storming of the Bastille. This act of rebellion was considered an integral part of the French Revolution. Grand Marnier is a French orange liqueur that has always embodied the revolutionary spirit. Created by Alexandre Marnier-Lapostolle in 1880, it's a distinguished spirit composed of gorgeous cognacs and a distilled bitter orange from the Caribbean called citrus bigaradia. There's no better way to celebrate the day than with an orange chiffon cake with Grand Marnier glaze.

BASTILLE DAY CAKE

Serves 6–8

Lemon Chiffon Cake (Mar. 29; sub oranges for lemons in the recipe)

2 cups powdered sugar

½ cup Grand Marnier

2–3 fresh oranges, segmented

1. Bake cake in a decorative mold, and cool.

2. Prepare glaze by sifting sugar, then add liquor and whisk in until smooth.

3. Drizzle glaze on cake and decorate with fresh orange slices. For extra fanfare, add a few sparklers to the cake before serving. That's always fun!

Tapioca Pudding Day

Did you know those little gemlike pearls you find in your pudding are not actually tapioca but a refined version of tapioca? Tapioca is a flourlike starch derived from the root of the cassava plant. In its raw state, it's liquid, but it's then dried into a flour and used for many things—from thickening sauces to firming up desserts and most commonly as pearl form. When cooked right, tapioca makes a wonderful pudding that can take on myriad flavors.

TAPIOCA PUDDING

Serves 4

½ cup small pearl tapioca (do not use instant)

3 cups whole milk

½ cup sugar

2 eggs

½ teaspoons vanilla extract

½ teaspoon butter

⅛ teaspoon salt

❶ Soak tapioca overnight in whole milk.

❷ The next day, bring milk to slow simmer, add sugar, and stir often, slowly, to make sure mixture does not stick to bottom.

❸ Cook until liquid thickens, tapioca has absorbed most of milk, and is tender when you bite into it, about 5–10 minutes depending on size of pearls.

❹ Add a little hot tapioca to eggs, then return entire mixture to main pot.

❺ Cook over low heat for 1–2 minutes until thick.

❻ Turn off heat and add vanilla, butter, and salt, and stir until dissolved.

❼ Serve warm or chilled. I like to add a little cinnamon on top.

Cook's Note

When tapioca pearls are cooked, the outside layers thicken the liquid they are in and form a barrier, not allowing the starch remaining to escape. This remaining starch within the bubble cooks and turns into little rubbery ball of starch.

Corn Fritters Day

JULY 16

Growing up, the mom of a good friend used to make these awesome little pancakes. She is from Indonesia and her name is Dee, or as her kids call her, Mamadukes. I've tasted a lot of her food and by far I thought these gems were the best. I don't know why, because she made a lot of great stuff, but for some reason these always struck my fancy. They're a simple combination of egg, scallions, and corn, fried and served piping hot. I just add a little ginger to them and that's it—simple, fast, and delicious!

MAMADUKES CORN FRITTERS

Serves 2

Oil for pan-frying

2 eggs

½ teaspoon salt

⅛ teaspoon ground ginger

⅛ teaspoon ground white pepper

2 tablespoons all-purpose flour

15 ounces canned corn kernels (drained well)

2 whole scallions (finely chopped)

❶ In large skillet, heat oil ¼" deep on medium-high.

❷ Combine eggs and spices, and sift in flour. Add corn and scallions, mix, and let rest until pan starts to smoke.

❸ With large spoon, scoop about 2 tablespoons of mixture into pan. Repeat until pan is filled, leaving at least ½" between each fritter. Cook on each side until golden brown, about 2 minutes, flip, and repeat.

❹ Drain on paper towels, and serve hot with a side of soy sauce.

Peach Ice Cream Day

Caviar Day

Peaches always remind me of Georgia. Georgia peaches are the best in the world, but it's a combination of the peaches themselves with the wonderful people and intoxicating Southern breezes that makes them spectacular. I never knew this until I met my friend Sarah—she is the sweetest Georgia peach I know. And when life gives you Georgia peaches, you make Peach Ice Cream, of course.

Caviar is salted eggs from the sturgeon fish. It is a delicacy of the sea and the best is said to come from Iran. For the longest time, wonderful caviar was available from the Hudson River when the sturgeon population was strong, but due to overfishing the American shortnose sturgeon is now on the endangered species list. Never fear, because there are many other fish in the world, and while our conservation efforts are in full effect, we have learned how to extract the caviar of other farmed fish. The traditional way of serving caviar is with blinis (simple pancakes) and sour cream, but here in the States we like crunch, so I serve it with fresh, warm potato chips.

SARAH'S GEORGIA PEACH ICE CREAM

Serves 3–4

2½ cups peaches (frozen or canned)

1 cup heavy cream

½ can condensed milk

1 cup evaporated milk

1 cup regular milk

½ teaspoon vanilla extract

❶ Combine all ingredients in a blender and process until smooth.

❷ Freeze according to your ice cream manufacturer's instructions. I like this best when served with fresh sliced peaches.

POTATO CHIPS

Makes 30–50 bite-sized servings

2 large russet potatoes

1½ quart vegetable or canola oil

Salt

❶ Scrub potatoes and pat dry. Using a mandolin, slice them as thin as possible and place in cold, salted water. Allow to soak for at least 15 minutes.

❷ Heat a pot with oil to 365°F (use a thermometer to keep temperature steady).

❸ Fry chips a little at a time until crisp. Remove from oil, salt lightly, and drain on paper.

FRESH SOUR CREAM

1 quart heavy cream

⅛ cup white vinegar

1 Bring cream to a boil, then turn off heat and stir in vinegar. Allow mixture to cool on stovetop, then refrigerate for at least 1 hour until cold. The best sour cream you'll ever taste!

2 Serve chips with caviar (I like American paddlefish or American hackelback—they're delicious, domestic, and a good bang for the buck), homemade sour cream, and chopped chives.

1 Combine all ingredients in a shaker, fill to the brim with ice, cover, and shake the hell out of it for 10 seconds.

2 Strain into a chilled martini glass or serve on the rocks. Garnish with cherry and a lime or grapefruit wedge.

Hot Dog Day

Whether covered in corn batter and fried, baked inside a pretzel, or drowned in chili, hot dogs are an American favorite. We can trace them back to Frankfurt, Germany, to the birthplace of frankfurters, where they were commonly served on a bun. In the States, we can trace the links to Coney Island, circa 1870. Fast-forward to today and my overactive imagination that came up with making a hot dog in the balloon-animal fashion of a pup!

BALLOON HOT DAWGS

Serves 4–5

Sheep or lamb casings

Group A

1½ pounds pork

1 pound chicken

⅛ pound beef

½ pound pork fat

1 egg white

1 ounce powdered milk

3–5 dashes of liquid smoke (if you don't have a smoker)

½ cup ice water

½ cup Chili Seasoning (July 21)

Daiquiri Day

Considered one of America's greatest authors, Hemingway's economic writing style made him iconic. But what I remember most about Papa's work is the way he describes food and drink—he makes you feel as if you're tasting daiquiris right next to him in a little dive bar in Cuba. You can almost taste the sweat from your lips as you lift the glass to your mouth. The folks in all the local watering holes knew him by name and in his honor named a daiquiri after him—the Hemingway Daiquiri, also known as the Papa Doble. Here it is.

HEMINGWAY DAIQUIRI

Makes 1 drink

1½ ounces 10 Cane or Bacardi rum

¼ ounce Luxardo Maraschino liqueur

¾ ounce fresh lime juice

½ ounce fresh grapefruit juice

Cook's Note

Add a little sugar or simple syrup if the drink is too tart for your taste.

Group B

½ onion (finely chopped)

½ cup parsley (finely chopped)

3–5 garlic cloves (finely chopped)

1. Soak sheep casings in room-temperature water. As water warms, casings should get soft and elastic.

2. Ask your butcher to pass the meat with the fat through a fine grinder. Make sure to keep it really cold (below 60°F). You will have to make the mix in two batches unless you have a very large food processor, which I don't.

3. Make slurry with egg white and milk powder and set aside.

4. Place half of ingredients from Group A in food processor and process for 5 minutes until smooth. Do the same with second half of Group A. Add the slurry to mixture and blend well.

5. In a large bowl, thoroughly combine meat mixture and all remaining ingredients, including those from Group B. Put everything in pastry bag with sausage attachment, or if you have a sausage-stuffing machine, use that. Slowly and gently lace the casings onto the attachment, tie end, and start stuffing, then form balloon animal dogs!

6. Cook in a 225°F oven for 1 hour or until hot dogs reach an internal temperature of 145°F. Refrigerate overnight. The next day, boil or grill and serve.

Junk Food Day

Chocolate-covered potato chips, donut burgers, deep-fried Twinkies, Oreos, candy bars, pizza . . . I could go on all day. Yep, I'm talking about artery cloggin', non-nutritious, fast, cheap, and downright delicious junk food. Definitely not something you should be eating every day, but that's why we have a day specifically designed to get your frustrations out and just indulge. The term "Junk Food" was coined in 1972 by Michael Jacobson, director of the Center for Science in the Public Interest. In honor of today, think of your favorite junk food and eat it! Or you can make these little gems.

PORK RINDS (A.K.A. PORK CANDY)

Serves 3

1 pound pork skin, fat removed

1 quart canola oil

Chili Seasoning

¾ cup brown sugar

¼ cup smoked paprika

¼ cup paprika

2 tablespoons freshly ground white or black pepper

⅛ cup kosher salt

1 tablespoon ground cumin

2 tablespoon chili powder

1 tablespoon cayenne pepper

2 tablespoon onion powder

2 tablespoon garlic powder

1 tbsp salt

Cook's note

I like to make the rinds from large pieces of the skin. If you have the space and ambition, this is more fun when it comes time for presentation.

❶ Remove the fat from the skin, then cut into 1" squares, and boil for 1 hour in a large pot with salted water. Remove the skin from the pot and see if there is extra fat attached, then remove that too with a sharp knife. Dry the skins with paper towels then place them either on parchment or aluminum foil in an oven set to 150–170°F and dry them overnight.

❷ Heat oil to 400°F in a 3-quart pot. Use a thermometer and keep it at a constant temperature. Fry pork skins for 1 minute, until puffy. Remove from oil and drain inside bowl lined with paper towels.

❸ In the meantime, mix remaining ingredients together to make Chili Seasoning. Toss with pork rinds and enjoy!

Penuche Fudge Day

JULY 22

Penuche Fudge is a big deal in New England and parts of the South. The word Penuche derives from the Mexican-Spanish panocha, which means "raw sugar," which in turn comes from the Latin panicula, which loosely translated means "cluster." So I guess we can call this fudge milk cluster. Yeah, let's call them Milk Candy Clusters.

MILK CANDY CLUSTERS

Serves 5–6

5 ounces evaporated milk

2 tablespoons powdered milk

½ cup light brown sugar

5 ounces butter

⅛ teaspoon salt

½ cup powdered sugar

1½ teaspoons vanilla extract

1. In a heavy-bottomed pot, combine all ingredients except powdered sugar and vanilla. Bring to soft boil over medium heat. Affix a candy thermometer to side of pot so tip is submerged in caramel but not touching the pan bottom. Heat mixture until it reaches 236°F, the soft ball stage.

2. Add powdered sugar to mixture in a bowl and combine slowly until it thickens.

3. Add vanilla, mix for a few more seconds, then pour into a 10–12" pan lined with aluminum foil that has been lightly sprayed with oil. Cool until hard, about 3 hours, then cut and serve. Store covered in a cool, dry place.

JULY 23 — Vanilla Ice Cream Day

Vanilla, an orchid native to Mexico, was brought to Africa and Asia by Portuguese and Spanish sailors. Attempts to cultivate vanilla were unsuccessful until it came to light that bees played a crucial role in the process. The flower opens just once a year for 12 hours, and if not pollinated it dies; but when pollinated, the beans grow. After harvesting, beans are cured and dried then sent off to markets around the world.

HOMEMADE VANILLA ICE CREAM

Makes about 4 cups

2 vanilla beans

2 cups heavy cream

2 cups milk

12 large egg yolks

1¼ cup sugar

Pinch of salt

1. Slice vanilla beans in half. Scrape insides into cream and milk and bring to a boil.

2. While waiting for vanilla cream to boil, beat yolks with sugar in a large bowl until you have golden ribbons.

3. When cream has come to a boil, turn off the heat, cover, and allow to steep for 30 minutes.

4. Bring cream back up to a boil. Temper yolks by adding hot cream a little at a time while whisking constantly. Return mixture to the pot. Continue stirring with a wooden spoon on medium heat for about 4 minutes. (The ice cream base is ready when you dip a spoon in cream, hold it horizontally, run a finger down spoon, and get a clean line that doesn't fill in immediately.)

5. Strain into plastic container with a lid and chill. Freeze according to ice cream maker's instructions.

JULY 24 — Tequila Day

Tequila is a type of liquor made from blue agave plants grown primarily in Jalisco, Mexico. Agave plants are planted and grown for several years until a finely skilled jimador determines it's time for picking. The plant must be mature enough so the starches have turned into sugars and young enough so that all these sugars haven't been used up to produce a long stem that puts out seeds for reproduction. This is a craft that has been honed for hundreds of years and is still done by hand today. Premium tequila sales are on the rise, and with much better quality spirits coming out of Mexico, it seems we can't get enough if this stuff.

ZESTY MARGARITA

Makes 1 drink

2 ounces white tequila

1 ounce orange liqueur (Cointreau or Combier)

1 ounce fresh lime juice

½ lime, zested

Ice

❶ Sometimes it's the simple things in life, my friends. Just a little bit of zest in your margarita will transform this cocktail! Combine all ingredients in shaker, fill with ice, and shake like crazy.

❷ Serve on the rocks in a salt-rimmed glass.

Hot Fudge Sundae Day

As noted on Strawberry Sundae Day (July 7), the history of sundaes is riddled with controversy. The debate centers on where the cool treat originated, but one thing we do know is that it was named because of God. A blue law was passed that prohibited the sale of ice cream sodas on Sunday, so shopkeepers started serving ice cream drizzled with soda syrups and a new dessert was born. The first record of a sundae was a "Cherry Sunday" sold in Ithaca, NY, in 1892. Local leaders objected to naming the dish after a day of worship, and so the name was ultimately changed to Sundae.

HOT FUDGE SUNDAE

Serves 3–4

Homemade Vanilla Ice Cream (July 23)

Perfect Chantilly Cream (Jan. 5)

Hot Fudge (June 16)

1 jar maraschino cherries

❶ Make ice cream and freeze. Make cream and keep chilled. Make hot fudge and keep warm.

❷ 1+3+1+3+2+cherry = Hot Fudge Sundae!

Coffee Milkshake Day

"I make my coffee so strong it wakes the neighbors!" America is a nation that lives and thrives on coffee. It makes us faster, sharper, and more productive when consumed—especially in the morning, when let's face it, none of us really want to go to work. Coffee milkshakes combine the best of both worlds when it comes to an afternoon cup-o'-pep or cooling off on a really hot day. And let's be honest, the legend of Starbucks is built around these. Call it what you want, but a Frappuccino is just a coffee milkshake with a fancy name. But a Joe by any other name is a still a Joe. Here's the all-American version.

REGULAR JOE COFFEE MILKSHAKE

Serves 1

  1 tablespoon instant coffee

  ½ cup milk

  2 cups really good-quality vanilla ice cream

  2 tablespoons sugar

Cook's Note

I make my milkshake with a vanilla base so I can make it as strong or light as I want by adding a little more or less instant coffee. Spray-dried coffee, like Nescafé Frappe powder, makes a really frothy and creamy milkshake or shaken cold coffee, but any other type will do.

❶ Combine coffee with milk and blend for 30 seconds on high.

❷ Add ice cream and sugar and blend until smooth. Serve immediately.

Scotch Day

Scotch whisky is whisky made in Scotland. Whisky, of course, is also whiskey—different origins, different spellings. Whiskey is the distillation of fermented grain mash, ranging from barley to malted barley, rye, malted rye, wheat, and corn. There are many rules that a whisky must comply with in order to be called Scotch whisky, but the most important is that it has to be made and matured in Scotland. Did you know that about .05–2% of the whiskey evaporates from the barrel while maturing? This is rightly called the angel's share.

ROB ROY

Makes 1 drink

  2 ounces blended Scotch whisky

  ¾ ounce Italian vermouth

  2 dashes Angostura bitters

  Ice

  Fresh cherries for garnish

❶ Chill martini glass in freezer or by filling with ice and water.

❷ In clean glass, combine liquors and bitters and fill with clean, fresh ice. Use a spoon to stir drink for 10 seconds.

❸ Empty martini glass and strain in cocktail. Garnish with fresh cherry. I also like smashing fresh cherry into it for extra zip!

Milk Chocolate Day

JULY 28

I grew up eating milk chocolate most every afternoon when my mom brought it home after work as a treat. There was a bakery nearby that made amazing sweet breads, very similar to challah, and she'd bring a small bag full of them and a bar of milk chocolate. We'd cut the chocolate in chunks and stuff it in the bread then put it in the toaster oven. In a few minutes we had amazing, crunchy, chocolate-filled bread that went perfectly with a cold glass of milk. These days, I swap coffee for milk, but the chocolate sandwiches remain the same.

S'MORES SAMICH

Makes 2 samiches

1 fresh baguette (cut in half)

Handful marshmallows

1 milk chocolate bar

❶ This is as simple as it can get. Just fill bread with marshmallows and chocolate and put in panini press until golden and gooey.

❷ You can also crisp in a 350°F oven for about 5–6 minutes.

Cheese Sacrifice Purchase Day

JULY 29

The Mayans had human ones, in the Caribbean they stick to goats and chickens, but apparently the ultimate sacrifice is cheese. Perhaps it's the sacrifice of making something so scrumptious you just want to shove your face right in, but instead opting to give away to someone so he may stuff his face. I think that's the ultimate sacrifice. But maybe the trick is to bring it to a potluck where you're able to sneak a bite or two.

SUNDRIED TOMATO CHEESE

Serves 4

2–3 sundried tomatoes

1 wheel soft cheese (such as epoisses or Camombert), preferably in a little wooden container

3 fresh basil leaves (finely chopped)

❶ Soak tomatoes in warm water for 10 minutes to hydrate and make easier to purée.

❷ Take small paring knife and carefully slice around top of cheese following the circumference (the goal is to remove the top, kind of like a can, and create a little container). Carefully scoop out cheese (warm in microwave for a few seconds if not malleable) and place in food processor, reserving empty container.

❸ Shake excess water off tomatoes, chop roughly, and add to cheese. Process until most tomatoes are incorporated (it's okay if you still see a few small pieces).

Cotton Candy Day, July 31

4 Add basil to food processor. Pulse 3–5 times until incorporated but not puréed. Return cheese mixture to empty container, replace lid, and top cheese with piece of sundried tomato and fresh basil. Bring bread with your offering.

Cheesecake Day

JULY 30

Cheesecake has been around a lot longer than you would have guessed—it dates back to Greco-Roman times! Yet to this day there is an ongoing debate about which kind of cheesecake is better. Italian-inspired ricotta crumbly cheesecake or ultra-creamy melt-in-your-mouth cream cheese cheesecake? In order to finally put an end to this cheesy battle, I've decided to make a hybrid. A coming together of two worlds if you wish. I call it the Italian-American Cheesecake.

ITALIAN-AMERICAN CHEESECAKE

Serves 6–8

2½ cups fresh whole milk ricotta (drained overnight)

1 8-ounce package cream cheese (at room temperature)

⅛ cup honey

1 tablespoon cornstarch

4 large eggs, room temperature

¼ teaspoon salt

2 teaspoons pure vanilla extract

1 Put ricotta in cheesecloth (I use a clean pillowcase) to drain overnight. Tie cheesecloth or case well and hang on top of container that will catch liquids.

2 The next day, whip room temperature cream cheese until smooth and fluffy (about 5 minutes). Add honey and ricotta, then mix until smooth. Add the cornstarch, followed by eggs one at a time, making sure to scrape down sides. Finish by mixing in salt and vanilla.

3 Pour cheesecake batter into 10–12" springform pan, wrap bottom with heavy-duty aluminum foil, and set inside a deeper pan filled with hot water. Bake at 350°F for 1 hour.

4 Remove cake from oven and cool while still in water bath, then refrigerate overnight.

Cotton Candy Day

JULY 31

Cotton candy was around as early as the eighteenth century when the sugar was melted and then spun by hand, which made it expensive and inaccessible to the common man. But that all changed in 1897, when William Morrison and John C. Wharton invented the first commercial machine. It was first introduced to a huge crowd at the 1904 World's Fair, and this Barb á Papa (dad's beard), candy floss, or fairy floss ended up being a crowd favorite selling 68,655 boxes!

COTTON CANDY CUPCAKES

Easy Chocolate Cupcakes (Oct. 18)

Sweet Dream Butter Cream (Apr. 22)

2 cups colored cotton candy

1 Make cupcakes and cool, until room temperature, then frost cupcakes.

2 Top frosting with lots of fluffy cotton candy. Enjoy!

AUGUST

Raspberry Cream Pie Day

Raspberries have got to be the most beautiful berries. Preferred in Europe and considered to be the strawberry's elegant sister, raspberries come in ruby red, black, orange, and golden colors, and when perfectly ripe in the peak of their season (as early as May, as late early July) they're short of life changing. Aside from being delicious, they're jam-packed with antioxidants and vitamins that can help ward off all kinds of diseases. I love strolling through the market with a small box of mixed raspberries, throwing them in the air and catching them in my mouth.

RASPBERRY CREAM PIE

Serves 6

⅛ cup bittersweet chocolate

4 tablespoons (½ stick) butter

1 cup Cocoa Krispies or Cocoa Pebbles

Pinch of salt

1 14-ounce can sweetened condensed milk

¼ cup sour cream

¼ cup fresh lemon juice

3 cups fresh raspberries

½ cup Perfect Chantilly Cream (Jan. 5)

Cook's Note

Make the crust with melted chocolate and your favorite cereal, or substitute cookies if you like. I prefer Rice Krispies, but feel free to use whatever you like. The chocolate coats the cereal and makes it stay crispy.

❶ Melt chocolate with butter, then mix in a food processor with cereal and salt until crumbly and moist. Press into pie shell, then refrigerate until hard.

❷ Whisk condensed milk with sour cream and lemon juice until smooth. Add half of raspberries and mix roughly until cream turns pink.

❸ Fold in whipped cream until everything is smooth. Pour into cereal shell and top with a few raspberries and dollop of fresh whipped cream.

Ice Cream Sandwich Day

Before there were Ice Cream Sandwiches there were ice cream cakes. Victorian-era chefs made lots of these cakes as well as myriad molded ice creams. The Ice Cream Sandwich as we know it today didn't actually come around until the late 1800s when they started popping up on the streets of New York being sold by street vendors. Apparently they fall under the category called "Novelties" that includes ice pops, ice cream cones, tacos, and many others. The earliest record we have of ice cream sandwiches is in the New York Times "New Hot-Weather Refreshments" published Aug. 31, 1928.

ICE CREAM DONUT SANDWICHES

Serves 4–5

Doughnuts (June 8)

Strawberry ice cream

½ cup pistachios (shelled and coarsely chopped)

1. Make doughnuts (with holes), cool down, then split in half.

2. Scoop strawberry ice cream in between doughnut halves, squish down so ice cream is even with the doughnut, then roll the ice cream edges all around the pistachios.

3. Dust doughnuts with powdered sugar and serve immediately or wrap and keep in the freezer.

Cook's Tip

For extra oomph, add chopped pistachios to the dough!

AUG. 3 Watermelon Day

I can eat watermelon all day and night, for lunch, dinner, as a late-night snack, and every other time in between. I like it as juice, in salads, with sushi, to cool my mouth off while eating chicken wings, as sorbet — and especially in cocktails. Watermelon is thought to have originated in Africa, and several watermelon seeds are said to have been recovered from King Tut! Nowadays, it's grown in 44 of our states. Watermelon flesh can be pink, orange, yellow, or white, and can range from less than a pound to more than 262 pounds! Now that's a lot of melon.

WATERMELON COOLER

Serves 5–6

1 large watermelon

1 750 ml bottle vodka

½ 750 ml bottle of orange liqueur

Fresh lemon juice

Ice

1. Make hole in top of the watermelon, stick in vodka bottle. Allow vodka to seep in overnight.

2. The next day, prop up watermelon on one end and slice top off. Scoop out insides and juice.

3. Taste and adjust flavor with orange liqueur and fresh lemon juice.

4. Fill watermelon with ice and drink, plop ladle inside, cover with top of watermelon, and serve.

   Or,

4. If you're feeling adventurous, buy a plastic spigot, the kind on a water cooler. With an apple corer (make sure it's as thick as the spigot) make a hole in front bottom of watermelon.

5. Screw in spigot, fill with ice and cocktail, and serve. Now isn't that more fun? Enjoy!

AUG. 4

Lasagna Day

An iconic dish consisting of baked layers of pasta with tomato sauce, cheese, meat, and béchamel, this dish—although attributed to Rome—has Greek roots. The Greek word lasanon *means cooking pot, and* laganon *means a flat sheet of pasta cut into strips. My cousin's going to kill me when he reads this, so I apologize in advance. He makes the best lasagna I've ever tasted but will not come within 100 feet of a vegetable. So Jess, if you're reading this—look away, look, a plane!*

LASAGNA PRIMAVERA

Serves 5–6

13 ounces whole-wheat lasagna sheets

Olive oil

1 red pepper

1 yellow pepper

1 large Spanish onion

1 small carrot

1 celery stalk

1 pound veal

1 pound beef

1 teaspoon salt

1 teaspoon pepper

1 teaspoon garlic powder

5 garlic cloves

1 28-ounce can San Marzano tomatoes

2 bay leaves

4 cups milk

1 10-ounce can tomato paste

5 tablespoons butter

¼ cup white flour

2 teaspoons salt

¼ teaspoon white pepper

¼ teaspoon nutmeg

1 cup ricotta cheese

1 pound mozzarella cheese (shredded)

Parmesan and fresh parsley (chopped) for finishing

1. Cook lasagna sheets in boiling salted water with a little olive oil for 8 minutes a piece, or until tender. Remove from water and chill in cold water, reserving 1 cup of pasta water.

2. Cut all veggies into ¼" chunks.

3. Drizzle olive oil into large pot, season meat with all spices (except white pepper and nutmeg), and sauté over high heat until browned but not dry, about 10 minutes. Break meat up

so it looks crumbly. Remove from pot and set aside.

4. Drizzle 4 tablespoons olive oil in pot and sauté veggies over medium heat, stirring often until wilted. Return meat to pot, add tomatoes (crush and work into sauce), bay leaves, 1 cup milk, and tomato paste. Give a good stir then simmer sauce for 1½ hours, stirring every 30 minutes.

5. Prepare béchamel. Melt butter in sauté pan over medium heat, add flour, and whisk. Cook over low-medium heat for 1 minute. Add 3 cups milk and whisk together; cook for another 3 minutes until sauce thickens. Turn off heat, season with salt, white pepper, and nutmeg, and set aside.

6. Once tomato sauce is ready, get ready to assemble the lasagna, baby! Take a large 12" roasting pan or casserole dish and brush with olive oil. Layer sauce, pasta, sauce, béchamel, little dollops of ricotta, and shredded mozzarella. Make as many layers as possible, until you reach the top. Finish with sauce, and drizzle with béchamel and shredded cheese.

7. Bake at 375°F for 45 minutes until bubbly and lightly burned on top.

8. Remove from oven and allow to cool for 15 minutes.

9. Cut into squares with a serrated knife trying to follow pasta seams. Remove and plate. Sprinkle with Parmesan and chopped parsley.

AUG. 5

Oyster Day

"It was a brave man who first ate an oyster," said Jonathan Swift. During the 1800s, Oysters were plentiful and cheap, mostly eaten by the working class. In the nineteenth century, the New York harbor was the largest source of Oysters worldwide! Oysters were popular in Manhattan where street vendors sold them on carts. Oysters are now considered a delicacy, but modern cultivation methods are producing more affordable and amazing varieties. Be sure to get yours from a respectable fishmonger and eat on the same day. Oysters should be tightly closed and kept on ice. I enjoy mine just with a little lemon juice, but if you're up for crunch, try this!

SOUTH OF THE BORDER OYSTERS

Serves 3–4

24 large oysters, shucked

1 lemon

2 eggs (lightly beaten)

1 cup all-purpose flour

1 cup bread crumbs

Vegetable oil for frying

Salt

Pinch of ground cayenne pepper

⅛ teaspoon pepper

Tequila Tartar

½ cup mayonnaise

2 tablespoons relish

1 lime, zested

½ tablespoon white tequila

❶ Place oysters in bowl and drizzle juice of half a lemon.

❷ Set up 3 little bowls—1 with eggs, 1 with flour, and 1 with bread crumbs.

❸ Fill pot about 4 fingers high with vegetable oil and heat to 375°F.

❹ Bread oysters 3–4 at a time in eggs, flour, and bread crumbs. Fry until golden and crispy. Remove from oil and drain on paper towels, sprinkle with salt, cayenne, and pepper.

❺ Prepare Tequila Tartar by combining all ingredients in a bowl.

❻ Serve oysters hot with a side of tartar.

AUG. 6

Root Beer Float Day

A genius gentleman by the name of Robert M. Green created the classic root beer float. The story goes like this: On a one hot summer day in Philly around 1874, Mr. Green ran out of ice. So in order to keep his sodas cold, he started serving them with ice cream. In his memory, the following is engraved on his tombstone "Robert M. Green, the originator of the ice cream soda." Now that's going out in style.

SPIKED ROOT BEER FLOAT

Makes 2 floats

1 pint good-quality vanilla ice cream

2 12-ounce bottles old-fashioned root beer (cold)

Splash rum or bourbon (optional, but drink would no longer be "spiked")

Perfect Chantilly Cream (Jan. 5)

1. Put 2 scoops ice cream into large chilled glass. Fill slowly allowing soda to pour down side of glass, then add rum or bourbon.

2. Garnish with whipped cream and serve.

AUG. 7 Raspberries and Cream Day

Doesn't need much more, does it. The thought of plump, tart raspberries dolloped with soft velvety cream with just a hint of sugar and the scent of vanilla seems to round out the perfect mouthful. When I was a young intern, I tasted my first panna cotta. Defined as cooked cream in Italian, this doesn't do this elegant dessert justice. The recipe for panna cotta calls for nothing but cream, sugar, and gelatin. With the addition of tart raspberries and a bit of buttermilk to the cream, you create an extraordinary dessert that will make any evening or late summer lunch unforgettable.

BUTTERMILK PANNA COTTA

Serves 3–4

2¼ teaspoons powdered gelatin

1 cup heavy cream

¼ cup sugar

2 cups buttermilk

½ teaspoon vanilla extract

½ cup fresh raspberries

1. Sprinkle gelatin over 2 tablespoons cold water in bowl and let hydrate for at least 3 minutes.

2. Bring cream to boil, then turn off heat as soon as it does. Add sugar and stir until dissolved, then add gelatin and whisk until completely dissolved. Add buttermilk slowly and whisk continuously until incorporated, add vanilla, then set mixture in a cool (but not cold) place for 1–2 minutes.

3. Take a few cups (size doesn't matter here too much, but I like ½–¾ cup ramekins) and cover lightly with nonstick spray. Once cream mixture has cooled, pour into ramekins and add a few raspberries to each. Cover with plastic wrap and refrigerate overnight.

4. When ready to serve, run tip of pairing knife around rim of panna cotta and invert onto plate. I like serving with a drizzle of elderflower cordial or St. Germain liqueur.

Cook's Note

If it doesn't come out easily, you need to break the air lock seal created in the container. Hold one corner of upside-down ramekin on the plate, take your pairing knife, insert it in the corner, and peel it from the side. The air will gush inside and the panna cotta will plop onto the plate.

Zucchini Day AUG. 8

Grated raw into a salad, baked into bread, or puréed into a soup, zucchini is always a people-pleaser that falls in between a cucumber and an eggplant. They're simple little creatures that grow on the vine like pumpkins and yield the most delectable and delicate flowers you will ever taste. We grow these in our backyard, and during the summer months it's easy to walk out and pick a few whether I'm making a simple omelet or a more complex dish of stuffed zucchini flowers with fresh ricotta and spaghetti. Stuffing the zucchini is also popular.

STUFFED ZUCCHINI

Serves 2

2 medium-sized zucchini

4 garlic cloves

3 vine-ripe tomatoes

3–5 fresh thyme sprigs

Olive oil

½ teaspoon salt

¼ teaspoon pepper

1 cup bread crumbs (seasoned)

½ cup Parmesan cheese (shredded)

2 tablespoons fresh parsley (chopped)

❶ Cut one side of zucchinis so they don't roll around. Slice other side so you can empty insides and fill. Scoop out and chop zucchini insides. Peel top you sliced off and chop also.

❷ Clean garlic and smash/chop. Chop tomatoes and peel the thyme so all that's left are leaves.

❸ Drizzle sauté pan with olive oil and cook garlic with zucchini and thyme over medium heat for 1 minute until soft. Add tomatoes, salt, and pepper and cook for 30 seconds, then remove from heat. Drain all but 2 tablespoons of liquid from pan.

❹ Add bread crumbs, cheese, and parsley, then toss together.

❺ Line small roasting pan with aluminum foil, drizzle with olive oil, and place zucchini shell inside. Fill with stuffing, sprinkle with cheese, and drizzle with a little more olive oil. Bake at 375°F for 30 minutes.

❻ Drizzle with more olive oil, sprinkle with parsley, and serve.

Rice Pudding Day

There's something nostalgic about rice puddings. It brings us back to an era when Jell-o was in every fridge across America and TV dinners in all freezers. Rice pudding is one of those desserts that has been adopted into virtually every culture across the world. Flavorings change depending on what part of the world you're in, but three things are always the same: milk, sugar, and, of course, rice. I prefer the mouth feel of the short-grain rice, and for me a little whipped cream seals the deal.

SIMPLE RICE PUDDING

Serves 2–4

5 cups whole milk

⅔ cup long- or short-grain rice

⅛ teaspoon salt

½ teaspoon ground cinnamon

2 whole star anise

2 teaspoons pure vanilla extract

¼ cup granulated sugar

Perfect Chantilly Cream (Jan. 5)

❶ Combine milk with rice, salt, spices, and vanilla in large pot and simmer for 25 minutes over low heat. Stir often with wooden spoon so rice doesn't stick to the bottom.

❷ Once rice is tender, turn off heat, add sugar, and stir until dissolved. Cool pudding in fridge and serve with whipped cream. Garnish with fresh cinnamon.

AUG. 10

Banana Split Day

The history of the Banana Split is somewhat unclear. The first account seems to date back to 1904 from David Evans Strickler, a twenty-three-year-old pharmacist in Latrobe, Pennsylvania. It is said that he invented this American favorite, and once word spread around the campus of Saint Vincent College, students just couldn't get enough of the super ice cream treat! However, Wilmington, Ohio (who share the claim for title of Banana Split creators in 1907) really takes the cake—or in this case, the sundae—with their annual Banana Split Festival held every year in mid-June.

CRISPY FRIED BANANA SPLIT

Serves 3

3 ripe bananas

Tempura Batter (Jan. 7)

3 cups vegetable oil for frying

Homemade Vanilla Ice Cream (July 23)

Chocolate Ice Cream (June 7)

Strawberry Ice Cream (Jan. 15)

Store-bought pineapple topping

Hot Fudge (June 16)

Store-bought strawberry topping

Perfect Chantilly Cream (Jan. 5)

½ cup chopped nuts

10 maraschino cherries

Cook's Note

You can use canned whipped cream, but it just won't be as good—that stuff melts really quickly and turns to goo. If anything, buy the ice cream and make the whipped cream (then try to get your hands on a piping bag to make it look fancy)!

1. Split bananas, dip in Tempura Batter, and fry until crispy.

2. Lay two halves on banana boat and fill with one scoop vanilla, chocolate, and strawberry ice cream. Top vanilla with pineapple topping, chocolate with hot fudge, and strawberry with strawberry topping.

3. Top with whipped cream.

4. Sprinkle 2 tablespoons of chopped nuts on top and finish with 3 maraschino cherries. Now dig in!

Raspberry Tart Day

AUG. 11

Raspberry tarts are fun desserts that are made for lazy afternoons. They're super easy and can last for a few days, although in my house this never happens. You can also make them individually and package for a picnic. I make mine with a simple short crust, some raspberry jam accented with lemon juice and chopped mint, and lots of fresh raspberries sprinkled with powdered sugar. Of course, if you have some ice cream and want to top it off, I won't object.

RASPBERRY-MINT TART

Serves 4–6

Shortbread Dough (Jan. 6)

1 12-ounce jar raspberry jam

3 cups raspberries and 4 more berries for garnish

1 teaspoon lemon juice

Powdered sugar

2 tablespoons fresh mint (chopped)

1. Cook dough in fluted tart shell, then cool.

2. Combine jam with the raspberries and lemon juice in a bowl and mash everything together, leaving little pieces of raspberries in jam.

3. Fill tart with jam to halfway point. Arrange raspberries on top and dust with powdered sugar. Garnish with mint sprig.

Julienne Fries Day

Julienne is a French term used to describe the cut that produces vegetables and other foods that look like matchsticks. This term is particularly popular when it comes to stir-fries and French fries, a.k.a. shoestring fries. I learned how to make these from Chef April Boomfield at The Spotted Pig. She fries beautifully thin shoestrings with garlic and rosemary that are just awesome! The thin potatoes crisp up perfectly and super fast, which allows you make these any night of the week. I make these a little different by frying up different veggies and then mixing them for a fun and colorful accompaniment to any meal.

MIXED VEGGIE SHOESTRINGS

Serves 4

1 small parsnip

1 small sweet potato

1 small yucca

1 small Idaho potato

1 small beet

Pot of cold salt water

4 cups vegetable oil

Salt

1. Wash all veggies thoroughly, using a brush if you have one. Cut into little matchsticks with a very sharp knife, keeping different veggies separate, and soak in cold, salted water while oil heats.

2. In a large pot (oil will rise when you add veggies), heat oil to 320°F.

3. Fry parsnip at 320°F for 1 minute, remove from oil, drain on paper towels, then sprinkle with salt.

4. Fry sweet potatoes at 340°F for 1 minute, remove from heat, drain, and season.

5. Fry yucca and potatoes at 360°F for 1 minute, remove from heat, drain, and season.

6. Fry beets (do last; they stain oil) at 350°F for 1 minute, remove from heat, drain, and season.

7. Combine all and serve hot. To reheat, pop in a hot oven for 3 minutes.

Filet Mignon Day

AUG. 13

My favorite food on this earth is a good, fat, juicy, bacon cheeseburger—cooked rare. Really, if it's my last meal on earth, I would want that . . . maybe two of them . . . cooked over an open grill and served piping hot. Filet mignon is normally not very good to make burgers with since it is lean, and when you're cooking burgers you want a little bit of fat (usually a 70:30 meat to fat ratio) to make a juicy burger. Thing is, I like my burgers rare, so I decided to create this little ditty in which I combine the smooth juiciness of steak tartar with the meatiness of a burger, then top everything with melted blue cheese and all the toppings of a burger.

TARTARE BURGER

Serves 2

2–3 tablespoons crispy bacon bits, cooled

12 ounces filet mignon (finely chopped and kept cold)

2 teaspoons brined capers

2 tablespoons red onion (finely chopped)

2 tablespoons parsley (finely chopped)

1 large egg yolk

4 dashes Worcestershire sauce

3 teaspoons Dijon mustard

3 dashes hot sauce

3 dashes liquid smoke

2 teaspoons bacon fat (cool)

Salt and pepper to taste

Blue cheese

Red onion (thinly sliced)

Ripe tomato (thinly sliced)

❶ Cut bacon into small bits and cook on baking sheet at 325°F for about 10 minutes, tossing twice to cook evenly. Once crispy and light brown, remove from oven and let cool.

❷ Chop filet mignon, capers, onion, and parsley. Add remaining ingredients except cheese, sliced onion, and tomato, and toss together.

❸ Scoop meat into rings and press lightly. Heat pan (if you have cast iron, use this) until it starts to smoke. Sear meat inside ring for 1 minute so a nice crust forms. Remove rings from pan, and top with flat piece of blue cheese that covers top of meat.

❹ Place tartar in broiler until cheese melts.

❺ Finish with slices of onion and tomato. Sprinkle with salt and pepper. Serve on a nice piece of lettuce with toast points.

Creamsicle Day

When Emeril tells his audience to get one of those frozen things from the freezer when he goes on break, this is what he's talking about. Creamsicles are a type of Popsicle manufactured by Unilever with vanilla ice cream in the center surrounded by flavored ice that come in a myriad of flavors. Did you know that Popsicles were invented by an eleven-year-old boy? One night he left a stick in a cup of flavored soda out on the porch, the temperatures in San Francisco dropped, and when he woke, he found the soda frozen on a stick! Hence the Popsicle was born.

ORANGE CREAMSICLES

Serves 2

3 oranges (have extras on hand in case you mess one up)

Homemade Vanilla Ice Cream (July 23)

Tangerine or orange sorbet

❶ Cut a slice across the top of oranges, then carefully remove the insides of each with spoon. Try not to puncture orange skin.

❷ Place 3 scoops vanilla ice cream on plate in freezer to harden. At the same time, allow sorbet to soften so it becomes easy to spread.

❸ Fill orange halfway up with sorbet then insert hard scoop of vanilla ice cream and press in so sorbet rises and vanilla is hidden. Finish filling up orange with additional sorbet so it fills orange.

❹ Place sliced cap of orange back on top and freeze. And the stick, you ask? Find a thicker one to use as a spoon!

Lemon Meringue Pie Day

Although lemon-flavored custards and pies have been consumed since Medieval times, it wasn't until the late seventeenth century that European bakers aced the meringue. And it wasn't until the nineteenth century that the Lemon Meringue Pie was born—the earliest recorded recipe was a simple farm pie. Today you can find this pie in its rightful place alongside banana cream pie and apple pie in any diner, glowing in its shining glory under fluorescent lights of the dessert display case.

LEMON MERINGUE PIE

Serves 5–6

¾ cup milk

¾ cup water

1 cup sugar

4 large egg yolks

⅛ cup cornstarch

1 tablespoon finely grated lemon zest

½ cup fresh lemon juice

¼ teaspoon salt

3 tablespoons butter (unsalted and at room temp)

1 Shortbread Dough (Jan. 6) or Pie Dough (Apr. 28) baked and cooled

Meringue (Feb. 1)

❶ Boil milk with water and sugar in a heavy-bottomed pot.

❷ Whisk yolks and cornstarch. Add hot milk to yolks a little at a time while whisking continuously. Return entire mixture to pot and cook over medium heat for 1 minute until thick.

❸ Remove from heat, add zest, lemon juice, and salt. Cover and chill in fridge for at least 30 minutes.

❹ When custard is cool, whisk in butter until smooth and shiny. Fill shortbread or Pie Crust with custard.

❺ Cover top of pie with meringue, making nice peaks, then bake for 10–15 minutes at 350°F. Serve.

Rum Day

A spirit made from the juice of sugarcane and molasses (a byproduct of sugar production), many Rums are now produced directly from the juice itself. Rum ranges in styles, with colors beginning with white and spanning to golden, spiced, and dark. In early America, elections were decided not on the quality of the candidates but on their generosity with the hooch—even Washington insisted on having a barrel of Barbados rum at his 1789 inauguration! Staten Island was site of the country's first Rum distillery. My favorite Rum drink has always been the mojito, one of Hemingway's favorites; it's the definition of a light, refreshing cocktail.

MOJITO

Serves 1

½ lime (cut into 4 wedges)

6–10 fresh mint leaves

2–3 tablespoons simple syrup (equal parts sugar and water, boiled and cooled) or agave syrup

2 ounces light rum (10 Cane, Bacardi, or Rhum Clement)

Ice

1 ounce club soda

❶ In glass shaker, add limes with mint and muddle.

❷ Add simple syrup, rum, then fill with fresh ice. Shake well for at least 10 seconds, add club soda and roll cocktail (pour from one glass to another to mix contents completely).

❸ Garnish with fresh mint and serve.

Cook's Note

Use a muddler, or thick stick, to firmly press limes and mint to squeeze out the juice and press the oils in the mint out to the surface. Make sure you don't crush the leaves and limes into oblivion so that every time you take a sip it feels like gritty pesto!

AUG. 17 — Vanilla Custard Day

Custards can be baked, steamed, cooked stovetop, or frozen to a deliciously smooth and dense consistency. Custards have been around since the fourteenth century and range from savory pairings with fish, meat, and vegetables to thin Crème Anglaise and thick pastry cream. Used as the base of many pastries from around the globe, from Galaktoboureko (Greece) and Napoleons (Italy) to Crème Brûlée (France) and Trifle (England), we recognize it in our very own Cream Pies. Basically, once you learn how to make custard, a world of awesome desserts is opened to you!

VANILLA VERBENA CUSTARD

Serves 3–4

2 cups whole milk

½ cup fresh lemon verbena

½ vanilla bean (split)

⅔ cup granulated sugar

6 egg yolks

¼ cup cornstarch

❶ Bring milk to boil over medium heat in a non-reactive pot. As soon it boils, turn off heat, add lemon verbena and vanilla, cover pot, and let steep for 15 minutes. After 15 minutes, bring milk back to a boil.

❷ In a large bowl, combine sugar, yolks, and cornstarch and whisk until smooth. Once milk comes to a boil, temper egg mixture by adding milk a little at a time while whisking until all is added.

❸ Return mixture to pot and cook over medium heat while whisking until custard is thick and glossy (about 2–3 minutes). Serve with ripe peaches or strawberries.

Soft Ice Cream Day

Soft ice cream has a very festive feel about it. You eat it at fairs, at ice cream parlors, or from an ice cream truck. This is what makes soft ice cream so much fun, because its not something you can just pull out of your freezer, there is an activity associated with it. So why make your own? It can be fun, economical, and if you incorporate it into a theme party it adds a festive little ending to a wonderful meal. Nowadays, there are many affordable home soft serve ice cream makers available. But if you don't have one, don't worry—adding a little alcohol does the trick.

PONCHE CREMA ICE CREAM

Serves 3–4

Homemade Vanilla Ice Cream (July 23)

2–3 ounces dark rum

Ice cream cones

Cinnamon

❶ Make vanilla ice cream base and add rum, then chill until cold, at least 2 hours.

❷ As soon as it's done, while still soft, serve on cones and top with cinnamon.

Potato Day

Potatoes are one of the corner-stones of the international diet, leading in fourth place as the largest food crop right behind rice, wheat, and corn. The birth-place of the potato can be traced back to Peru where they nourished the Incas, but most potatoes we see on the market today are descendants of the Chilean potato. Brought to Europe by way of Spain in the early 1500s, and finally to America in the 1800s, the humble potato is now consumed at an average of 73 pounds per person, per year. And although the world largest potato grown in the Tyre area of Lebanon by Khalil Semhat weighed in at 24.9 pounds, no one can deny that America is the international face of the potato, just ask Mr. Potato Head. He's an American? Right?

POTATO GRATIN

Serves 4–6

1½ cups heavy cream

3 tablespoons butter, plus more for buttering casserole

1 sprig fresh thyme

2 pounds waxy potatoes (washed, peeled, and cut ⅛" thick)

Salt and fresh white pepper

½ pound Gruyère, Cheddar, or Swiss cheese

❶ Bring cream, butter, and thyme to boil then set aside.

❷ In a buttered casserole dish, layer potatoes in scalloped pattern. Sprinkle with salt and pepper and cover with cream mixture. Layer cheese, then repeat process with 2 more layers.

❸ Cover with aluminum foil and bake for 40 minutes at 375°F then uncover and bake for 5–10 more minutes until golden and bubbly.

AUG. 20

Lemonade Day

Before we had what we now know as Lemonade, Native Americans mixed up a drink from sumac berries that was sweetened with maple syrup. This drink came to be known as pink lemonade. Today, pink lemonade is simply made with lemons, sugar, water, and some kind of red drink like cranberry juice or grenadine. Pete Conklin, a lemonade stand vendor at a carnival, ran out of water one busy day, and in desperation he made his drinks with water a rider had used to wash his red tights. He called the concoction strawberry lemonade, and apparently doubled his sales. You know what they say: When life gives you lemons . . . .

PINK LEMONADE

Serves 4–5

  1 cup hot water

  2 cups sugar

  1cup hibiscus flowers

  1 gallon cold water

  2 cups fresh lemon juice

  1 lemon, sliced

  Ice

❶ Combine hot water with sugar and hibiscus flowers, then stir until dissolved. Let cool at room temperature.

❷ Add cold water, lemon juice, and sliced lemon (strain hibiscus leaves if you want).

❸ Serve in glasses filled with ice. Enjoy!!

Pecan Torte Day

Tortes are categorized as being made up of mostly eggs, sugar, and nuts instead of flour. Although many modern recipes bend the rules and incorporate a bit of flour here and there, tortes traditionally don't contain flour. The word torte *seems to come from the Italian word* torta, *meaning round cake or bread. In this Pecan Torte I tried to keep it as simple as I could, but feel free to add any kind of frosting you like or serve alongside some nice warm peaches with vanilla ice cream. Tortes remain nice and moist and age well in the fridge.*

PECAN TORTE

Serves 4–5

  2½ cups pecans (chopped)

  1½ cups granulated sugar

  7 eggs

  ¼ teaspoon cream of tartar

  ½ teaspoon vanilla extract

  Pinch of salt

❶ Combine pecans with sugar in a food processor, and pulse until mixture is fine and smooth.

❷ Separate 4 eggs and set whites aside. Add remaining eggs to yolks and whip until fluffy. Transfer whipped eggs to a larger bowl, clean whipping bowl and wipe dry, then whip whites. Begin on slow, beat until a little frothy, add cream of tartar, and beat on medium high until soft peaks form.

❸ Add pecan mixture a little at a time to whipped eggs folding everything together gently, then add vanilla and salt.

4 Add half of whites to mixture, folding in until smooth. Repeat with other half.

5 Pour into a lightly greased and floured 10–12" springform pan and bake at 350°F for 35–45 minutes or until knife inserted in middle comes out clean.

6 Let cool on a wire rack, unmold, and serve.

Spumoni Day

I'm sure you've cruised by the ice cream case at the supermarket and in the midst of browsing the plethora of flavors spotted a carton called Spumoni. You might have picked it up and read that it contained chocolate, cherry, and pistachio-flavored ice cream with fruit! Or Italian-style ice cream with real fruit and nuts! Let's break it down . . . Spumoni, spoo-MOH-nee, spoo-MOH-nee . . . isn't it fun to say? It's a pretty festive treat that only takes about 15 minutes to prepare with store-bought ice cream.

SPUMONI CAKE

Serves 5–6

Devil's Food Cake (May 19)

1 pint cherry ice cream

½ cup cherries (dried and chopped)

1 pint pistachio ice cream

½ cup pistachios (chopped)

2 batches Perfect Chantilly Cream (Jan. 5)

Extra pistachios and maraschino cherries for garnish

1 Bake cake in Springform pan and chill.

2 Cut it into 2 equal parts horizontally and set the bottom back into the pan. Layer cherry ice cream, sprinkle cherries on top, and freeze for at least 15–20 minutes.

3 Add pistachio ice cream as another layer, sprinkle pistachios, then set cake on top. Press down firmly, but not crushingly. Freeze until hard (about 3 hours).

4 Unmold cake and decorate with whipped cream. Garnish with pistachios and cherries.

Sponge Cake Day

Sponge Cake is one of the first things you should make if you want to learn to bake. Knowing when to stop whipping, knowing how to fold, knowing when a cake is done—all these things are integral to making you a better cook, and they are inherent in this recipe. Sponge cakes were the first cakes to be leavened without yeast—they got their rise from air whipped into the eggs.

SPONGE CAKE

Serves 4–5

4 large eggs, separated plus 1 yolk (at room temp)

½ cup granulated sugar

¼ teaspoon cream of tartar

3 tablespoons cornstarch (sifted)

⅛ cup cake flour (sifted)

1 teaspoon vanilla extract

Pinch of salt

Zest of 1 lemon

1 Prep a jelly roll pan with nonstick spray and line with wax paper.

2 Separate eggs into two bowls. Beat yolks first (if using a stand mixer, make sure yolks are in bowl you will use to whip). Add half of sugar and whip yolks for about 5 minutes on high until pale and glossy. Pour yolks into another bigger bowl.

3 Clean mixing bowl and dry thoroughly, then begin whipping whites. Once they are frothy, add cream of tartar and continue beating. Once foamy, add half of remaining sugar, then beat again. Once soft peaks form, add remaining sugar and beat on high until stiff peaks form.

4 Combine cornstarch and flour, then sift mixture half at a time into yolks. With rubber spatula, fold together gently until smooth and fluffy, then add vanilla, salt, and lemon zest. Add half of whites, folding gently, and finish with remaining whites.

5 Pour batter into pan, tapping several times firmly on a hard surface to release large air bubbles in batter. Bake at 450°F for 7 minutes. Cool and serve with jam.

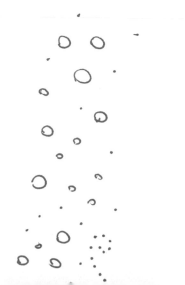

Peach Pie Day

In most of the country, you start to see the first peaches of the season in early July. It's a magical period that always reminds me that good things take time. Peach season is long-awaited, and for good reason! Sun-ripe peaches at their peak explode with luscious juices as soon as you bite into them. Normally pies are a wonderful way to feature a bounty of fresh fruit, and this pie is no exception. So why not make a day of it? Find a farm that allows you to pick your own fruit, take the kids along, and bake yourself and a few lucky neighbors some tasty Peach Pie.

PEACH PIE

Serves 5–6

1½ pounds fresh peaches (washed and cored, skin on)

2 tablespoons sugar

Pie Dough (Apr. 28)

1 Prepare peaches by slicing and covering them with sugar in bowl. Let sit at room temperature.

2 Bake pie crust and chill until room temperature.

3 Fill with peaches and cover with pie topping, then bake pie at 375°F for about 15 minutes. Cool and serve with whipped Devonshire cream if you can find it.

Cook's Note

Devonshire cream is a double cream, kind of like heavy whipping cream but a bit denser and more buttery. It has the richness of ice cream but the lightness of whipped cream.

Whiskey Sour Day

Cherry Popsicle Day

All bourbon is whiskey but not all whiskey is bourbon. Got that? Whiskey is the distillate of mash, which is fermented grain. But bourbon is whiskey that's comprised of at least 51 percent corn, which makes it sweeter. Lately there's been a revolution of sorts with small-batch whiskey distilleries, and we, my friends, are very fortunate to be a part of this. Whiskey is by far my drink of choice—it is robust, piquant, complex, and oh-so versatile. A whiskey sour tastes good in any season; however, this drink is best when you can get your hands on fresh, ripe blackberries.

It's August, which means it's hot. Really hot! Wouldn't it be great to hit the beach with your cooler, and when the kids come out of the water, you magically whip out some delicious Cherry Popsicles? Well, it's not magic; I'm going to show you how it's done. Most beer wholesalers or ice distributors sell dry ice—which is compressed carbon dioxide. Because there's no water in it, it doesn't melt; instead, it turns directly into a gas, bypassing the liquid phase altogether by sublimation. Anyway, that's why whenever you see an ice cream cart in a hot place and the cooler is opened you see a little bit of smoke. Its from the dry ice.

BLACKBERRY BOURBON SOUR

Makes 1 delicious drink

Ice cubes

2 ounces high-quality bourbon whiskey (Tuthilltown, Makers Mark, or Bulleit)

⅔ ounces lemon juice

5 fresh blackberries, plus 3 for garnish

1 teaspoon superfine sugar (or simple syrup)

Fresh mint

CHERRY POPSICLES

Serves 4–5

2 cups fresh strawberries

2 cups cherry juice

1 cup granulated sugar

2 tablespoons lemon juice

Popsicle sticks

❶ In a shaker half-filled with ice cubes, combine bourbon, lemon juice, blackberries, and sugar. Shake well. As you shake, the blackberries will get mashed and flavor the drink.

❷ Pour into a rocks glass and garnish with mint and remaining blackberries.

❶ Combine all ingredients in blender and process until smooth. Pour into Popsicle mold, stick in sticks, and freeze overnight until hard.

❷ You can also use frozen cherries in place of cherry juice, just add ½ cup water to the mix to loosen things up a bit.

❸ Feel like having a little fun? Add a splash of vodka for the strictly grown-up version.

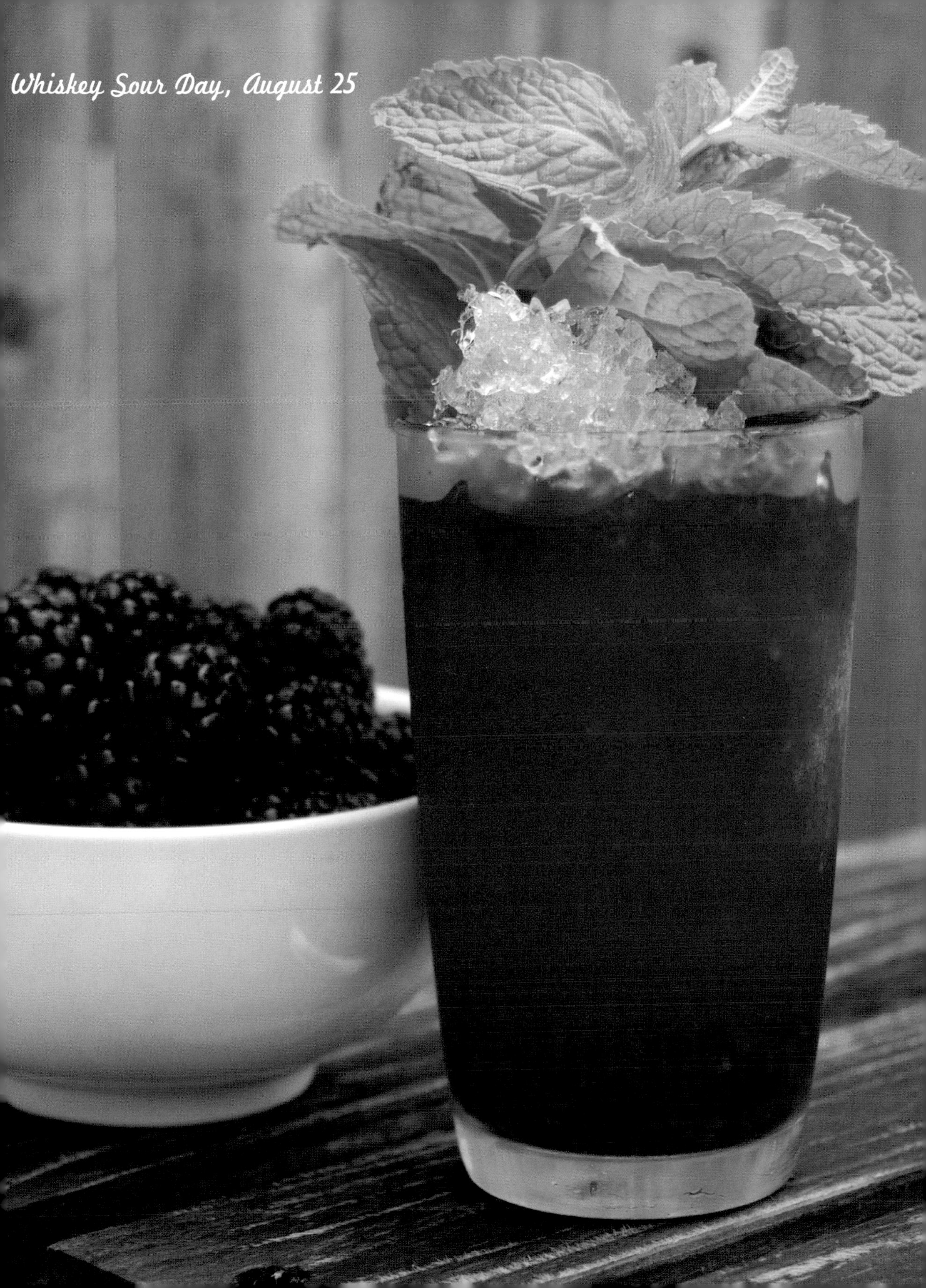
Whiskey Sour Day, August 25

AUG. 27 — Pots de Crème Day

Pots de Crème [Poh-duh-KREHM] literally translates into "pots of cream." The name refers both to the little ramekins as well as the dessert itself. Pots de Crème are the ancestors of crème brûlée, flan, and pudding. I adore banana shakes with a little cinnamon and vanilla—I drink one just about every day. There is something very comforting about the combination, so I turned it into a Pot de Crème. And since Banana Lovers Day shared the day, it works out even better! I hope you enjoy it.

BANANA POTS DE CRÈME

Serves 5–6

2 cups heavy cream

6 egg yolks

¼ cup sugar

2 tablespoons 99 Bananas (banana liquor)

½ teaspoon vanilla extract

½ teaspoon cinnamon

❶ In a small pot, bring cream to a boil.

❷ Process yolks, sugar, and 99 Bananas in blender until smooth.

❸ When cream comes to a boil, add it slowly through hole at top of blender while blending on slow. Once cream is incorporated into eggs mixture, cover the hole and blend on high for 10 seconds. Add vanilla and cinnamon and blend again for 5 more seconds.

❹ Place a few small ramekins or coffee cups in a roasting pan that is taller than the cups themselves. Pour the banana mixture into ramekins, filling them ¾ full.

❺ Fill the outside pan with hot water, cover the whole thing with aluminum foil, poke a few small holes into foil, and cook at 300°F for 45 minutes.

❻ Cool and serve. Preferably with a dollop of whipped cream and a little more cinnamon!

Cherry Turnover Day — AUG. 28

Frithsden, together with the neighboring hamlets Nettleden and Potten End in England, lay claim to this beautiful pastry. The area is home to some of the most amazing black cherries, and every July townspeople gather to celebrate at their annual cherry fair! A turnover is normally made from puff pastry and either a sweet or savory filling. Growing up there was a deli that sold fresh bagels with cream cheese and jelly for $0.99 (when you're a broke kid, this is an awesome deal)! I always loved the combination of sweet and savory and replicated it in this pastry.

CHERRY & CHEESE TURNOVERS

Makes a dozen turnovers

1½ cups cherries (frozen)

3 tablespoons sugar

2 tablespoons cherry juice or cranberry juice

1 tablespoon cornstarch

Zest of ½ lemon

1 17-oz package of frozen puff pastry

1 egg

1 8-ounce package cream cheese

1. In a heavy-bottomed pot, combine frozen cherries with sugar over low heat, and cook for 1 minute, until cherries thaw and are hot. Combine cornstarch with juice and add to pot. Cook on low while stirring for 1 minute, then add lemon zest, stir, and cool.

2. Lay puff pastry out and cut into 4 square pieces. Whisk egg with a little water and wet edges of the puff pastry squares with pastry brush. Spoon on 1 tablespoon of cherry mixture and ½ teaspoon of cream cheese.

3. Close squares and press firmly to close edges. Trim edges with a knife to make them clean, or press with fork to create ridges.

4. Place turnovers on cookie sheet lined with wax paper or nonstick-spray-covered aluminum foil. With a sharp knife, make 3 slits across top of pastries and bake at 400°F for 10 minutes until golden.

5. Remove from the oven, brush with remaining egg wash, and return to bake for another 5–10 minutes until golden and glossy. Allow to cool until warm and enjoy.

AUG. 29 Chop Suey Day

A favorite among Chinese-American immigrants, Chop Suey seems to have originated in Taishan, a district of Guangdong Province. Quick to whip up, it's served with noodles or rice. I prefer noodles, and the best I've tasted included a sunny-side-up egg on top, so that's what I make here. The formula is simple: Go to the market and buy the freshest vegetables—a good contrast of crunchy, soft, and chewy—pair with enough broth to create a sauce that holds it together.

SUNNYSIDE CHOP SUEY

Serves 3–4

1 pound fresh wonton pasta (or Asian noodles)

2 garlic cloves

Olive oil

1 cup mini-corn (cut in thin 1" pieces)

1 cup oyster mushrooms (or white mushrooms, cut in thin 1" pieces)

1 cup carrots (cut in thin 1" pieces)

1 cup bamboo shoots (cut in thin 1" pieces)

1 cup broccoli (cut in thin 1" pieces)

1 cup fresh bean sprouts

¼ cup water chestnuts (cut in thin 1" pieces)

½ cup chicken (or vegetable) stock

Hot sauce

5 tablespoons soy sauce

1 tablespoon cornstarch

1 egg

Scallions for garnish (green part, thinly sliced)

1. Follow package instructions, but cook noodles 3 minutes less than you would if you were going to eat right away. Drain and set aside. (When you add veggies and broth later, noodles will suck up juices and cook a bit more.)

2. In a large skillet or sauté pan over super-high heat, sauté garlic with a little olive oil, then add veggies and sauté until soft.

3. Add ½ cup chicken (or vegetable) stock, hot sauce, and soy sauce, and cook for 30 seconds until boiling. Combine 2 tablespoons of water with the cornstarch to make a slurry, Add the slurry and cook for another minute, then spoon everything over noodles.

4. In another pan, quickly crack an egg in a little oil and cook so it's sunny-side up. Place on top of chop suey. Garnish with scallions.

Toasted Marshmallow Day, August 30

Toasted Marshmallow Day

Toasted marshmallows remind me of camping as a kid! There's something about putting that big ball of fluff on a long stick and toasting it over a campfire that makes me giddy. That's why everybody loves s'mores—it brings you back. It's a mini-vacation to simpler times. The other day, I heard of a place called Stand in NYC that makes a Toasted Marshmallow Milkshake, which inspired me to create this S'mores Milkshake.

S'MORES MILKSHAKE

Serves 1

1 large graham cracker

1 cup milk

2 cups vanilla ice cream

3½ tablespoons Hot Fudge (June 16)

½ cup mini marshmallows

❶ In a blender, combine graham cracker with milk and ice cream until smooth.

❷ Pour into large glass, top with about 3 table-spoons hot fudge and mini marshmallows.

❸ Being careful not to stay in one place for too long and trying to not stay on the glass, burn the top of the marshmallows with hand torch until toasted. Garnish with a 2" piece of graham cracker and a little more fudge drizzled on top. Serve with a straw and a long spoon.

❹ Enjoy!

Trail Mix Day

It can be hard to live an active lifestyle with the runaround of kids, meetings, work, and school—it's always run, run, run. What's harder yet is maintaining energy to do all this. It's no wonder we end up grabbing something crappy and scarfing it down while running errands. I've found the best way to keep from eating junk is to have something good to eat prepared in advance. Enter Trail Mix. Trail Mix was invented around 1968 by two surfers when they blended peanuts and raisins for a quick energy boost. Now you can make your own on-the-go snack and kick butt!

TRAIL MIX

Serves 3–4

3 cups dried fruit (have fun, try bananas, apples, apricots, etc.)

1 cup mixed nuts (cashews, almonds, peanuts, brazil nuts, etc.)

1 cup granola (something crunchy with maple or honey for a touch of sweetness)

❶ Combine all ingredients and keep in a sealable bag or container.

❷ Store in a dry place.

SEPTEMBER

Cherry Popover Day

If you read about Blueberry Popover Day in March or you've ever made these little goodies, you already know why the name fits. When cooking they inflate to reveal a puffy shell with buttery moist pastry inside. When making cherry popovers, the concept is the same except I've made these savory and substituted cherries and a little rosemary.

CHERRY AND ROSEMARY POPOVERS

Serves 4–5

1 cup all-purpose flour

1½ tablespoons granulated sugar

2 eggs (at room temperature)

1 teaspoon kosher salt

1 tablespoon unsalted butter (melted but just warm)

1 cup milk

½ tablespoon rosemary (chopped)

1 cup cherries (thawed and chopped in quarters)

Salt and pepper for topping

1 Sift flour and sugar into a bowl. Make a well in the middle and add eggs, salt, and butter. Whisk everything together slowly, allowing eggs to drag flour into the middle—do not force.

2 When batter starts to harden, add milk a little at a time while whisking. When milk has been completely incorporated and the batter is smooth, mix in rosemary. Coat a muffin pan with nonstick spray and pour batter in so it fills cups ⅔ of the way up.

3 Add 1 teaspoon of thawed and chopped cherries to each popover and sprinkle a little salt and pepper on top of each. Bake for 40 minutes at 400°F.

4 Allow to cool until they are warm and serve.

Blueberry Popsicle Day

My friends Todd and Tim Cella own a store called SubtleTea in Manhattan. Todd came in one day raving about blueberries and how amazing they are. But they've been around forever and sometimes they are overshadowed by the new "it" superfruit. When making Popsicles I always try to use real fruit and real fruit juice instead of fake flavorings. Then you get more of a fruit bar than a sugar bar. All during the summer, I go on a smoothie kick. Blueberry-banana is one of my faves. In this recipe I do the same thing, only I turn 'em into Popsicles.

BLUEBERRY POPSICLES

Serves 2–3

3 tablespoons honey

1 banana

1 cup Greek yogurt

1 pint fresh blueberries

1 cup milk

Popsicle sticks

1. Combine all ingredients in a blender.

2. When mixed well, pour into Popsicle molds, insert sticks, and freeze until hard, about 6–7 hours.

3. To unmold, fill a container bigger than the mold with hot water.

4. Dip mold into water for 7 seconds, remove, invert, and pop out cool treats.

Cook's Note

No Popsicle mold? Don't sweat it, just use plastic cups. Pour in mix, cover with plastic wrap or aluminum foil, poke a hole in the center, and insert the stick. Freeze and enjoy!

SEP. 3

Welsh Rarebit Day

No, no rabbit. Welsh Rarebit is similar to a fondue that's been poured over toast. The biggest difference in a Welsh Rarebit is that the base cheese is Cheddar as supposed to the classic Gruyère, Emmenthaler, or Swiss cheeses found in fondue. It originated in Wales, and the first mention we have of the name is from 1785 by Francis Grose. I like this dish on hearty country bread that's been toasted and served with a slice of ham, a sunny-side-up egg, and cheese sauce drowning the whole shebang for a perfect tavern-esque meal.

WELSH RAREBIT

Serves 4–6

2 tablespoons unsalted butter

2 tablespoons all-purpose flour

2 teaspoons Dijon mustard

¼ teaspoon cayenne pepper

¼ teaspoon paprika

½ teaspoon salt

½ teaspoon freshly black pepper

1 teaspoon Worcestershire sauce

½ cup double white or witbier (beer) such as Southampton or Blue Moon

¾ cup heavy cream

½ pound Cheddar cheese (shredded)

Crusty country bread cut into 1" slices

Butter (room temp)

3 tablespoons olive oil

Eggs

½ pound deli ham (sliced)

Hot sauce

1. Make roux by heating butter over medium heat in a heavy-bottomed pot until completely melted. Add flour and whisk for one minute to cook out starch.

2. Add mustard, spices, and Worcestershire sauce, followed by beer, cream, and cheese. Allow sauce to come to a boil while whisking until smooth. Remove from heat, cover, and set aside.

3. Slice and butter bread, arrange on baking sheet, and toast in oven at around 350–400°F for about 3–4 minutes.

4. Heat 3 tablespoons olive oil in a skillet, and over medium-high heat, crack a few eggs (as many as you want; one per slice or one for every other). Cook the eggs sunny-side up.

5. Remove bread from oven, lay slices of ham on top, and then top with eggs. Reheat cheese sauce if needed, then pour on top of toast, ham, and eggs. Garnish with a little parsley. I like to add a few dashes of hot sauce for an extra oomph!

SEP. 4 — Macadamia Nut Day

The world's most expensive nut is the macadamia. Macadamias are large white nuts that got their name after a German-Australian botanist named the genus after his friend, Dr. John McAdam. The plant where the nuts come from are native to Australia and the story goes that aborigines used these nuts as currency. The plant itself resembles a holly and takes seven whole years to begin bearing fruit. Around 1922, Ernest Van Tassel organized the Hawaiian Macadamia Nut Company in Hawaii, and that helped this delicious nut gain popularity in the States.

MACADAMIA NUT ICE CREAM

Serves 4–5

3 cups whole milk

1 cup heavy cream

1 vanilla bean, split lengthwise

2 cups macadamia nuts

9 large egg yolks

¾ cup granulated sugar

Pinch of salt

1. Combine milk and cream in a heavy-bottomed pot, then scrape vanilla bean insides into milk and bring to a simmer. Turn off heat and infuse for 30 minutes.

2. Toast macadamia nuts, and as soon as they come out of the oven, place half in a food processor and blend until smooth and buttery. Allow remaining nuts to cool and chop coarsely into chunks about half the size of peanuts.

3. Give yolks a good whisk with the sugar.

4. Bring milk mixture to boil again and temper eggs by drizzling milk slowly while whisking constantly.

5. Once half of milk is incorporated into yolks, return entire mixture to pot with remaining milk. Cook on low-medium heat while scraping bottom of pot with heatproof spatula until custard coats it.

6. Add macadamia nut butter and salt, strain mixture, and chill thoroughly for at least 2 hours in the refrigerator. Remove vanilla bean, rinse off and pat dry, then reserve to infuse into oil or sugar.

7. Freeze ice cream according to your ice cream maker's instructions. When ice cream is done add chopped macadamias, stir in, and freeze for at least another hour.

Cook's Note

Make sure nuts are cold when you add them to the finished ice cream. Place them in the freezer until ready to add them.

SEP. 5

Cheese Pizza Day

Originating in Naples, Italy, pizza-style foods can be traced back to the ancient Greeks, who topped their flatbreads with cheese, olive oil, and herbs. Pizza is inexpensive, easy, delicious, and one of Americas greatest addictions. So bad is our craving that if you laid down all the pizza Americans eat in a day you would have 9 acres. That's huge!

CHEESE PIZZA

Serves 4–5

⅔ cup warm water (about 100°F)

4 teaspoons fresh yeast, or 2 teaspoons dry yeast plus 1 teaspoon instant yeast

¾ teaspoon sugar

1 ½ cups flour

1 teaspoon salt

1 tablespoon semolina plus more for rolling the dough (optional, but it adds a nice crunch)

1 tablespoon fresh rosemary (finely chopped)

Olive oil, as needed

1 cup pizza sauce

2 cups shredded mozzarella

Optional toppings: red pepper flakes, garlic powder, oregano, Parmesan cheese, and fresh basil

❶ Mix water with yeast and sugar until dissolved. In stand mixer, combine dry ingredients while slowly adding yeast mixture. Add rosemary. Mix until dough forms sticky ball around hook.

❷ Place dough in oiled bowl and let rise about 1 hour.

❸ Punch down, remove from bowl, and roll into a nice ball.

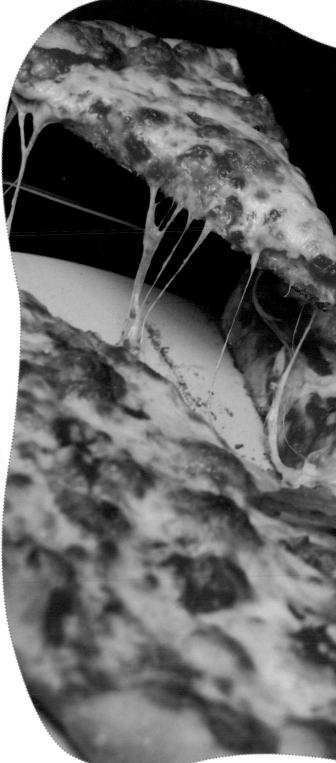

4. Place in a clean, lightly oiled container with a lid and refrigerate overnight. (You can skip this step if you want, but it'll be easier to roll out if refrigerated.)

5. Take out dough and leave at room temperature while oven warms and ready to use.

6. Preheat oven to 450°F, and place pizza stone in middle.

7. Roll out dough. Dust surface of clean countertop with either flour or semolina. Take dough and place in middle of work area and with fingertips push out rim of pizza. Press down, leaving about ¾" around circumference of dough.

8. Using rim as your guide, spread dough by using balls of hands (the part on the side of your hand from pinky up to your wrist; the part used to karate chop!). Put your hands in rim grooves on opposite sides of dough, spread dough a little, then rotate and repeat until dough is as big as stone.

9. Place dough on floured parchment paper. You can either cover dough and let rest for 30 minutes for a fluffier crust, or if you're like me and can't wait, spread sauce on dough lightly. (You don't have to spoon it on and circle it around like they do at the pizzeria, I prefer it chunky.) Top with shredded mozzarella and slide pizza onto stone in oven.

10. Bake until hot and bubbling, 12–15 minutes. Garnish with red pepper flakes, garlic powder, oregano, a dash of Parmesan, and a fresh basil sprig in the middle.

Coffee Ice Cream Day

SEP. 6

In case you've been living under a rock for the past thirteen centuries, coffee is the popular beverage made from small roasted beans of the coffee plant. After it was first brewed in Yemen, it spread to Italy, the rest of Europe, and then to the Americas. Brazil is now the largest producer of coffee in the world, trailed by Vietnam and Colombia. Did you know the most expensive coffee in the world is called Kopi Luwak and it comes from Indonesia?

COFFEE ICE CREAM

Serves 4–5

2 cups whole milk

¾ cup sugar

1 vanilla bean, split lengthwise

9 large egg yolks

Instant coffee (this depends how strong you like your coffee, and the strength of the instant coffee, but I like about 1 heaping teaspoon per cup of mix)

2 cups heavy cream

Pinch of salt

1½ teaspoon pure vanilla extract

1. In a heavy-bottomed pot, combine milk with sugar, then split vanilla bean in half and scrape insides into milk, and bring to a simmer. Turn off heat and allow vanilla to infuse into the milk for 30 minutes.

2. In the meantime, separate the eggs, combine with the coffee, and give them a good whisk.

3. Fill a bowl with ice water place another bowl on top. Fill top bowl with the heavy cream, salt, and vanilla. This ice bath stops the custard from overcooking.

④ Bring the milk to a boil and temper the eggs by drizzling the milk slowly while whisking constantly. Once you have added half the milk into the egg yolks, return the mixture to the pot with the remaining milk. Cook on low to medium heat while scraping the bottom of the pot with a heatproof spatula until the custard can coat the spatula. Strain the mix into the heavy cream and chill thoroughly, for at least 2 hours in the refrigerator. Remove the vanilla bean, and rinse off and pat it dry, then plop it into a bottle of wine for vanilla wine, into oil, or into sugar for vanilla sugar.

⑤ Freeze the ice cream according to your ice cream maker's instructions. When the ice cream is done, add in the chocolate-covered coffee beans and freeze until hard, about 2 hours.

Chocolate-covered Coffee Beans

Makes 1½ cups beans

1 cup bittersweet chocolate

1 cup roasted coffee beans

① Melt ¾ of the chocolate in a microwave by pulsing 1 minute at a time. Once the chocolate is completely melted, add the remaining chocolate and stir. Take the temperature of the chocolate and make sure it's about 90°F.

② Wrap the coffee beans in a towel. Roll over the towel with a rolling pin with a little pressure. Put the cracked beans in a large metal bowl.

③ Pour in a few tablespoons of the melted chocolate and using a wooden spoon coat all the cracked beans. Place the bowl in the fridge for 30 seconds, remove, then using the spoon stir the beans until the chocolate has cooled and dried. Repeat the process twice more. Place bowl in fridge so the chocolate solidifies well.

Acorn Squash Day

SEP 7

Every time my mom and I go out for lunch or dinner I can bet on one thing. If they have soup on the menu, she's ordering it. Growing up, we ate soup constantly—my mom loved to make it, from the übersimple to truly complicated varieties! Having to feed a large family with little time, energy, and money can be trying at times, but for the smart cook, soup can be the answer. Since my mom loves soup so much I came up with this little ditty for her.

"I LOVE YOU, MOM" SOUP

Serves 3–4

3 acorn squash

2 carrots (peeled and chopped into 1" pieces)

1 onion (cleaned and chopped into 1" pieces)

Olive oil

Salt

Pepper

3 cups vegetable stock

1 cup heavy cream

¼ teaspoon ginger

⅛ teaspoon allspice

⅛ teaspoon nutmeg

2 tablespoons butter

Sour cream

½ cup toasted pumpkin seeds for garnish

① Cut squash in half and remove seeds, then cut halves in half again. Place squash pieces along with carrots and onions on baking sheet, drizzle with oil and salt and pepper, cover with aluminum foil, and roast at 400°F for 45 minutes, or until soft.

② Remove from oven and carefully remove flesh from squash with a spoon.

③ In a large stockpot, heat vegetable stock with heavy cream. Thoroughly blend squash flesh, onions, and carrots with a hand emulsion blender or in a food processor while adding hot stock little by little. Continue blending, adding more stock if needed until desired thickness. (For thicker soup, add less stock, and vice versa.)

④ Add spices and adjust salt and pepper to taste. Add butter, and blend one more time then return to pot to keep warm.

⑤ When ready to serve, ladle soup into bowls, place dollop of sour cream in the middle, top with a few toasted pumpkin seeds, and sprinkle with your mom's favorite herb (my mom loves cilantro, so that's what I use).

Cook's Note

To win extra brownie points with Mom, get creative and serve soup in a roasted and hollowed-out squash!

Date Nut Bread Day

SEP. 8

Date nut bread is a quick bread, as such, it's leavened with baking powder and baking soda as opposed to yeast. There are three basic methods when making quick bread batters: the muffin method, in which dry and wet ingredients are mixed rapidly; the creaming method, in which the butter is "creamed" to incorporate air into it; and the biscuit method, in which cold fat is "cut" into the flour, a method called "shortening." The main ingredient in this bread is the date, a sweet fruit originating in Africa and a food staple for ancient Egyptians going back as far as 6000 BCE.

CHOCOLATY DATE NUT BREAD

Serves 3–4

¾ cup boiling water

¼ cup cocoa powder

2 tablespoons butter

1½ cups dates (chopped)

¼ cup molasses

2 large eggs

¼ cup brown sugar

¾ cup unbleached all-purpose flour

1½ teaspoons baking powder

¼ teaspoon baking soda

½ teaspoon salt

1 cup walnuts (chopped)

½ cup chocolate chips

❶ Grease loaf pan with butter and dust with flour.

❷ Boil water and add cocoa powder and butter. Pour mixture over dates. Let sit for 15 minutes.

❸ Purée half the mixture and return it to the rest of the date mix. Mix in molasses and eggs and beat well.

❹ In another bowl, sift remaining dry ingredients and add in egg-chocolate-date mixture. Mix slowly to incorporate until batter is smooth. Stir in nuts and chocolate chips then pour batter into prepared pan.

❺ Bake at 350°F for 50–60 minutes until a knife inserted in middle comes out clean. If top starts to get too brown, place a piece of aluminum foil to cover, and continue to bake. Cool and serve.

Wiener Schnitzel Day

SEP 9

Just about every nation enjoys breaded, fried meat. Why shouldn't they? It's amazing! Wiener Schnitzel is popular all over the world and is often served with lingonberries or lemon potatoes. Variations include our ever-popular chicken fried steak and veal cutlet parm with tomato sauce and melted mozzarella. Though in Austria, Wienerschnitzel technically only applies to veal, nowadays it is just as common for it to be made with chicken, pork, or lamb. And trust me, they're all awesome. Again, what's not to like about breaded and fried meat?

LEMON WIENER SCHNITZEL

Serves 4

4 veal fillets

Garlic powder

Paprika

Salt and pepper

Juice of 1 lemon

2 cups plus 1 tablespoon flour

4 eggs (lightly beaten)

2 cups seasoned bread crumbs

2 cups vegetable oil

❶ Place cutlets into a large Ziploc bag and pound them thin with a mallet or tenderizer (until about ¼" thick). Lay out flat and season both sides with spices and lemon juice.

❷ Set up a breading station with one deep plate or bowl with flour, one with eggs, and one with bread crumbs.

3 In a deep skillet, bring oil to 365–375°F. One by one, dip cutlets into flour, then eggs, and finally bread crumbs. Add to skillet, fry about 3–4 minutes until golden, remove from oil, and drain on paper towels.

4 Serve with a nice salad and enjoy! This makes a wonderful lunch or a quick sandwich.

TV Dinner Day

In 1953, TV was all the rage. It was a grand event—not everyone owned one so people would gather at each other's houses to watch "the tube." Since TV was a main event at the time, American ingenuity followed suit. Enter the TV Dinner. Originally marketed by C.A. Swanson & Sons as "TV Brand Frouncesen Dinners," they normally included some sort of starch, veggies, and meat. We've come a long way with technology, and thankfully so have our frozen meals. But why not take it up a notch and make your own? The quality will be better and you can relive some good-old Americana.

CLASSIC MEATLOAF TV DINNER

Serves 3–4

Cheesy Mashed Potatoes (Oct. 27)

Ma! the Meatloaf! (June 13)

Heavenly Biscuits (May 14)

Peach Cobbler (Apr. 13)

1 The trick to this bad boy re-enactment is finding those nifty little TV dinner trays. The web is awesome, and you can find them and have them shipped right to your home.

2 Once you have the trays, bake the biscuits and peach pie. Then make potatoes and meatloaf. You can fill the trays with anything you like really. Just make sure to eat them in front of the TV—it makes all the difference!

Hot Cross Bun Day

SEP 11

Nothing beats the smell of fresh baked bread except the smell of fresh baked sweet bread. It's quite serendipitous that as I was about to write this, I walked by a bakery in Maspeth, NY, and saw a huge sign advertising HOT CROSS BUNS! What luck! I walked in and asked for some, but they were out. I kept walking and entered the next bakery, where the girl behind the counter ushered me toward a litter of petite, golden, eggy buns featuring frosting crosses. I bought one, ate it, and ran home to make my own. Now you can, too.

HOT CROSS BUNS

Makes a dozen buns

½ cup milk (warm)

1 teaspoon instant yeast

1 teaspoon granulated sugar

1⅛ cups bread flour

1 large egg lightly beaten

⅔ teaspoon salt

3½ tablespoons honey

1 teaspoon grated orange zest

2 tablespoons unsalted butter (soft)

½ cup dried cranberries

1 egg (beaten with 1 tablespoon water)

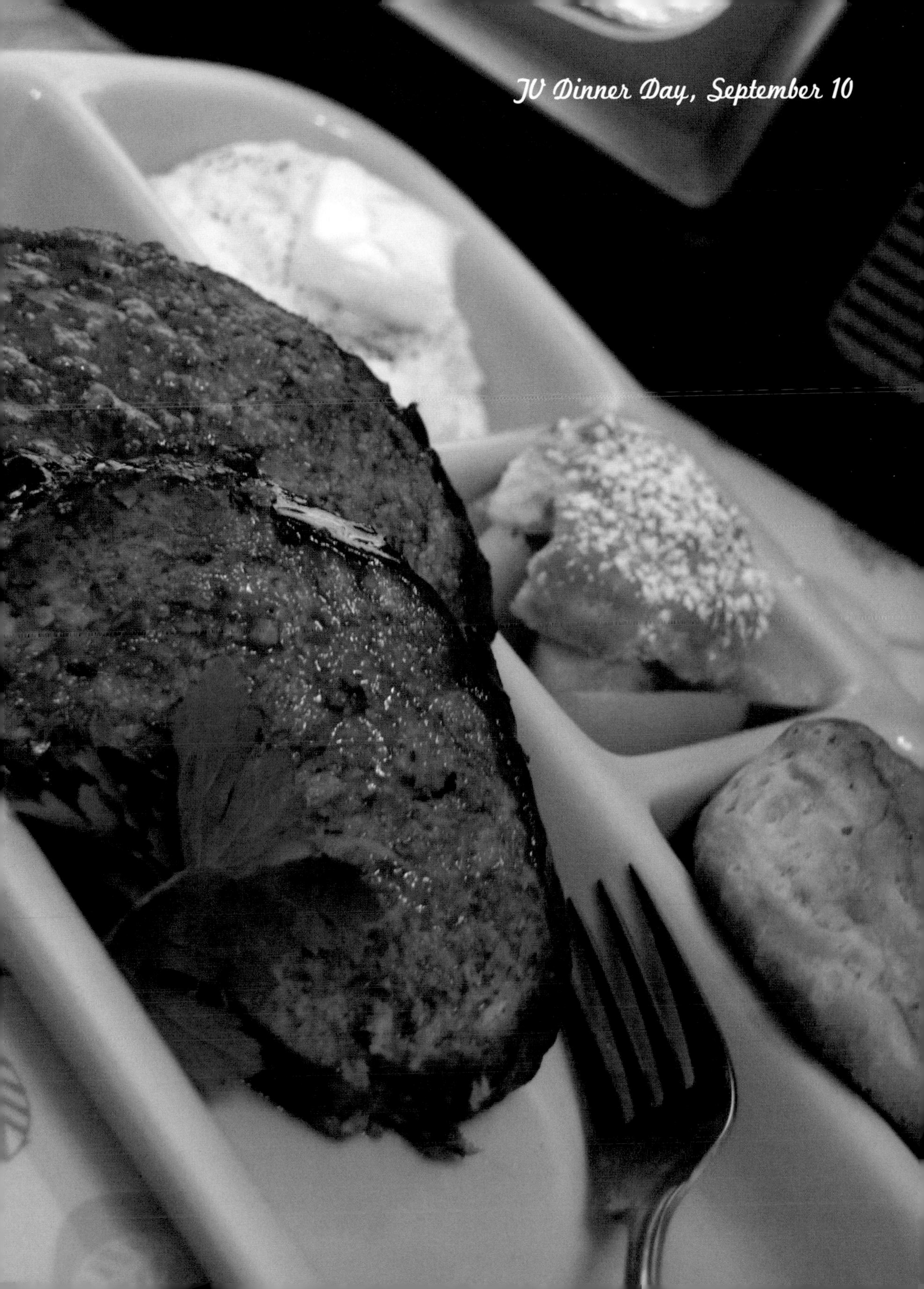
TV Dinner Day, September 10

Cream Cheese Frosting

1 cup (8 ounces) cream cheese (at room temp)

¾ cup butter (soft)

2 cups powdered sugar

2 teaspoons vanilla extract

❶ Mix milk with yeast and sugar until dissolved. Cover with plastic wrap and let rise for 5 minutes.

❷ Set up your stand mixer with the hook attachment, Sift flour then slowly add milk/yeast mixture followed by egg, salt, honey, and zest.

❸ Add butter a little at a time and mix until dough is elastic and hardly sticks to bowl, about 8 minutes. Add cranberries and combine well.

❹ Place dough in an oiled bowl and let rise 1 hour, punch down, remove from bowl, and roll into 2" balls. Arrange in a buttered pan (springform works well). Cover with plastic wrap and refrigerate overnight. (If you want to cook sooner, don't refrigerate overnight, simply let rise for 1–2 hours at room temp until double in volume.)

❺ The following day, remove from fridge and let rise for 2 hours. Glaze with egg wash and bake at 375°F for 15–20 minutes until golden.

❻ To make the frosting simply whip cream cheese with butter, sugar, and vanilla until light and fluffy. Once the buns have cooled, decorate the tops by piping the frosting through a little tip or simply place it inside a Ziploc bag, seal, and snip the tip of the corner. Make cheesy crosses on top of the buns and serve.

Chocolate Milkshake Day

SEP. 12

As you probably already know, chocolate is awesome. When you're craving a quick pick-me-up, or feeling sad, or just need to quench that nagging sweet tooth, chocolate is always there. Like a good friend, chocolate is around to console you, to make you feel better, and tell you everything's going to be all right. Most of all, chocolate doesn't judge you. It just provides unconditional and fulfilling love. So forget calling your best friend to cry or watching Oprah; instead, whip up a nice, cold, smooth and delicious chocolate shake. (Okay, maybe watch Oprah, too.)

MOLTEN CHOCOLATE MILKSHAKE

Serves 1

2 cups really good-quality chocolate ice cream

1 teaspoon vanilla extract

4 tablespoons chocolate syrup

½ cup milk

Whipped cream

Hot Fudge (June 16) or chocolate shavings made with peeler or zester

Lava Mousse (Apr. 3)

❶ Combine all ingredients except cake and blend until smooth. Bake the little cakes in small ramekins the same size as the top of the glass and pop right on top of the milkshake.

❷ Top with a scoop of vanilla ice cream, drizzle with chocolate syrup, top that with whipped cream, and finish by taking a solid chocolate bar at room temperature and, using a peeler, make little chocolate shavings. Serve with straws. And napkins. Lots and lots of napkins.

SEP. 13

Snack on a Pickle Day

One of my favorite bars is this place in Astoria called Sweet Afton. Their food is awesome, people are cool, and the scene is great. However, if you go, you must, and I mean you must, ask my boys behind the bar to make you a pickle martini. Simple ingredients, but this martini is sick made with Brooklyn's McClures spicy pickles. That's where I got the idea for these little puppies. With this recipe grab your favorite pickled veggie (it doesn't have to be a pickle) and fry it up. The acid cuts the fat perfectly and keeps you coming back for more. I know you'll love them!

FRIED PICKLES

Serves 2–4

1 cup flour

¼ cup cornstarch

1 teaspoon garlic powder

1 teaspoon baking powder

¼ teaspoon salt

1 cup beer

1 egg

Gherkins or cornichons

Vegetable oil for frying

1. Combine all ingredients (except pickles and oil) until smooth batter forms. Let rest for about 10 minutes.

2. Pat pickles dry and set out on paper towels to fully dry. Once dry, dunk pickles in batter.

3. Heat skillet with 1" oil to 375°F.

4. Dip coated pickles in hot oil a handful at a time and fry until golden.

5. Drain on paper towels and serve right away, ideally with a side of hot sauce and an ice cold beer or martini.

Cream-Filled Doughnut Day

SEP. 14

The doughnut began as the olykoek, meaning oil cake, coming from Dutch settlers who had already brought us cookies and cobblers. It is said that the shape of the doughnut came from a man named Hansen Gregory who, while aboard a ship and frustrated of frying these little cakes and the dough always coming out raw, cut a hole in the middle—the rest is sweet-fried history. Of course, no hole is necessary here since we'll be filling the center with yummy goodness. And you're not thinking just sweet fillings, right? Think of a savory cheese-filled donut, or how about chili-filled!!?? Now that's what I'm talking about!

DOUGHNUTS

Makes a dozen doughnuts

5 tablespoons warm water (about 90°F)

3½ tablespoons fresh yeast

2 cups powdered sugar

6 cups flour

3 whole eggs (at room temp)

1½ cups whole milk (warm)

5½ tablespoons butter (unsalted and soft)

1 teaspoon salt

Oil for frying

Pastry Cream (Feb. 20) or Vanilla Pudding (May 22)

1. In a bowl, combine water with yeast until dissolved, and add 1 tablespoon powdered sugar and ½ cup flour. Cover with plastic wrap and set atop stove or in oven (while turned off) and let rise for 10 minutes.

2. Sift remaining flour and powdered sugar, then combine remaining ingredients, except oil and Pastry Cream, in a bowl. With paddle attachment on stand mixer, combine all ingredients until dough forms.

3. Add yeast mixture and thoroughly combine. If dough is sticky, add more flour until dough hardly sticks to your hands. Cover with plastic wrap again, and let rise for 1 hour, undisturbed.

4. In large stockpot, heat 5–6 cups of oil to 350°F, using a thermometer to keep temperature constant. Put dough on clean, floured work surface, and pat down until 1" thick. Cut doughnuts with ring cutter (don't make hole in the middle, remember we're stuffing these). Fry on each side until golden, about 2 minutes on each side, drain on paper towels.

5. Using chopstick or something similar, prick a hole in doughnut, push in and make a little hole in center for filling.

6. Scoop Pastry Cream in piping bag with metal or plastic tip, and squeeze as much cream into doughnut as you like. Dust with powdered sugar before serving.

Linguini Day

You know, pasta is extremely easy to make from scratch,
and the coolest part is that once you've got great-quality homemade pasta, you don't have to add much more to it for it to taste incredible. A good drizzle of extra-virgin olive oil and a few shavings of Parmesan cheese and you have yourself a nice dinner. This is not a traditional pasta recipe, but more like a formula. Normally pasta is made with eggs and semolina flour, but here we use purées as the liquid and mix it with flour to create wonderful vegetable-flavored pasta.

VEGETABLE LINGUINI

Serves 1–2

1 cup vegetable purée (preferably of a root vegetable, cooked, puréed and cooled)

Salt and pepper

Flour

1. Scoop purée into bowl and season with salt and pepper. Little by little, sift flour into purée while mixing with other hand until semifirm dough forms. Wrap with plastic wrap and let rest for 15 minutes on counter.

2. Roll dough onto clean, floured surface, and using a sharp knife, slice into thin strips. Cook in boiling water until tender, about 2–4 minutes.

3. Finish with simple tomato sauce, a drizzle of olive oil, and plenty of Parmesan cheese.

Cook's Note

You'll need to add more or less flour depending on the moisture content of your veggie purée.

Guacamole Day

What can be more representative of fresh Mexican cuisine that the simple preparation of guacamole? Stemming from a–huacatl, which means "avocado," plus molli, which means "sauce or milled," this delicious staple can be made as a dip, a filling, or thinned out to a wonderful saucy consistency. The Aztecs are accredited with the invention of guacamole, and thanks to the conquistadors, avocados became a popular food of the New World. Avocados are a fruit and can even be enjoyed with a little sugar or salt. In Asian countries they make avocado milkshakes, and in the United States, ice cream and even cocktails feature the fruit. But we'll stick to this delicious dip for now. . . .

GUACAMOLE

Makes 2–3 cups

1 small ripe tomato (chopped into ¼" cubes without the seeds)

2 tablespoons finely chopped white onion

1 jalapeño (minced)

2 large ripe Haas avocados

2 teaspoons freshly squeezed lime juice

½ teaspoon salt (preferably kosher)

¼ teaspoon freshly cracked pepper

2 tablespoon finely chopped cilantro leaves

❶ Clean and chop veggies. Remove seeds and veins from jalapeños and mince finely.

❷ Slice avocados in half, scoop out flesh into a bowl, take out seeds and reserve one. Immediately add lime juice and with either a potato masher or a whisk, break and mash avocado until it's a rough paste (I like mine a little chunky).

❸ Add remaining ingredients and stir well. Taste and adjust seasonings if necessary. Return one of the seeds to guacamole and place a piece of plastic wrap directly on top, then refrigerate, or if you can, serve immediately.

Cook's Tip

How do you know when an avocado is ripe? First, choose an avocado that's dark, not one that's vivid green. Second, take the avocado and hold it in the palm of your hand. Gently press it with your thumb, if it gives way, do it again in another spot, if it gives way again, it's ripe. If you're really uncertain, buy three and choose the two best ones. Before you begin to make your guacamole, refrigerate the avocados. Avocados start to turn brown as soon as the air hits the flesh. By refrigerating them, you slow down the oxidation process making for a greener end product.

Apple Dumpling Day

If you can imagine little crusty bites of apple pie, lovingly nestled in a cinnamony butter-sugar sauce topped with a scoop of ice cream, then today is your day! Apple dumplings can take many shapes and forms, from boiled to pastry-filled little morsels and crispy fried snacks. The traditional dumpling is thought to have originated in the Northeast, with the Amish.

APPLE DUMPLINGS

Serves 2

Pie Dough (Apr. 28)

Apple Pie filling (Dec. 3) (drained, liquid reserved)

1 egg (beaten)

1cup brown sugar

5 tablespoon butter

1. Roll Pie Dough out to about ⅛". Create several rings with 3" cookie cutter. Place some pie filling in middle, brush edges with egg, and fold up both flaps of dumpling to form. Using fork, crimp edges all the way around. Repeat until you have used up all dough and/or filling.

2. Place dumplings in casserole dish greased with butter. Sprinkle brown sugar all around, drizzle remaining liquid from apples, and dot tops with dollops of butter. Bake at 350°F for 20–25 minutes until sugar has melted and dumplings are bubbling.

3. Serve hot with sauce and a scoop of vanilla or rum raisin ice cream.

Cheeseburger Day

SEP 18

Cheeseburgers are the perfect food, bar none. They are everything you could ever want in a meal all nicely arranged to be devoured together. My rule is if you can eat a Cheeseburger with one hand, then you're doing something wrong. Burgers should be big enough that you need to use both hands in order to eat them. What makes Cheeseburgers so great? I think it's the combination of textures and flavors, temperatures, and the little burst of juiciness that explodes in your mouth as you bite in.

DA BOMB

Makes 6 delicious burgers

6–10 thick-cut bacon slices

Simple Burgers (Dec. 21)

6 eggs

American sliced cheese

2 cups potato chips or potato sticks

1 tomato (sliced)

4–5 lettuce leaves (washed and dried)

1 bag potato chips (crushed)

Salsa Rosada (a.k.a. Pink Sauce)

½ cup ketchup

½ cup mayonnaise

½ teaspoon chili powder

2 tablespoons pickle relish

❶ Cook bacon on baking sheet in one layer in 350–375°F oven for 10–15 minutes until golden and crispy,

❷ Make Simple Burgers. Then toast or warm buns in either a steamer or on the stove over medium heat.

❸ Spread Pink Sauce on both parts of the buns.

❹ Fry eggs in hot skillet, sunny-side up.

❺ Top burger with cheese and melt in broiler, then add a couple bacon slices and one sunny-side egg, a few tomato slices, and the lettuce. If you're feeling a little frisky put a handful of crushed potato chips on top. It's a perfectly balanced breakfast for any time of the day!

Butterscotch Pudding Day

SEP 19

Similar to toffee, kind of like caramel, thick or thin, butterscotch does not get its name from the scotch added into it. As a matter of fact, scotch is not normally used in the recipe—until now. Butter plays a mayor role in the creaminess of this pudding. What's really cool about this recipe is that you can freeze it and you'll have mouthwatering butterscotch pudding pops!

BUTTERSCOTCH PUDDING

Serves 4

½ cup granulated sugar

2 teaspoons scotch whiskey

4 tablespoons butter

½ cup packed dark brown or Muscovado sugar

2½ cups whole milk

2 large eggs plus 1 egg yolk

3 tablespoons cornstarch

½ teaspoon kosher salt

1 teaspoon vanilla extract

❶ In a heavy-bottomed 2-quart pot, melt granulated sugar over medium heat. Using wooden spoon, stir until it starts to smoke. Add scotch whiskey, then butter, and remove from heat. Stir until butter is dissolved and a caramel forms. Add brown sugar, followed by milk and bring back to boil over medium heat. Stir until all has dissolved and formed a caramel milk.

❷ Mix eggs with cornstarch until smooth.

3. Add hot milk to cornstarch mixture a little at a time to temper eggs. Add half of milk, return entire mixture to remaining milk in pot, and cook over medium heat whisking continuously until thick, about 2 minutes. Remove from heat, add salt and vanilla, and stir well.

4. Pour pudding into individual cups or one large, decorative bowl. Refrigerate until cold, at least 3 hours. Serve with dollops of whipped cream or freeze for butterscotch pudding pops.

SEP 20
Rum Punch Day

The term punch *has a colorful history that leads us back to Indian* Panch, *coming from* Paantsch, *stemming from the Persian word* Panj *for five. This is because traditional punches usually contained five ingredients. The drink was spread into European culture by sailors returning from India, by the British East India Company around the seventeenth century. The modern rum punch came around 1655 when Jamaica started producing the spirit. There are three major rum punches widely consumed: Bajan Rum Punch, Caribbean Rum Punch, Planter's Punch. Here, we'll mix up a batch of the latter. . . .*

PLANTER'S PUNCH

Serves 1

2 ounces dark rum

2 ounces fresh orange juice

2 ounces fresh pineapple juice

½ ounce fresh lime juice

Dash grenadine

Orange slice and cherry for garnish

Ice

1. Combine all ingredients in shaker, fill with clean ice, shake well, and serve in a tall glass or a hurricane glass. Serve with a straw.

Pecan Cookie Day

SEP 21

If you're ever driving around in Brunswick, Missouri, and happen to drive by what looks to be a giant bus-sized pecan on the side of the road, I suggest immediately stopping. As you drive up to it, you will behold the worlds largest pecan; measuring 7' x 12' and weighing in at more than 12,000 pounds, it's quite a nut! Alongside you'll see a sign leading you to The Nut Hut. George and Elizabeth James have run this wonderful pecan farm for over 60 years, and now their kids are helping run things. When I find a wonderful ingredient like pecans I keep it simple—it's either pie or cookies. Here is the cookie recipe.

PECAN COOKIES

Makes about 2 dozen cookies

¾ cup butter (unsalted)

1 cup brown sugar

½ teaspoon salt

¾ cup all-purpose flour

½ teaspoon baking soda

½ teaspoon ground cinnamon

1 large egg

2 cups instant oats

1 teaspoon vanilla extract

1 cup pecans (chopped) and ½ cup whole

1. Cream butter and sugar for about 8 minutes on high speed until fluffy. Sift all dry ingredients except oats.

2. Add egg to butter mixture. Combine for 10 seconds, then add dry ingredients in 2 parts. Mix thoroughly, then add oats, vanilla, and chopped pecans. Combine well for at least 10 seconds.

3. Spoon mixture (if you have a small 1–2 tablespoon ice cream scoop, use it) onto greased cookie sheet about 1 tablespoon at a time, leaving 1" between each cookie.

4. Wet hand a little with oil or water and press cookies down a bit. Place one whole pecan on top of each.

5. Bake at 350°F in middle rack of oven for 10–12 minutes or until golden. Cool and enjoy!

Ice Cream Cone Day

The story starts at the St. Louis World Fair, circa 1904. More than 50,000 gallons of ice cream were served to fairgoers, and next to one of those ice cream vendors was a humble man making a humble waffle. And when the gentleman serving ice cream ran out of serving dishes, Ernest A. Hamwi had the bright idea to serve the cool treat inside one of his rolled-up waffles. Eureka! One of the greatest creations your sweet tooth has ever come in contact with was born. After the fair, manufacturers caught wind of this and started producing them, making cones available to every home and ice cream truck across America!

HOMEMADE ICE CREAM CONES

Makes about a dozen cones

½ cup all-purpose flour

½ cup powdered sugar

3 large egg whites

⅛ teaspoon salt

¼ teaspoon vanilla extract

4 tablespoons butter (melted)

½ cup dark chocolate (melted)

1. Sift flour and powdered sugar, making a well in middle.

2. Add egg whites, salt, and vanilla. Whisk all together, add butter, and whisk again.

3. Allow batter to rest overnight or at least for an hour.

4. Line baking sheet with Silpat or nonstick aluminum foil.

5. Drop 1 tablespoon batter onto sheet and using a spatula, flatten to thickness of a quarter.

6. Cook for 6–8 minutes at 350°F until edges are slightly browned.

7. Remove from oven and loosen by running spatula underneath cookies.

8. Roll them into cones and place in deep glasses to dry and cool.

9. Drizzle melted chocolate inside cones to prevent leakage.

White Chocolate Day

What is White Chocolate? When the cacao bean is picked, dried, and roasted, the nuts are ground and the oil or butter is squeezed out. As a result of this process you end up with cocoa butter and cocoa powder. To make White Chocolate, the cocoa butter is emulsified with milk powder, sugar, lecithin, and some-times vanilla then cooled into bars or pellets. I think the best way to highlight the richness of white chocolate is with mousse. There's also a great White Chocolate Cheesecake (Mar. 6). So hopefully people will stop picking on white chocolate—it's delicious!

WHITE CHOCOLATE MOUSSE

Serves 4–5

½ tablespoon powdered gelatin

¼ cup ice cold water

½ cup heavy cream

1 cup white chocolate (chopped small)

1 teaspoon vanilla extract

1¼ cups heavy cream (chilled and whipped to stiff peaks)

❶ To hydrate gelatin, sprinkle over water.

❷ Bring cream to a boil over medium heat. Place white chocolate in a large bowl and pour hot cream over it. Wait 40 seconds and whisk together. Add gelatin and whisk again until gelatin melts and incorporates, add vanilla, and whisk again.

❸ Place bowl in fridge to cool for about 2–3 min-utes. Mixture should turn into a smooth thick cream called ganache.

❹ Wait 5 minutes and whisk ganache. Repeat every 5 minutes until ganache is as thick as soft custard. (If it becomes hard, microwave for 5–10 seconds at a time until smooth.)

❺ Add half of whipped cream. Whisk in cream until smooth mixture forms. Add remaining whipped cream and fold together.

❻ Pour mousse into individual cups or one big glass bowl. It's best served right away, but it also keeps in the fridge for a few days.

Cherries Jubilee Day

Queen Victoria decided to throw a Diamond Jubilee on her sixtieth year. In honor of this celebration, the famed Chef Aug. Escoffier created a dish made with fresh cherries cooked with Kirschwasser (a cherry brandy) and served over vanilla ice cream. This is a simple dish I like to serve over pound cake or in a waffle shell.

CHERRIES JUBILEE

Serves 4–5

1½ cups frozen cherries

3 tablespoons sugar

⅓ cup plus 1 tablespoon cherry juice

½ lemon zested

1 tablespoon cornstarch

3 tablespoons kirsch

Buttery Pound Cake (Mar. 4)

Homemade Vanilla Ice Cream (July 23)

❶ In a heavy-bottomed pot, combine frozen cherries with sugar and ⅓ cup juice and zest over low heat, cook for 1 minute or until cher-ries thaw and are hot.

② Combine cornstarch with 1 tablespoon juice and add to pot, along with kirsch. Cook on low for 1 minute.

③ Place pound cake slice in bowl with scoop of vanilla ice cream, pour hot cherries over, and serve immediately.

Crab Meat Newburg Day

I used to work at a restaurant that made an incredible lobster newburg. Every day we'd make lobster sauce, and since there was always some left over at the end of the night I'd serve it on top of jasmine rice. One day we were making ravioli and I thought it'd be incredible to pair it with the lobster sauce. One thing led to another and these little babies were born.

CRAB NEWBURG DUMPLINGS

Serves 2 dozen

1 pound fresh or frozen crabmeat (thawed if frozen)

3 scallions (finely chopped)

½ red bell pepper (finely chopped)

3 tablespoons mayonnaise

1 egg

½ teaspoon dry mustard

½ lemon, juiced

¼ teaspoon garlic powder

1 teaspoon salt

Dash cayenne pepper

½ lemon juiced

1 package wonton wrappers

1 egg for wash

Newburg Sauce

1 medium Spanish onion (finely chopped)

Pinch of saffron

1 tablespoon tomato paste

2 tablespoon dry sherry

2 tablespoon Cognac or brandy

1½ cups heavy cream

Salt to taste

1 dash white pepper

3 tablespoon butter

① In large bowl, mix all ingredients (except wonton wrappers) until combined well.

② Place 1 teaspoon crabmeat mixture in middle of wonton wrapper. Brush sides with egg wash. Seal tightly by closing all sides to create a small purse.

③ Set aside and repeat process with remaining mixture.

④ To make sauce, sauté onion with saffron over medium heat until translucent. Add tomato paste and stir for 1 minute, then add sherry and brandy. Whisk until dissolved then follow with cream.

⑤ Season with salt and pepper and cook for 1–2 minutes until thick. Remove from heat and finish with butter. Whisk until butter is completely dissolved.

⑥ Boil dumplings in simmering water for 1–2 minutes, gently strain and serve piping hot with sauce.

Pancake Day

Hot, fluffy, light-as-clouds pan-cakes, stacked sky-high, with a pad of soft butter lightly melting, sprinkled with salt, and drizzled with warm maple syrup. Can you think of anything better? In the United States, pancakes are sometimes called hotcakes, griddlecakes, or flapjacks, and they range from savory to sweet and are served with everything from simple fruits to pickles, fish, but mostly syrups such as maple, condensed milk, and marmalade. Whichever way you like them, just make sure to stack them high and eat them right off the pan, piping hot, until you can't eat any more.

SIMPLE PANCAKES

Serves 3–4

2 cups all-purpose flour (sifted)

2½ teaspoons baking powder

3 tablespoon white or brown sugar

½ teaspoon salt

2 eggs

1½ cups milk

3 tablespoons melted butter

❶ Sift flour with the baking powder, then make a well in the middle of the mix.

❷ Add sugar, salt, and eggs. Start mixing the eggs, allowing the flour to be incorporated little by little.

❸ As the mix becomes thicker add milk and butter little by little until you have a smooth batter. If the batter looks too thick, add a little more milk.

❹ Cook pancakes in a griddle or sauté pan over medium-high heat with a little vegetable oil.

❺ Cook each pancake for about 30–40 seconds until little bubbles form on top. Flip each pancake with a spatula and cook for another 20 seconds on the other side. Repeat with remaining batter. You can keep the pancakes hot in the oven with aluminum foil over them, or simply reheat them in the microwave. Serve with room temperature butter and warm maple syrup.

Corned Beef Hash Day

Diners are the one place you can go to have pan-cakes, next to pork chops, next to a gyro, with fresh waffles. This is the home away from home where you can always find good Corned Beef Hash. A wonderfully nourishing pairing of a good breakfast, lunch, or dinner, I like this dish with sunny-side eggs, so that when you break the yolks the golden river of lava flows into the hash making a wonderful sauce that goes perfect on crusty toast. Here I incorporate a little pork and go with sweet potatoes instead of regular potatoes.

SWEET POTATO HASH

Serves 3–4

1 large gold potato (shredded)

2 medium sweet potatoes (shredded)

Salt

Olive oil

1 Spanish yellow onion (thinly sliced)

1 teaspoon butter (unsalted)

3 cups corned beef (cooked and shredded)

4 bacon strips (finely chopped)

2 teaspoons fresh minced parsley

1 teaspoon fresh minced chives

Salt and pepper to taste

1. Toss potatoes with salt and olive oil, then arrange on a baking sheet lined with aluminum foil and bake at 375°F for 12 minutes.

2. In a large sauté pan, cook onions in butter with a little olive oil over medium-high heat until tender and translucent.

3. Add corned beef and bacon and cook until warmed through.

4. Add potatoes and cook over high heat until caramelized and crusty.

5. Serve with over-easy eggs, garnish with parsley, chives and a side of toast.

Drink Beer Day

SEP 28

Did you know beer is the most consumed alcoholic beverage in the world? It's not only the oldest alcoholic beverage, it is one of the cornerstones of Americana. In fact, when the colonists first came to the States, they thought beer was safer to drink than water. Today, the United States has more than 1,500 breweries, producing upwards of 6 billion gallons of beer annually—which makes sense since each person consumes on average 23 gallons per year! Beer has inspired art for as long as it's been consumed, including this quote from our very own Benjamin Franklin, who said, "Beer is proof that God wants us to be happy."

BEER SANGRIA

Serves 10

1½ cups fresh mango (cut into ½" cubes)

1½ cups watermelon (cut into ½" cubes)

1½ cups orange (segmented, no pith)

1 cup fresh pineapple (cut into ½" cubes)

1½ cups strawberries (halved)

3 kiwis (peeled and sliced)

½ cup orange liqueur (such as Combier or Cointreau)

10 12-ounce beers

Ice

① Clean and cut fruit.

② Mix orange liqueur in a large container with 3 beers and fruit then refrigerate overnight. The next day, mix in remaining beers. Allow mixture to marinate in the fridge in a sealed container for at least 20 minutes.

③ Serve chilled, with ice.

Coffee Day

It's amazing how far coffee has come since it first arrived in Europe under the guise of Arabian wine. Did you know that in some African countries coffee is actually soaked in water with spices and chewed instead of brewed and drunk? Served strictly dark and straight for hundreds of years, a French physician was responsible for recommending it with milk as café au lait for medicinal purposes. In the last three centuries, 90 percent of all people living in the Western world have switched from drinking tea to drinking coffee. In America we are coffee fanatics, and we drink it any way we can get it!

NOT YOUR AVERAGE CUP OF JOE

Makes 5 Cuppa Joe

5 8-ounce coffee cups

6½ tablespoons ground coffee beans

Optional cardamom pods, cinnamon sticks, or a simple peel of orange

① A few things before we begin. . . . First, make sure coffee pot is clean of all debris. Old coffee tastes like old stale coffee. Second, use fresh coffee beans, purchasing only what you need for the week and grinding right before brewing. Finally, make sure your water has no off odors or flavors; if it does, don't use it.

② Filter water before you put it in your coffee pot or bring to a boil.

③ Use 2 tablespoons for every 8-ounce cup, this makes strong solid coffee. If you like coffee a little stronger, add ½ tablespoon more.

4. Brew coffee with water just below boiling. Remember, espresso has just about ½ the caffeine of regular drip coffee, and the stronger (longer/darker) the roast, the less caffeine it has as the oils evaporate due to the heat.

5. After brewing, keep hot in a thermos until ready to enjoy.

Cook's Note

I'm a huge iced coffee fan; I like mine with a little sugar and milk. The trick is to put all ingredients in a cocktail shaker with ice and shake vigorously. Shaking dissolves sugar and makes the whole drink a little frothy, which in turn makes it taste much better.

SEP 30 Hot Mulled Cider Day

During the cold days of winter, hot beverages are as nourishing to the body as they are to the soul. However, the weather in September (especially on the East Coast) can be hit or miss—when you are least expecting it, the cold arrives. For that reason it's good to have some frozen cider in the freezer. That way, all you need is a quick heating of chilled spiced cider and you've got yourself a cozylicious cup of warm mulled cider! This recipe is an adaptation of a cider I learned to make from my friends Ryan Harris and Chef Kevin Lasko of Park Avenue Winter restaurant. Thanks guys!

HOT MULLED CIDER

Serves 4–5

1 gallon apple cider

1 3" piece of fresh ginger

3 whole star anise

3 whole cloves

3 cinnamon sticks

½ cup maple syrup

Peel of ½ orange

3 Bartlett pears

2 cups cranberries

1. Heat cider in a big pot.

2. While cider heats, add ginger, spices, maple syrup, and orange peel. Allow it to come to a boil and infuse for 10 minutes.

3. Peel, core, and cut pears into quarters and then into chunks.

4. Strain hot cider into another container, mix in pears and cranberries, and let chill.

5. This cider is better reheated the next day, but you can also serve right away if you want. The next day, reheat on stovetop and garnish with rosemary sprig.

OCTOBER

World Vegetarian Day

At some point I think everybody considers becoming a vegetarian. Seriously, what's not to like? It's good for you both physically and morally. Vegetarianism is defined as the practice of following a plant-based diet including fruits, vegetables, cereal grains, nuts, and seeds, with or without dairy products and eggs. However, vegetarians that tell you eating any kind of animal product is against their beliefs are actually vegans. The bottom line: it is good to eat your vegetables! My buddies Joe and Dhanny Palma who own NYCcaterers .com in NY are awesome cooks and make a killer veggie burger, so here's their recipe.

JOE AND DHANNY'S VEGGIE BURGERS

Serves 3–4

1 medium carrot (shredded)

1 large yellow squash (shredded)

1 large zucchini (shredded)

¼ cup cut corn kernels

¼ cup frozen green peas

¼ cup red bell pepper (diced)

1 cup cracked bulgar wheat (soaked overnight)

1 cup egg whites (about 6 eggs)

Freshly ground black pepper to taste

Salt to taste

Plain bread crumbs (enough to soak up liquid)

❶ In a large bowl, combine all ingredients then add bread crumbs until you are able to form patties. Patties should be about 4–4.5 ounces each.

❷ Coat baking sheet and patties with nonstick spray and bake at 400°F for about 20 minutes or until patties start to set and brown.

❸ Serve on lightly toasted potato rolls with a little guacamole and ketchup.

Fried Scallops Day

My uncle Chalo owns a Peruvian restaurant called Pio Pio Riko. He serves beautifully golden rotisserie chicken and a great assortment of traditional dishes, but one plate that drives me bananas is an authentic dish reminiscent of fried calamari on steroids. It's called jalea de mariscos, which translates from Spanish into "seafood jam," and it's a fitting name because the dish is jam-packed full of flavor! It features a combo of shrimp, scallops, and calamari battered and fried crisp then served with a pickled slaw of tomatoes and red onions. In honor of the day, we'll make it with just scallops.

SCALLOP JAM & RED ONION SLAW

Serves 2–3

15 small scallops (bay or diver)

2–3 cups milk (enough to cover)

1 sprig fresh rosemary

1 tablespoon dried oregano

2 garlic cloves (sliced)

1 tablespoon garlic powder

2 large red onions

2–3 limes

1 tablespoon white balsamic or apple cider vinegar

2 tablespoons olive oil

2 teaspoons salt

1 teaspoon pepper

2 large ripe tomatoes (sliced ¼")

3 cups vegetable oil for frying

2 cups flour

½ cup bread crumbs

1 tablespoon cilantro (finely chopped)

1 Clean scallops under cold water, removing the little connector muscle on the side.

2 Combine milk with rosemary sprig, oregano, sliced garlic, garlic powder, and scallops; cover and refrigerate overnight or at least for 3 hours.

3 The following day clean onions, cut in half, slice ¼", and place in a bowl.

4 Roll limes, cut in half, and squeeze juice onto onions. Add vinegar, olive oil, salt and pepper, and tomatoes. Toss everything together, cover, and refrigerate for at least 20 minutes.

5 Heat oil to 350°F in a deep pot.

6 In a large bowl, combine flour with bread crumbs and set aside.

7 Pour milk-scallop mixture into a fine mesh colander and shake lightly.

8 Dump strained scallops with garlic and rosemary into flour mixture and toss for at least 10 seconds, allowing milk to soak up the flour. Return mix to colander and shake off excess flour.

9 Add scallops to hot oil and fry until golden and crispy, about 1 minute. Using a fine mesh strainer, transfer scallops with little chunks of garlic and rosemary onto paper-towel-lined plate. Salt lightly and serve with slaw on top and garnish with fresh cilantro.

Caramel Custard Day

OCT 3

There are many names for caramel custards. As you travel across the world you will encounter little ethnic nuances on the basic custards. From flan to crème brûlée, and crème caramel to caramel latte cotta, they are all creamy egg-based custards cooked in a water bath at a very low temperature until the eggs set. Once cooled, custard has a delightfully ethereal texture that melts when it touches the warmth of your mouth.

CARAMEL CUSTARD

Serves 4–5

1½ cups granulated sugar (divided)

3 tablespoons water

2½ cups milk

3 large eggs

2 egg yolks

1 tablespoon vanilla extract

1. In a saucepan, combine ½ cup sugar with water and cook until caramelized.

2. Divide caramel into small ramekins, sprinkle with salt and let cool.

3. Bring milk to boil. Beat eggs and yolks lightly with 1 cup sugar. Temper eggs by adding milk a little at a time while whisking. Add vanilla.

4. Once all milk is combined with eggs, pour mixture into ramekins.

5. Cook in a water bath at 325°F for 1 hour until custard sets. Let cool and serve in ramekins or invert onto plates. Serve with whipped cream.

Taco Day

Tacos! When you say tacos, you don't just say tacos, you proclaim tacos! Tell people you're making tacos, and I'm never surprised when they respond with a quick "arriba arriba!" It's just the effect they have on people—they're a jam-packed, fun-filled meal. Originating in Mexico, and considered everyday peasant food, simple tacos are composed of corn tortillas wrapped around meat and are eaten without utensils. The fillings are endless, but the tortilla is what makes the taco. In that department you have either flour or corn, soft or crispy. My favorite taco is the "Puffy Taco," which originated in San Antonio, Texas, and has since exploded!

PUFFY TACOS

Serves 2–3

Taco Toppings

Shredded lettuce

Shredded queso blanco

Ripe tomatoes (chopped into small cubes)

Radishes

Lime wedges

Guacamole (Sept. 16)

Sour cream

Hot sauce

Chorizo Filling

1 pound chorizo (removed from casing and crumbled)

1 large Spanish onion (chopped small)

2 garlic cloves (minced)

Fresh cilantro

❶ Over high heat, sauté chorizo for 3 minutes, add onions, and cook for an additional 4 minutes, finish with garlic and cook for 40 seconds.

❷ Remove from heat and add cilantro.

Puffy Taco Shells

3 cups corn tortilla mix (which you can find next to the regular flour in the supermarket)

½ tablespoon salt

2¼ cups warm water

3–4 cups vegetable oil for frying

*You can skip the first two steps and just buy either corn or flour tortillas and fry 'em up!

❶ Combine ingredients and mix well with hands. Let dough rest for 3 minutes.

❷ Take a small piece of dough (about the size of a golf ball) and press in a Ziploc bag that has been cut into a flat piece or in between two pieces of plastic wrap. Press dough with a tortilla press or rolling pin.

❸ In a heavy, deep pot, heat at least 2" of oil to 250°F and fry tortilla while holding it down with tip of a flip spatula, and cook until puffy. Keep warm in oven.

❹ Line up ingredients, fill up tortillas, and enjoy. *Olé!*

Apple Betty Day

Apple Betty is simply a variation on the traditional American dessert, Brown Betty. Brown Betty was popular in colonial times and is similar to bread pudding or cobbler, made with brown sugar. It is easy to make and, like most apple desserts, is best served straight out of the oven with a large heaping of vanilla ice cream.

APPLE BETTY

Serves 5–6

2 pounds Granny Smith apples

3 cups challah bread (cut into ¼" cubes)

½ cup brown sugar plus 2 tablespoons

1 teaspoons freshly grated nutmeg

1 teaspoon cinnamon

Zest of 1 lemon

½ cup applejack

3 tablespoons butter (melted)

1. Peel and core apples, then slice into thick slices. Toss bread cubes in half of sugar, half of spices, lemon zest, and half the applejack. Toss apple slices in the remaining sugar and spices.

2. Butter a casserole dish and line bottom with half of bread mixture. Top with half of apples, followed by remaining bread and remaining apples. Top with 2 tablespoons brown sugar, remaining applejack, and butter drizzled over the top.

3. Cover with a lid or aluminum foil and bake at 375°F for 40 minutes. Remove cover and continue to bake for 15 more minutes until brown and toasty.

Cook's Note

You can also cook in individual little ramekins and serve each with a scoop of vanilla ice cream.

Noodle Day

At some point it seems we've all lived on noodles. Those slippery buggers that are inexpensive, totally filling, and a snap to prepare by boiling water. They're a staple in most college dorm rooms and bachelor pads, because, let's face it: After returning home from a long day at school or work, it's all the energy you can muster when it comes to dinner. But making noodles from scratch isn't that hard, and it's even cheaper than store-bought (plus you get to add whatever you want)! With fresh noodles all you need is broth, soy sauce, and a little scallion to make a satisfying meal.

UDON NOODLES

Serves 2–3

1 teaspoon salt

⅔ cup water

2½ cups wheat flour

Fresh ginger (grated)

Soy sauce

Scallions (thinly chopped)

1. Combine salt with water, then add to wheat flour little by little.

2. Mix with hands until a nice dough forms, then knead for 10 minutes solid. (During this time glutens develop in dough that make it elastic and give it a nice "chew.")

3. Flatten dough to the size of a plate, cover with plastic wrap, and allow dough to rest for at least 1–2 hours.

4. With a floured rolling pin, roll dough out, then roll dough onto itself. With a sharp knife, cut out noodles ⅛" wide.

5. Boil noodles in salted water until tender, about 3 minutes.

6. Toss with fresh ginger, soy sauce, and fresh scallions to taste.

OCT 7
Frappe Day

A hallmark of summer in Astoria, Queens (where I lived for some time), are packed sidewalk cafes that line the avenues. As Astoria is a predominantly Greek neighborhood, frappes are a given on most tables. In today's world of ultrapremium coffees, sophisticated roasting techniques, and dramatically elaborate drinks, the Frappe stands above the rest—tall, iced, and delicious. Jam-packed with caffeine, frappes are made with spray-dried instant coffee. These coffee crystals contain practically no oil, and when shaken create a frothy creamy head similar to that found in espresso. It can be served sweetened or unsweetened and can include milk, ice cream, and even Coca-Cola!

FRAPPE

Makes 1 frappe

2 teaspoon frappe instant coffee (like Nespresso)

¾ cup cold water

Ice

1 teaspoon sugar (optional)

Milk (optional)

1 ounce rum (optional)

❶ In a shaker, combine coffee powder with ¼ cup water, and a few ice cubes.

❷ Shake vigorously until nice and foamy, add sugar, and shake for another minute until sugar dissolves.

❸ Pour into a tall glass, add remaining water and milk, and top with ice. If you're feeling frisky, add a little rum. Enjoy!

OCT 8
Fluffernutter Day

Bread, Marshmallow Fluff, and peanut butter, all schmeared and pressed together so some of the Fluff starts oozing out the side. The thought of that while sitting at my breakfast counter, perhaps still in pajamas, is one of the most comforting to cross my mind in the morning. Unofficially the state sandwich of Massachusetts, Fluffernutters are popular in the northeastern United States with kids of all ages and in diners across the country. Add crisp bacon and sliced bananas and you've got a Fluffmonster!

FLUFFMONSTER

Serves 1

2 slices potato bread (or brioche, challah, or white bread)

Peanut butter

1 banana (thinly sliced)

Crisp and cooled bacon (cool is optional)

Marshmallow Fluff

Butter (soft)

❶ Spread 2 slices of bread with peanut butter. Fill middle with the banana, bacon, and Fluff. Put sandwich together without pressing down too much.

❷ Spread soft butter on outside of sandwich and cook in a skillet over medium heat (like a grilled cheese) until golden. Flip and grill on other side.

❸ Remove from skillet, trim crust with a serrated knife, and serve.

Submarine-Hoagie-Hero-Grinder Day, October 9

OCT 9

Submarine-Hoagie-Hero-Grinder Day

The Hoagie—named after workers on Hog Island who brought these sandwiches to work—is the official sandwich of Philadelphia. Subs got their name around WWI after Submarines, and when New York Herald Tribune *writer Clementine Paddleford wrote that you would have to be a "Hero" to finish this gigantic sandwich, the name was born.*

NAME-YOUR-OWN-SANDWICH SANDWICH

Serves 2

4 crusty French baguettes

4 tablespoons mayonnaise

Salt and fresh ground pepper

¼ pound Prosciutto di Parma (thinly sliced)

¼ pound capicola (thinly sliced)

¼ pound Genoa salami (thinly sliced)

¼ pound sopreassata salami (thinly sliced)

¼ pound provolone cheese (thinly sliced)

¼ head lettuce (thinly sliced)

1 small onion (thinly sliced)

1 large ripe tomato (thinly sliced)

2 tablespoons olive oil

2 teaspoons red wine vinegar

1 tablespoon dried oregano

I know, I know, you just read the ingredients and gasped. I call for baguettes instead of traditional hoagie rolls because I happen to love my sandwiches on French bread. If you're a purist, go for a classic hoagie.

❶ Slice bread in half and spread mayo on both sides, this will act as a protective layer and keep the bread crispy. Salt and pepper mayo.

❷ On bottom slice, lay meat, folding each slice in half and overlapping. After you layer meat, layer cheese, followed by lettuce, then onions, and topping with tomatoes.

❸ In a small bowl, whisk together olive oil, vinegar, a little salt and pepper, and oregano. Drizzle vinaigrette over sandwich. Place bread on top and get prepared to open wide!

Angel Food Cake Day

OCT. 10

It's thanks to the development of rotary egg beaters developed in the late 1800s that this cake became so popular. Before that Mr. Two Forks, steadfast hands, and a whole lot of patience was needed to create the meringue base for the cake. Very popular in the nineteenth century, it is said that this cake was actually created by the Pennsylvania Dutch, those wonderful bakers who gave us such indispensable inventions as the cake pan. In this case, the tube cake pan (although a Bundt pan also works in a pinch).

ANGEL FOOD CAKE

Serves 4–5

8 large egg whites (room temperature)

1 teaspoon cream of tartar

½ cup sugar plus ⅛ cup sugar

1 cup cake flour (sifted)

1½ teaspoons pure vanilla extract

⅛ teaspoon salt

1. Place whole eggs in a bowl of warm water for 5 minutes until room temperature. (Why? Because your eggs were probably in the fridge; that's where I keep mine.)

2. Separate eggs and whip whites on medium speed. Once frothy, add cream of tartar and ¼ cup sugar.

3. Continue to whip on medium until soft peaks form.

4. Add another ¼ cup of sugar and whip on medium high until stiff peaks form.

5. Sift flour with remaining sugar and salt. Fold into egg mixture. Add vanilla and fold in well.

6. Pour into an ungreased tube cake pan and bake at 350°F for 30–35 minutes.

7. Flip pan upside down onto wire rack and let cool. (This keeps the cake light and airy, and prevents it from collapsing under its own weight).

8. To serve cake, run a knife along the sides of the pan and transfer a plate.

Cook's Note

Why not serve with fruit in the middle? My top choice is strawberries tossed in a little simple syrup with thinly sliced fresh mint and whipped cream.

World Egg Day

OCT 11

What came first, the chicken or the egg? I have the answer for you! Technically speaking, dinosaurs laid eggs, but modern chicken didn't evolve from the jungle fowl until many years later. So that settles it—the egg came first. Which figures, as eggs are by far some of the most amazing foodstuffs; they are a great source of nutrition, inexpensive, but most of all, they can be used for so many diverse applications! Sometimes the simplest things really are the best, and I think one of the best ways to prepare an egg is to soft boil it.

PERFECT SOFT-BOILED EGGS

Serves 3

6 eggs

Ice

Coarse salt

1. Take a thumbtack and pierce each egg at the bottom. Bring a big pot of water to a boil. Once boiling, gently drop in eggs with a spider or slotted spoon. Boil the eggs for 5 minutes.

2. Fill a bowl that is big enough to hold all the eggs with cold water and some ice.

3. Remove eggs carefully and drop into cold water for 20 seconds and then strain the cold water. This shocking of the eggs makes them a little easier to peel and stops them from overcooking. Once you peel the tops off of the eggs, you can reheat in microwave or put back in boiling water for a few seconds.

4. Sprinkle salt on top; serve on an egg holder or inside shot glasses with toast points, caviar, or if you're feeling really adventurous, salmon roe.

Gumbo Day

Soul-nourishing, robust, full of flavor, and satisfying in every sense of the word, this stew is the great national dish of New Orleans! Gumbo represents the creation of an American classic through a merging of cultures. It brings together a bouquet of flavors from French bouillabaisse, Spanish sofrito, sticky West African okra, Italian tomatoes, Native American Choctaw filé powder (ground sassafras) in addition to the natural bounty from the region—Andouille sausage, crawfish, shrimp, and tasso, sometimes thickened together with a little roux (flour and lard). There are many variations, but it usually comes down to preparing Creole or Cajun.

❶ In Dutch oven or thick pot, sauté chorizo with onions and peppers with a little olive oil over medium heat until golden and lightly browned. Set aside.

❷ Season chicken around skin and under it with Cajun seasoning. Raise heat to medium-high and sauté chicken with a little olive oil until golden and slightly browned on both sides (about 6–8 minutes). Set aside with chorizo.

❸ Return to medium heat, add ½ cup vegetable oil and flour, mix thoroughly, and cook for about 10–15 minutes until browned like chocolate.

❹ Add celery and bay leaves and drizzle in chicken stock. Return veggies and chorizo to pot, raise heat to high, bring to boil, then lower heat and cook for 1 hour, stirring often.

❺ Return chicken and continue to cook on low for another hour. Remove chicken pieces from pot, discard skins and bones, shred meat and return to pot along with filé powder, and stir.

❻ Serve on top of rice and garnish with green onions and chopped parsley. Hot sauce is an *absolute must* on the side.

MUMBO GUMBO

Serves 4–5

1 pound chorizo (cut crosswise into ½" thick pieces)

2 cups Spanish onions (chopped into ¼" pieces)

½ cup red peppers (chopped into ¼" pieces)

½ cup green peppers (chopped into ¼" pieces)

½ cup poblano chiles (¼" pieces)

3 tablespoons olive oil

3½ pounds chicken thighs

3 tablespoons Cajun seasoning (mix of paprika, cayenne, black pepper, onion powder, garlic powder, thyme, and chili powder)

½ cup vegetable oil

1 cup all-purpose flour

1 cup celery (chopped into ¼" pieces)

2 bay leaves

9 cups chicken stock

1 tablespoon filé powder

Green onions (finely chopped)

Fresh parsley (finely chopped)

Hot sauce, lots!

Yorkshire Pudding Day

Cooking throughout time has been more about making something with ingredients on hand, and how to reuse and preserve ingredients to prevent waste. It was in that spirit that people first preserved fish in salt, cured and dried meat in the sun, and pickled vegetables so as to have veggies during the winter. Yorkshire pudding originated in Yorkshire, England. It's not a pudding in the traditional sense, it's more of a popover. I add fresh herbs and Parm, but if you're really feeling creative, bake an egg inside it or fill with mashed potatoes and cover with gravy when it's done!

YORKSHIRE PUDDING

Serves 4–5

2 eggs

1 cup all-purpose flour

1 cup whole milk

½ teaspoon salt

3 tablespoons Parmesan cheese (grated)

2 tablespoons fresh thyme (chopped)

1 cup beef drippings (or lard, bacon fat, or butter)

❶ The most important thing is a hot oven. What am I trying to say here? Trust your oven as far as you can throw it, and unless you're baking with an EZ bake oven, I bet that's not very far. Use an oven thermometer. Heat oven to 450°F.

❷ Beat eggs until foamy, about 2 minutes, then sift in flour, and add remaining ingredients except beef drippings.

❸ Put about 1 tablespoon beef drippings or fat in each cup of a muffin tin and put in the oven for 4 minutes. Remove pans from oven and pour in batter until tins are halfway filled.

❹ Return to oven and bake for 15 minutes. Reduce temperature to 350°F and bake for another 10 minutes until golden and dry.

Chocolate-Covered Insects Day

Yes, we're going to go there. First we need to define what constitutes insects, then we'll see how far we can take it. I'm just kidding, but we do have to tackle this holiday so we'll use gummy worms, not technically an insect but close enough! In this ridiculously simple snack, the tartness of the gummy worms with the sweet chewy filling nestled in a dark chocolate shell makes for a grand taste combination.

CHOCOLATE-COVERED GUMMY WORMS

Serves 2

1 cup gummy worms

½ cup dark chocolate (melted)

1 cup chocolate cookies (crumbled into dirt)

2–3 mint sprigs

❶ Dip gummy worms in chocolate using a barbecue fork, tap bowl to remove excess chocolate, and lay on parchment paper, aluminum foil, or plastic wrap.

❷ Refrigerate until hard, about 20 minutes. Serve intermingled with the chocolate dirt; use the mint sprigs to look like weeds. Enjoy!

Chicken Cacciatore Day

OCT 15

Cacciatore means "hunter" in Italian, and although that carries throughout the land, there are a few variations that change with the region. Chicken Cacciatore is a stewed dish served in the "style of the hunter," and in southern Italy red wine is used, as supposed to the preferred white wine in northern Italy. It's the kind of good delicious meal that you can make any day of the week, feeds a big family for little money—plus, whatever is left over can be reheated the next day and it will taste even better!

CHICKEN CACCIATORE

Serves 3–4

7 chicken thighs

Salt and pepper

½ tablespoon dried oregano

Onion powder

Garlic powder

Olive oil

1 large Spanish onion (sliced)

1 green pepper (sliced)

1 red bell pepper (sliced)

4 garlic cloves

1 28-ounce can San Marzano tomatoes

1 cup white wine

1 cup chicken stock

1 tablespoon capers

2 large fresh basil sprigs

1½ tablespoons honey

❶ Season chicken with salt, pepper, oregano, and onion and garlic powder. Sauté in deep pan over medium-high heat until brown on both sides, then set aside.

❷ Add a little more olive oil to pan and sauté sliced onions with the sliced peppers until slightly charred, then add sliced garlic and sauté for 30 more seconds.

❸ Add tomatoes, using your hand to crush coarsely. Stir with a wooden spoon (wooden spoons make rustic dishes taste better), scraping bottom of pan.

❹ Add wine, stock, capers, basil, and honey and return chicken to pan with skin-side up.

❺ Cook for 30–40 minutes on low until sauce reduces by half. Serve over rice or pasta. Garnish with fresh basil.

Liqueur Day

OCT 16

It's hard to believe that early ancestors of liqueurs were used for medicinal purposes. Flavored with spices, herbs, honeys, and flowers, these spirits were almost always sweetened and meticulously made in order to prevent sickness and heal ailments. At an ABV (alcohol by volume) of 15–30 percent, liqueurs are not very strong and are meant to be sipped or enjoyed with dessert. Liqueurs also play a main role making many cocktails memorable by adding a distinctive sweet and/or colorful note. Limoncello, an Italian lemon-based liqueur, provides the perfect ending to a meal or the punch needed in a citrus martini. Best of all, it's a breeze to make.

LIMONCELLO

Serves 2–3

9 lemons (throw an orange in there too if you want)

1 (750ml) bottle of high-proof alcohol (Everclear or just vodka works well)

4 cups granulated sugar

4 cups water

❶ Wash lemons thoroughly under running water and dry.

❷ Use a microplane or zester to remove zest, making sure not to get to the bitter white pith beneath.

❸ Combine alcohol with zest and cover. Place container in a cool, dark place for a month. (You can also keep in the fridge, but you'll need about 2 months.)

❹ After a month, blend mixture in a blender.

❺ Now, bring sugar and water to a boil. Stir into lemon alcohol, replace lid, and let Limoncello mature and develop its flavors for at least 1 week in fridge.

❻ Serve chilled. I like to drink with iced tea for a fancy Arnold Palmer.

Pasta Day

OCT 17

Pasta is a generic term used when talking about noodles made with any type of flour mixed with water and sometimes eggs. In Italian, the term Pasta simply means paste or dough. However, under Italian law dry pasta can only be made with durum wheat semolina—this is the only way to get pasta to cook to perfection, or as they say, al dente. Pasta has always been about simplicity, so here I marry two all-American faves, mac and cheese with tomato soup, to make a truly comforting combo!

TOMATO BOWTIES 'N' CHEESE

Serves 4

½ pound bowtie pasta (½ 1-lb box)

2 tablespoons butter

10 ounces sharp Cheddar cheese (shredded)

2 eggs

1 8-ounce can tomato soup

Fresh chives for garnish

❶ Boil pasta until al dente. Drain and return to pot.

❷ Add butter and coat pasta thoroughly.

❸ In the meantime, grab another bowl, combine cheese with eggs and tomato soup, give it a good stir, then add to the hot pasta.

❹ Cook over medium heat while stirring with a wooden spoon or heatproof spatula until creamy, about 3 minutes. If sauce breaks up, remove from heat, it's done! (To fix it, add a little cold cream, milk, or a bit of an egg to re-emulsify.)

❺ Serve with hot sauce, crusty toasted bread, and a sprinkle of fresh chives.

OCT. 18
Chocolate Cupcake Day

The cupcake didn't actually come around until the nineteenth century when the ingredients for them were measured in cups instead of weighed, as had originally been the custom. The term "cup" also had a double meaning as this sweet cake was baked in small gem pans, the cast iron ancestors of the modern muffin tins. In the beginning, cupcakes were sometimes called "number" cakes, because they were easy to remember by the measurements of ingredients it took to create them: One cup of butter, two cups of sugar, three cups of flour, four eggs, one cup of milk, and one spoonful of baking soda if they had it around.

EASY CHOCOLATE CUPCAKES

Makes one dozen cupcakes

¾ cup unsweetened cocoa powder

¾ cup granulated sugar

¾ cup light brown sugar

1½ cups all-purpose flour

½ teaspoon baking powder

1½ teaspoons baking soda

¼ teaspoon salt

⅛ cup vegetable oil or melted butter (olive oil also works)

2 large eggs (at room temperature)

¾ cup buttermilk

¾ cup water

1 teaspoon good-quality vanilla extract

1 cup mini chocolate chips

❶ Sift dry ingredients.

❷ Whisk together oil, eggs, buttermilk, water, and vanilla.

❸ Add egg mixture and chocolate chips to the flour and mix until smooth.

❹ Prep a cupcake tray with a dozen cupcake liners and lightly spray with vegetable spray.

❺ Scoop batter into prepared cupcake molds, filling about ¾ full, and bake at 350°F for 12–15 minutes. Cool and frost or eat right away with a cold glass of milk.

Cook's Note

Sometimes I like to underbake and call them Cake Batter Cupcakes. Too many hurt my tummy, but I like the taste . . . it's just like licking the beaters!

OCT 19 — Seafood Bisque Day

A delightfully creamy seafood soup with excessive amounts of cream and liquor is how I describe this little number. Lobster is the most popular bisque, but there's also crab, mixed, and even root vegetable soups called bisques (even though we know they shouldn't be). This soup was actually created to use less-than-pristine crustaceans, and make them taste spectacular! Of French origin, it's thought to have come from the Bay of Biscay, where seafood is aplenty. For this recipe, go to the market and simply see what they have; as long as you have either shrimp, lobster, or crab, you're good. Whatever else you add is up to you!

IMPRESS YOUR FATHER-IN-LAW SEAFOODPALOOZA

Serves 3–4

½ pound large shrimp (shelled and deveined—save shells!)

½ pound scallops

10 clams

10 mussels

2 small crabs

¼ pound calamari (cleaned and cut)

Garlic powder

Onion powder

Paprika

Cayenne pepper

Salt and pepper

Olive oil

2 cups vegetable stock

1 medium Spanish onion (¼" slices)

2 garlic cloves (thinly sliced)

2 tablespoons Goya sofrito

2 cups whole tomatoes in sauce

2 cups white wine

2 tablespoons cognac

1 bay leaf

❶ Clean seafood and season with spices.

❷ In a 2-quart pot, drizzle 2 tablespoons olive oil and sauté shrimp over high heat on each side for 30 seconds, then set aside in bowl. Follow with scallops, cooking for 1 minute. Then set aside with shrimp. Add clams, mussels, and the crabs with ½ cup vegetable stock, cover, and cook until all open, about 2–3 minutes. Remove shellfish set aside with other cooked fish.

3 Add shrimp shells along with remaining vegetable stock to pot, and simmer until liquid reduces to 1 cup about 10 minutes.

4 In the meantime, in a 4-quart pot, sauté onions over low heat for 4 minutes, stirring often until translucent. Add garlic and cook until translucent. Add sofrito and tomatoes with sauce, crushing in your hand. Add wine, Cognac, and bay leaf, and cook for 20 minutes, barely simmering until liquid reduces to 1½–2 cups. Blend. (I like my bisque smooth, so I use a hand blender because I can blend directly in the pot and not dirty the blender—and it only costs twenty bucks!), but a regular blender works just fine.

5 Return sauce to pot, add cream and strain in shrimp stock. Add seafood and bring to a rapid boil over high heat. Season calamari and add to pot. Cook over high heat for 1 minute and you're done!

6 Serve with country style bread and garnish with fresh parsley for presentation points.

Brandied Fruit Day

Brandy and fruit go together like peanut butter and jelly. Not only is the pairing a great way to preserve fruits, it's a wonderful way to flavor brandy! There are a few "definitions" when it comes to brandying fruit: One uses no alcohol whereas the other is all about the brandy. I will explain both to follow. The first method takes six weeks.

UN-BRANDY BRANDIED FRUIT

Makes 5 cups of fruit

2 cups fresh peaches (pitted and cut into ½" pieces)

6 cups granulated sugar

2 cups fresh pineapple (peeled and cut into ½" pieces)

2 cups fresh cherries (pitted)

1 This method ferments fruit with sugar, creating residual alcohol, and when done, it can stay indefinitely in the fridge. Combine peaches with 2 cups sugar, stir, cover, and leave at room temperature for 2 weeks, tossing daily.

2 After the two weeks, add pineapple along with 2 more cups of sugar, toss everything together, and again cover and leave at room temperature for 2 weeks, tossing every day.

3 Add cherries along with remaining sugar, toss everything together, cover and leave at room temperature for 2 weeks, tossing every day.

4 At the end of the 6 weeks, fruit is ready and may be refrigerated. You can also spice things up by adding a little brandy to the mix at this point.

BRANDIED FRUIT

Makes 6 cups of fruit

6 cups of your favorite ripe fruit (I use cherries)

2 cups sugar

3 lemon peels

Brandy

1 Combine fruit with sugar and lemon peels in a container with a lid and cover with brandy. Use plate to weigh down fruit so remains submerged.

2 Keep at room temperature and out of sun for 1 month, or if you can, a few months. This is great spooned on top of ice cream!

Caramel Apple Day

I love caramel apples! They're so fun and colorful, they add a special touch to any occasion. Nowadays, candy apple toppings range from toffee, peanut butter, and that colorful red candy coating to a whole range of other rainbow colors. Apparently, William W. Kopound invented the red candy apple in Newark, New Jersey, around 1908. Story goes that one night while making red cinnamon candies, he got the idea to dip apples in it. He set them up in his window sill and an American classic was created.

CANDY APPLES

Makes 8 Candy Apples

2 cups granulated sugar

1 cup light corn syrup

1 cup water

8 drops red food coloring

½ teaspoon cinnamon extract (or any other flavor you want)

8 apples with sticks inserted (choose firm apples with no spots; at room temperature)

1 Combine all ingredients, except extract and apples, in a heavy-bottomed nonreactive pot. Mix evenly with a wooden spoon and set on stove over high heat. Use a pastry brush to wipe down sides where sugar syrup meet sides of pot.

2 Fill a bowl (wide enough for the pot to fit inside) with warm water and set aside.

3 Boil mixture until the candy thermometer reaches 300°F.

4 Once syrup reaches temperature, turn off heat, remove pot from stovetop, add extract and coloring, and stir with clean wooden spoon until color is even.

5 Dip pot into warm water for 2 seconds to prevent syrup from cooking further.

6 Line baking sheet with waxed paper. Using kitchen gloves, dip each apple into syrup one at a time, then stand them on the tray. Allow to cool and dig in!

Nut Day

When I reach for a cup of coffee in the morning, sometimes I get in the mood for a little something special. A little dash of cinnamon is nice, vanilla is pretty tasty, and I sometimes even throw an orange peel in the pot for a little hint of summer in my Joe. But when I go to the fridge for some milk, normally the only choice I have is regular milk. But when I make ice creams I have so many different choices! So yes, I have to say, sometimes instead of reaching in the fridge I go to the freezer and pull out my favorite ice cream, add a few tablespoons into my coffee and, presto!: chunky monkey cuppa joe. If this is a little weird for you, you can simply make nut milks to add to your coffee or to enjoy with your cereal. They're simple and add a little variety to your morning routine.

NUT MILK

Makes 3½ cups

1 cup nuts (blanched, raw, or roasted almonds, cashews, or hazelnuts)

3 cups milk or water

1 tablespoon honey

1 Toast nuts in a 350°F oven for 6 minutes until golden. Combine with milk or water and honey and soak them overnight.

2 Blend everything together on high speed for at least 6 minutes. Strain through a fine mesh (I use a clean towel) into your container of choice and refrigerate.

1 Bake two 9" cakes and let cool.

2 Make Pastry Cream and let cool.

3 Stack cakes on top of a rack and spread cream on one. Place second cake atop cream and glaze the whole thing with ganache.

Bologna Day

Bologna has the same makeup as hot dogs except the sausage is much wider and it's traditionally sliced as cold cuts. It gets its name from the Italian city of Bologna, whose famous pistachio-dotted mortadella is quite similar except for the fact that with bologna the fat is blended into the meat. Although traditionally made with pork, nowadays we're seeing bologna with turkey, beef, or chicken added as well.

Boston Cream Pie Day

This is what happens when the French try their hand at American pastries. Boston cream pie is not even a pie at all! By definition, a pie has to have some kind of pastry shell, but this Boston delicacy is actually composed of two layers of sponge cake filled with pastry cream with a topping of decadent chocolate ganache. Concocted at Boston's Omni Parker House hotel by French chef M. Sanzian, this delicious anomaly is the official dessert of the Commonwealth of Massachusetts.

BOSTON CREAM PIE

Serves 4–5

Sponge Cake (Aug. 23)

Pastry Cream (Feb. 20)

Ganache (Mar. 28)

BAKED BOLOGNA

Serves 4–5

4 garlic cloves

1½ cups brown sugar

2 cups Dijon mustard

½ cup bread crumbs

1 tablespoon hot sauce

1 6-pound bologna

1 In a food processor, blend all ingredients (except bologna) to make a paste.

2 Slice bologna in a cross-hatch pattern on top, going about ½" deep. Rub paste all over and bake at 300°F until toasty and brown, about 40 minutes. Think of this as barbecue food and serve with coleslaw and cornbread.

Greasy Foods Day

Normally when you think of greasy foods, it's sparked by drinking or perhaps walking around the county fairgrounds. It's as if fairs and amusement parks are full of naughty foods to enhance the fun, and while visiting we get a free pass to eat any number of cheese-covered fried goodies without suffering an ounce of guilt. The same thing applies today, so in honor of the day I came up with this delicious grease bomb. Enjoy!

NACHO FRIES

Serves 2

Chili (prepare your favorite recipe!)

Beer Cheese (Dec. 10)

½ cup lettuce (shredded)

2 cups salsa

1 cup sour cream

¼ cup pickled jalapeño slices

2 cups Cheddar cheese (shredded)

Good Karma Fries (July 13)

❶ It's greasy foods day, okay? So don't hold back! Make Chili, make Beer Cheese, and set up ingredients.

❷ Make French fries, pile everything up, and go to town! Yummmm. . . .

Pumpkin Day

It's October, right before Halloween, so I'm sure there are a few pumpkins lying around ready to be carved. In my house, we like to make pumpkin soup, pumpkin pie, and roasted pumpkin. Normally, we have a lot leftover since it's customary for us to overcook for holidays. This is a great way to use any leftover pumpkin and recycle it for a brand-new meal. My little sister Beatriz has become a master at making this pasta. I think she now makes it better than me!

PUMPKIN PASTA

Serves 2–4

All-purpose flour

1 cup pumpkin purée

Salt and pepper to taste

Olive oil

❶ I know you're probably thinking, "What kind of recipe is this?" The thing is, making pasta relies less on recipe than craft.

❷ Add flour to pumpkin purée along with salt, pepper, and olive oil and combine with hands until a nonsticky dough forms. That's it! Cover with plastic wrap and let rest at room temperature for 20 minutes (this relaxes gluten in the dough and lets you roll out thinly).

❸ Flour a clean work surface and roll out pasta. Using a pizza cutter, cut pasta into long strands ¼" thick.

4. Cook pasta in salted boiling water for 1 minute. Strain and toss with a little olive oil. Serve with tomato sauce or more pumpkin purée. Garnish with Parmesan cheese.

OCT 27 — Potato Day

Although there are many varieties of the common potato, they can all be traced back to the indigenous potato of Peru. However, the most commonly grown potato is actually from Chile and from there has grown to propagate throughout the world and become our fourth-largest grown crop right behind corn, wheat, and rice. The etymology of the potato tells us that before we had the white potato there was the sweet potato, and the word potato *actually comes from the Spanish word* batata *(sweet potato) and* papa *(potato). I can still remember one of the first restaurants I ever worked in made the most ethereal and velvety mashed potatoes. The trick was a ton of butter, cream, and lots of epoundow grease to get the potatoes though a fine mesh strainer. This process produces the smoothest mashed potatoes you will ever behold.*

CHEESY MASHED POTATOES

Serves 4–6

2 pounds potatoes (peeled and cut into ½" cubes)

Salt

¼ cup butter

1 cup heavy cream

White pepper

1½ cups mozzarella cheese (shredded)

1. Peel and cut potatoes and put them in a pot that is at least 2" higher than the potatoes. Cover with cold water, add salt, and cook over high heat for 20–30 minutes, until tender.

2. Strain the potatoes into a colander and return the pot to the stove. Fill it with butter and heavy cream and bring to a boil.

3. Once the cream has come to a boil, place the colander over the pot and, using a flat-bottomed cup, press the potatoes through. Make sure to do this fast, because when the potatoes cool they will be harder to pass through. Stir the potatoes in with the cream until smooth, season with salt and pepper to taste.

4. Stir in about 1 cup shredded cheese, put potatoes into a casserole dish, top with remaining cheese, and broil until golden and bubbly. Enjoy!

OCT 28 — Wild Foods Day

In case you read this and have no idea what it's all about, "Wild Foods" simply refers to unadulterated, wholesome, and naturally grown foods. There are many theories on what is best when it comes to eating, but one thing's for certain: Nothing is better than food you grow yourself! We have a garden at my house, albeit a small one, where we grow squash, apples, pears, apricots, a ton of herbs, but mostly tomatoes. From the second they start growing we get so much fresh fruit we don't know what to do with it all. So I started jarring Tomato Confit, so I know I can revisit the wild flavors of summer long after the plants are gone and the snow has fallen.

TOMATO CONFIT

Serves 6–8

20 plum or Roma tomatoes

¼ cup olive oil

10 cloves garlic (peeled and finely chopped)

3 sprigs fresh rosemary

10 sprigs fresh thyme

Salt and pepper to taste

❶ Bring pot of water to a boil.

❷ Take tomatoes and with a small pairing knife score the bottom of each making an x. Next to pot, place a bowl with ice water. Blanch tomatoes in batches (as to not overcrowd) for 1 minute then remove and place in ice bath. Peel tomatoes and set aside.

❸ Cut tomatoes in half and with spoon remove seeds. Discard seeds and skins.

❹ Drizzle baking skeet with olive oil followed by some garlic, rosemary leaves, and thyme leaves (remove from sprigs).

❺ Place tomatoes face down on top of herbs followed by remaining garlic, and drizzle with more olive oil, salt, and pepper.

❻ Cover with aluminum foil and bake at 200–225°F for 2½ hours.

❼ Remove from oven, give a gentle toss and transfer to a lidded container, then fill to top with more olive oil, and stick in the fridge. This is great on salads and pasta, but *especially* as a sandwich spread!

OCT. 29

Oatmeal Day

Oatmeal, porridge, peasant meal, or stirabout all refers to the same thing: a meal composed of oats. Oatmeal can be ground coarsely, cut into small pieces to make steel-cut oatmeal, or rolled or quick oats. Instant oatmeal is usually cut into small pieces, cooked, then dried. It seems like a wonder food! They say a cup of oatmeal a day can significantly lower your blood pressure and keep your cholesterol in check. And oatmeal can be used to thicken soups, flavor pastries and cookies, and as a cream to soothe your face or reduce eye puffiness! Here, we make it into a delicious treat.

OATMEAL CHILLER

Serves 3–4

- 1 cup instant oatmeal
- 2 cups milk
- 2 cups water
- ¼ cup honey
- Splash vanilla extract

1 Combine oatmeal with milk and water. Refrigerate for at least 1–2 hours.

2 Remove from fridge and blend until smooth, add honey and blend again for at least 3 minutes.

3 Strain through cheesecloth or a towel to remove any bits. Splash the vanilla and serve over ice. Garnish with a little cinnamon and serve.

OCT. 30

Buy a Doughnut Day

When Krispy Kreme came to Manhattan they caused quite a commotion. They set up their doughnut machines behind large windows—practically on the street. I'd like to know what the city was thinking when they let them do this. You need a permit to have lighted signs, but no one considered the mayhem that would ensue from placing perpetual doughnut-making machines that produce warm, sweet treats in front of innocent bystanders on the sidewalk? I'm just thankful that after I claw my way through the crowd I can get my hands on a nice box of sugar glazed to scarf down with my coffee.

CLASSIC CAKE DOUGHNUTS WITH MAPLE BACON GLAZE

Serves 3–4

- 3¾ cups all-purpose flour
- 1 tablespoon baking powder
- ¾ teaspoon salt
- ¾ cup granulated sugar
- 1 teaspoon ground cinnamon
- 1cup fine applesauce
- 3 eggs
- 2 tablespoons butter (unsalted and melted)
- Vegetable oil for frying

1 Sift flour and baking powder into a bowl, then whisk in salt, sugar, and cinnamon. Add applesauce and eggs and mix until thoroughly combined. Add butter and mix for 1 minute.

2 Invert dough onto clean, floured work surface and roll out to ¼"–½" thick. Using a cookie cutter, cut out the doughnuts and holes.

3 Fry at 375°F until golden brown, about 3–4 minutes. Drain on paper towels.

GLAZE

1¼ cup powdered sugar (sifted)

1 teaspoon pure vanilla extract

⅛ cup pure maple syrup

Pinch of salt

Cooked bacon bits (optional for topping)

1 Combine all ingredients until smooth. Once doughnuts have cooled, dip them in the glaze and top with bacon bits.

OCT 31 Trick or Treat for UNICEF Day

One year on Halloween, while trick-or-treating with my little brother and sister, we saw a young witch swinging a little box on a string that said, "Trick or Treat for UNICEF." I plopped a dollar in the box and looked up UNICEF. Turns out, the organization helps the world's most vulnerable children gain access to essentials like water, food, education, and medicine—simple things that truly changes their lives. So this Halloween before getting ready for the costume party, take your box and collect a little something to help the kids (www.unicefusa.org). And in return, maybe you can give out these spooky ghost cupcakes.

GHOST CUPCAKES

Serves 4–5

Easy Chocolate Cupcakes (Oct. 18)

Chocolate Frosting (Dec. 15)

Fondant (from Cherry Chocolates recipe, Jan. 3)

1 Make cupcakes in little cups. Allow to cool.

2 Make the frosting and frost cupcakes.

3 Roll out fondant and cut into circles. (The size disks will depending on the size of your cupcakes.) Use a straw to cut two little holes right next to each other in the middle; these will be the ghost eyes. Drape fondant disk on top of frosted cupcakes so it looks like a sheet with two little holes on top of the cupcake. Repeat with remaining cupcakes.

NOVEMBER

NOV. 1

Deep-Fried Clams Day

When in New England, don't walk, RUN to the nearest seaside clam shack and order yourself a basket of piping hot, whole-belly fried clams! Sit down, squeeze fresh lemon over them, and scarf down every single one until you are completely happy and full. This is a must when you're in the area. You simply won't find a better basket of fried clams anywhere, perhaps because these states have been cranking out killer clams for a long time and have it down to a science. Or maybe it's smelling the salty sea air while you eat this perfect food.

CRISPITY CLAMS

Serves 3–4

20 littleneck clams (shucked)

1 cup buttermilk

dash of onion powder

dash of garlic powder

dash of oregano

Vegetable oil for frying

1 cup all-purpose flour

1 cup cornmeal

Salt and pepper

Old Bay seasoning

Lemon wedges

1. Soak clams in buttermilk, onion powder, garlic powder, and oregano leaves overnight.

2. After clams soak, heat oil in large pot to 350°F. Combine flour with cornmeal, drain clams, shake off excess buttermilk, and toss in flour mixture. Dump into fine mesh colander to remove excess flour. Fry until golden and crispy, about 3 minutes, drain on paper towels, and season with salt, pepper, and seasoning. Serve with tartar sauce and lemon wedges.

NOV. 2

Deviled Egg Day

Great as a party snack, Deviled Eggs are inexpensive and a breeze to make. The term deviled dates back to the eighteenth and nineteenth centuries, and it refers to the spiciness of the yolk fillings; however, these eggs are said to have originated back in Roman times!

LITTLE DEVILS

Makes 14 spicy snacks

1 shallot (sliced thinly)

¼ cup white vinegar

¼ teaspoon black pepper

½ cup beet juice (or 1 medium raw beet peeled and blended with the vinegar and strained)

7 large eggs (hard-boiled and peeled)

¼ cup mayonnaise

½ cup fresh goat cheese

1½ tablespoons Dijon mustard

Coarse salt and freshly cracked pepper

Couple of dashes of hot sauce

Smoked paprika

Chives or scallions sliced thinly (for garnish)

Chili flakes (for garnish)

1. In a plastic container with a lid, combine shallots, vinegar, black pepper, and beet juice and set aside.

2. Bring a pot of salted water to a rapid boil over high heat. Use a toothpick or thumbtack to prick a small hole in long pointy tip of each egg. Carefully drop eggs into boiling water using a strainer or slotted spoon and cook for 6 minutes. In the meantime, set up an ice bath for eggs. After 6 minutes, remove eggs one by one and place into ice water. Allow eggs to chill for 10 minutes.

3. Crack each egg gently all around and place back in water (this will help peels come off easily). Peel eggs carefully, rinse to remove any excess shell, and set aside.

4. Gently drop eggs into beet and vinegar mixture. Allow whites to soak in the fridge overnight until they have turned reddish-purple.

⑤ The next day, split eggs in half and scoop yolks carefully into a bowl. In a mixer, whip yolks with mayonnaise, cheese, and Dijon mustard. Season with salt, pepper, and hot sauce, then mix thoroughly.

⑥ Place white-turned-ruby eggs on a plate. Spoon or pipe mixture into crevice of egg and garnish with sprinkling of coarse salt, paprika, and chives or scallions. For extra oomph, sprinkle with chili flakes, drizzle with a little olive oil, and serve.

Sandwich Day

I've said it before, and I'll say it again—sandwiches are my favorite food in this world. What's not to love? They feature all the major food groups, wrapped into one convenient package. The story of the word "sandwich" goes back to the eighteenth century when John Montagu, the fourth Earl of Sandwich, ordered his valet to get him some cold meat between two pieces of bread. The idea caught on and people started to order the hand-held meal by simply saying "give me the same as Sandwich." If only he knew what he started!

PULLED PORK SAMICHES

Serves 4–5

2–3 pounds pork shoulder

Barbecue sauce

1 12-ounce bottle of beer

Potato rolls

❶ Cover pork shoulder with barbecue sauce (use your favorite), then place in roasting pan. Pour beer into pan, cover with aluminum foil, and braise at 300°F for 4–5 hours. Every hour flip shoulder, spread more barbecue sauce on top, cover pan, and return to oven (you'll do this 3 times).

❷ Once cooked, use two forks to pull pork from bone. Remove bones and any cartilage, then toss pork in juices left in the pan, taste, and adjust seasoning with either salt and pepper, a little apple cider vinegar, or a tad more barbecue sauce. Let pulled pork sit in the juices; the pork will absorb all those delicious flavors and make the filling really moist.

❸ Serve on warm potato rolls topped with cole slaw and potato chips.

Candy Day

Candy is traditionally made from sugar that is dissolved in water (or some other soluble liquid) and then boiled until the desired consistency is achieved. As the sugar syrup cooks, moisture evaporates creating a denser sugar that changes texture depending on the temperature. Monitoring these stages prior to the advent of thermometers was tricky but not impossible; it's much easier to measure with the use of a thermometer. Here's a guide:

> *thread 230–233°F*
> *soft ball (a.k.a. fudge stage) 234–240°F*
> *firm ball 244–248°F*
> *hard ball 250–266°F*
> *soft crack 270–290°F*
> *hard crack (a.k.a. toffee stage) 300–310°F*
> *clear liquid 320°F*
> *brown liquid (a.k.a. caramel) 338°F*
> *burnt sugar 350°F*

MARSHMALLOWS

Serves 3–4

3 tablespoons gelatin

1 cup water (separated into 2 ½ cups)

1½ cups sugar

1 cup light corn syrup

¼ teaspoon salt

1 tablespoon vanilla extract

Nonstick spray

Powdered sugar

1 Combine gelatin with ½ cup cold water and allow to hydrate.

2 Meanwhile, combine remaining ½ cup water with sugar and corn syrup in a heavy-bottomed pot, and bring to a boil over high heat.

3 Cook syrup until it reads 245°F on a candy thermometer. Remove from heat and pour syrup into the bowl of your stand mixer.

4 Add gelatin mixture, attach the balloon whip to your stand mixer, and whip on high for about 10 minutes until light, white, and fluffy.

5 Add salt and vanilla, then mix for another minute.

6 Spray a 10 X 12" square cake pan with nonstick spray. Pour in marshmallow mix and refrigerate in the fridge until hard, at least 4 hours.

7 Cut marshmallows with a lightly oiled knife. Roll marshmallows in powdered sugar and serve.

8 Keep stored in an air-locked container in powdered sugar.

Doughnut Day

NOV. 5

I learned to make these while working with Jacques Torres at Le Cirque 2000. Every morning I would walk in and smell the dough. To this day, I can't decide which I like better: the smell of sweet fermenting dough or the smell of frying dough. Actually, I think I like the smell of fried dough much better, but it's only because that smell means doughnut-eating time is quickly approaching! Warm, plump, sugary, and filled with cold, smooth, and eggy sweet cream—OMG—I can't think of anything more amazing than one of these. (Okay, maybe two, or three, or four. . . .)

OMG BOMBOLONIS

Serves 3–4

¼ cup fresh yeast

¼ cup cold water

3½ cups bread flour

4 eggs

⅛ cup sugar

1½ teaspoons salt

1 cup plus 2 tablespoons butter (cubed)

Vegetable oil for frying

Pastry Cream (Feb. 20) or Vanilla Pudding (May 22)

1 Dissolve yeast in water and set aside.

2 In stand mixer, combine flour with eggs, sugar, and salt for about 1 minute until smooth. Change to dough hook, add yeast mixture, and combine again for 2 minutes until smooth.

3 Add butter and mix, this time for about 5 minutes, stopping twice to scrape down the sides of bowl.

④ Once dough no longer sticks to sides and has formed a ball (if it hasn't happened after this time, add a little more flour), remove bowl from mixer and cover with plastic wrap. Let dough rise for 30 minutes in a warm place.

⑤ Smack dough to release air, and scrape out onto lightly greased baking sheet or baking dish. Cover with plastic wrap and refrigerate overnight or for at least 1 hour.

⑥ Remove from fridge and roll out on clean, lightly floured surface (use your hands for this) until dough is 1" thick. Using a 2" round cutter, cut out rounds and place on lightly greased baking sheet. Spray lightly with vegetable spray and let rise for 2 hours in a warm place.

⑦ Fry at 330°F until golden, about 2–3 minutes on each side. Using method described in the PB&J Doughnuts recipe (June 8), fill dough-nuts with Pastry Cream. Roll in granulated or powdered sugar right before serving.

Nachos Day

I've mentioned already that my little brother Johnny is a crazy fan of nachos, and every time I think of these, I think of him. Nachos represent simple everyman food, best enjoyed while watching the game on the couch! They're essential when watching football games, or the big fight on TV. My good friend Eric is a phenomenal chef, but he's never been able to perfect the art of making nachos. I suspect it's because he's has excellent training in professional kitchens and overcomplicates his nachos a bit. My trick? The microwave.

PERFECT MICROWAVE NACHOS

Serves 2–3

1 9-oz bag flavored nacho chips

½ cup pepper jack cheese (shredded)

½ cup mozzarella cheese (shredded)

½ cup Cheddar cheese (shredded)

½ cup salsa

¼ cup sour cream

½ lime

Fresh cilantro (finely chopped)

① Lay chips on a large, flat microwavable plate (the larger the better, so cheese gets on all the chips).

② Sprinkle with cheeses and microwave on high for 1½ minutes.

③ Remove nachos from microwave and dollop on salsa.

④ Return to microwave and cook on high for 1 more minute.

⑤ Remove from microwave, drizzle sour cream on top, follow with a good squeeze of lime, and garnish with cilantro.

Bittersweet Chocolate with Almonds Day

Today celebrates the second-most favorite chocolate-nut combo in America! The hint of bitterness that comes from the almond complements the bitterness and complexity of the chocolate, lending a perfumy note before you bite in, and the crunch steals the show. When I first learned how to make chocolate bars, we created two kinds: plain and almond. It's a fun endeavor and best of all, you end up with great holiday gifts or special treats for your kid's lunch.

HOMEMADE CHOCOLATE BARS

Serves 5–6

16 ounces bittersweet chocolate

1 chocolate bar mold

½ cup whole almonds (toasted and cooled)

Coarse salt (I like Fleur de Sel or Maldon sea salt)

Aluminum foil and customized printed paper (for wrapping bars)

❶ Before you begin, design a customized candy bar wrapper. It can be as simple as saying "Happy Birthday, Suzie!" or "Happy Halloween from the Andersons." (This can be easily done with a bunch of different computer programs. If you aren't familiar with them, just ask your kids, chances are they'll know.) Once that's done, print 5 6 of them (they should be half the size of an 8½" x 11" piece of paper, or two up on a page) cut in half, and set aside. And onto cooking. . . .

❷ Temper chocolate by melting ¾ in microwave then adding ¼ in whole pieces back to mixture and stirring until melted. Take the temperature; chocolate should be at 90°F. (If it's not, nuke again a few seconds at a time until it reaches 90°F.)

❸ Pour chocolate into mold, top with a few almonds, press them down, and sprinkle coarse salt all around.

❹ Place mold in freezer for 1 hour until ultra-hard and edges pull from molds just a little. (If unsure, tug on a corner of the mold. If chocolate peels off immediately, then they're good.)

❺ Pop bars out carefully by inverting onto a cold plate lined with parchment paper. Using gloves or otherwise making sure not to touch chocolate, wrap bars in aluminum, then wrap in preprinted customized labels.

❻ Seal in the back with a small piece of tape and that's it. You're ready to hand out your very own chocolate bars.

NOV. 8

Harvey Wallbanger Day

Cold, bright, and super refreshing, this drink is accredited to a famous world champion mixologist Donato "Duke" Antone, who came up with the concoction in 1952. The drink exploded onto the scene when a Galliano salesman took this spiked screwdriver on the road introducing it to a number of different bars across the country. To this day it is the most famous drink ever made with the sweet herbal Galliano liqueur from Italy.

HARVEY WALLBANGER

Serves 1

1½ ounces orange-infused vodka

6 ounces fresh orange juice

Ice

½ ounce Galliano

1 orange slice

❶ Combine vodka and OJ over ice in a highball glass.

❷ Top with Galliano and orange slice.

NOV. 9

Scrapple Day

This combination of pork scraps, cornmeal, buckwheat flour, and spices is cooked and molded into a loaf. This is then sliced and heated and served. Who should we thank for this delicious meat loaf? That'll be the famous Pennsylvania Dutch.

CHICKEN-FRIED SCRAPPLE WITH ROSEMARY APPLESAUCE

Serves 3–4

1 pound scrapple (cut into ½" slices; I like High Hope Hogs)

1 cup all-purpose flour

3 eggs (beaten)

2 cups bread crumbs

Vegetable oil for frying

❶ Dredge scrapple in flour, then dip in egg wash and bread crumbs.

❷ Pan fry in the vegetable oil until golden.

❸ Serve with rosemary applesauce.

ROSEMARY APPLESAUCE

Makes about 1 cup of applesauce

3 apples (peeled, cored, and cut into chunks)

1 rosemary sprig (leaves only)

1 teaspoon olive oil

2–3 teaspoons sugar

❶ Combine all ingredients in a microwave-safe bowl and cook for 3–5 minutes until tender. Remove from bowl and purée.

Vanilla Cupcake Day

Sundae Day

Imagine with me for a second a blast of warm, buttery air as cupcakes come out of the oven. . . . Slowly, you place the pan down, take in the fruits of your labor, then close your eyes and take a deep breath—the kind that lifts your shoulders and makes you feel as if you're floating . . . and in this heavenly cloud you're greeted with the sweet scent of vanilla . . . then you ask yourself: Do I wait until they cool down a bit, or do I need to try a piece now to see if they're done right? Go ahead, I won't tell.

If you read Strawberry Sundae Day (July 7) or Hot Fudge Sundae Day (July 25), you know what a great story this delightful dessert has. So many varieties, and yet, the simple fact remains, it's not the toppings that make the sundae. When you get down to it, a good-quality ice cream is the main actor in this musical, and yes my friends, it is a musical. Musicals are colorful, fun, and vibrant. So I called my friend, Cristina, who is the biggest lover of musicals and she said Gypsy was her favorite. Here's a tribute to that.

GYPSY'S SUNDAE

Serves 2–3

Hot Fudge (June 16)

½ cup smooth peanut butter

Homemade Vanilla Ice Cream (July 23)

Perfect Chantilly Cream (Jan. 5)

Peanuts

Cherry

VANILLA CUPCAKES

Makes about 1 dozen cupcakes

½ cup plus 1 tablespoon butter (soft)

1¼ cups sugar

2½ teaspoons baking powder

1¾ cups plus 2 tablespoons cake flour

½ teaspoon salt

3 egg whites

¾ cup buttermilk

2 teaspoons pure vanilla extract

❶ Prepare Hot Fudge, heat, and whisk in peanut butter until smooth.

❷ Scoop ice cream and top with warm fudge.

❸ Garnish with whipped cream and peanuts. Top with a cherry, of course!

❶ Whip butter with sugar until fluffy. Sift dry ingredients and set aside.

❷ In another bowl, whip egg whites and gradually add buttermilk. Combine.

❸ Go back to butter mixture and intermittently add buttermilk with flour, stopping every once in a while to scrape down the sides. Finish by mixing in vanilla. Pour batter into lined muffin tins and bake at 350°F for 15–20 minutes.

Pizza with Everything Day (Except Anchovies)

What? No anchovies? What kind of holiday is this? If that's what you're thinking, you're on my team. If not, like the rest of the people I know, either you don't like anchovies or never tried them. But anchovies have gotten a bad rap over the years. The old anchovies you once found on the bottom of supermarket shelves covered in dust are being replaced with light, succulent, and lightly brined white anchovies that blow the others out of the water. So whether you like anchovies or not, give them a try; if not, you can just pick 'em off and put them on my slice.

PIZZA TOPPINGS

Pizza dough (Sep. 5)

Pizza sauce (your favorite brand)

Shredded mozzarella

¼ cup red peppers (sliced)

¼ cup pepperoni (sliced thin)

¼ cup button mushrooms (sliced)

¼ cup red onions (sliced thin)

2 tablespoons black olives (sliced)

¼ cup prosciutto or ham (sliced thin)

❶ Make and prepare dough. Preheat oven to 450°F degrees, and put pizza stone inside.

❷ Spread sauce over dough and top with shredded mozzarella and remaining toppings.

❸ Bake until slightly charred and the cheese is bubbling, about 12–15 minutes.

Guacamole Day

Fork in hand, I found myself looking at a bowl full of ripe avocados while my dog Lucas looked on. I had cut my tomatoes and they sat on the cutting board alongside cilantro, limes, and onions, juices dripping onto the floor. No way would I buy a "bottle" of guacamole. Homemade guacamole is such a super-healthy, überdelicious dip, and then it dawned on me. . . . Wasn't September 16 Guacamole Day? Are we so obsessed with the green stuff we have two holidays?

SHRIMP ROLLS

Serves 2–3

1 medium carrot (peeled)

½ cucumber

1 package rice paper

½ pound shrimp (peeled, boiled or steamed, and cooled)

Guacamole

3 fresh mint sprigs

Baby greens (or shredded lettuce)

❶ Grate carrot and cut cucumber into little sticks.

❷ Fill pot with hot water. Dip one sheet of rice paper into hot water for 5–10 seconds until hydrated. Place rice paper on plate and put 1–2 shrimp (depending on the size), a little guacamole, a little mint, greens, some cucumber and carrots in middle, then roll by folding two sides in then rolling from the bottom up. The rice paper is sticky and will seal the roll up.

❸ Repeat process with remaining rolls. Serve with soy sauce and duck sauce.

NOV. 14

Pickle Day

My friend Lisa reached into the refrigerator; we were both parched and needed a drink. She looked inside and pulled out a small thick glass container. When I came closer I noticed to my horror that she was holding a pickle jar! A pickle jar! And she had just removed the lid and was holding it up to her lips! Did I mention this was a pickle jar? I shrugged and reached for a beer. A few years later I saw a Pickletini on a bar menu. Curiosity got the best of me and I tried it. It was wonderful.

PICKLETINI

Serves 1

2½ ounces good-quality vodka

½ ounce good-quality pickle juice

Ice

❶ Combine ingredients in a shaker filled with fresh ice. Shake like crazy for at least 5 seconds and strain into a chilled martini glass.

❷ Garnish with a pickle on a skewer. Or serve with Fried Pickles (Sep. 13)!

Raisin Bran Cereal Day

You remember those singing raisins commercials with the California Raisins? Whatever happened to them? That's what I always think of when I think of raisin bran. This delicious combination is most commonly known as a great cereal and is praised for its high-fiber content. Introduced to the United States in 1926 by U.S. Mills, it has become one of America's longest-standing cereals.

RAISIN BRAN CLUSTERS

Serves 2–3

½ cup dark chocolate (finely chopped)

2 cups raisin bran cereal

❶ Melt ¼ cup chocolate and temper by melting in a microwave, bring it up to 112–115°F. Add remaining chocolate. Stir until dissolved, then bring temperature to 88°F, making sure to keep it below 90°F.

❷ Add cereal, stir everything together (you may need to add a little more cereal if it's too broken; try to use the largest flakes).

❸ Scoop mixture into little clusters on cookie sheet lined with parchment paper or aluminum foil. Freeze for about 20 minutes until hard enough that it peels from paper or foil cleanly and when you take a bite it snaps.

Fast Food Day

In theory I love fast food. In theory you should, too. In theory we should all be living in perfect harmony not paying taxes and have a lawn that automatically cuts itself. In theory children should come with mute buttons, healthy food should be cheap, and all kitchens should have an "auto clean" option. In a world that moves at the speed of communication, fast is good. Fast food was developed to do just that. However, we tend to think that fast food is simply burgers and fries, when in fact fast food has been around as far back as Roman times when they had little stands that sold wine and flatbread. Throughout the world you can find different kinds of foods that can be bought for little money and served fast. Such foods can include a bowl of noodles in Asian countries, kebabs in Africa and the Middle East, pizza, chilled shellfish, and hundreds of other great choices. My little siblings, however, prefer chicken nuggets.

CHICKEN NUGGETS WITH MAPLE MUSTARD

Serves 2

2 skinless chicken breasts

3 eggs

1 cup all-purpose flour

2 cups bread crumbs

2–3 cups oil (if frying)

Salt and pepper

3 tablespoons Dijon mustard

4–5 tablespoons maple syrup

❶ Cut up chicken into small 1" cubes. In food processor, purée chicken until smooth, then add 1 egg and blend again until smooth (about 30 seconds).

2 Slowly add enough bread crumbs so a manageable chicken dough forms (think meatball consistency).

3 You can go two ways on this: Either take chicken and press it into a baking sheet that has been lined with a piece of parchment or aluminum foil, then place another piece on top and flatten with a second baking sheet and use cookie cutters to get different shaped nuggets; or make little balls and flatten.

4 Refrigerate nuggets until firm enough to handle.

5 Set up dredging station with three bowls: one for flour, one for eggs, and one for bread crumbs. Dip the nuggets into flour, then eggs, then bread crumbs. Repeat with all nuggets.

6 Either bake at 375°F for 15 minutes, or fry at the same temperature until golden. Season with salt and pepper.

7 Make maple mustard by mixing Dijon and maple syrup until smooth. Serve with nuggets.

NOV. 17

Baklava Day

Baklava is recorded as being one of the first desserts consumed by the human race. Composed of simple ingredients—honey and crunchy nuts—it should be one of the wonders of the world. When it came to making it, I got in touch with my friend Reno Christou because I remembered him going on and on about how wonderful his mom's recipe was so I had to try it. Then I reached out again to see if he'd let me share the recipe with you. He called his mom and she said okay. Here it is. . . .

HOMEMADE BAKLAVA

Serves 3–4

2 cups toasted almonds (coarsely chopped) (if you get raw almonds, toast in oven until browned)

2 cups toasted walnuts (coarsely chopped) (you can use ONLY walnuts, or mix almonds and walnuts or even add pistachios—all of which are toasted before being chopped)

2 teaspoons cinnamon

1½ cups unsalted butter, clarified and heated (discard the creamy solids)

1 pound ready-made phyllo dough (use a thinner gauge of phyllo; any Greek grocery store should carry it)

3 cups sugar

2 cups water

½ cup good-quality honey

Rind of one lemon

1 Mix together almonds, walnuts, and cinnamon in a bowl. Set aside.

2 Grease bottom of a baking dish the same size as the phyllo generously with the clarified butter. Lay four phyllo sheets on bottom of pan, one on top of the other, while brushing each one with clarified butter.

3 Distribute nut mixture evenly over pastry. The multiple layering of a baklava is achieved by spreading nuts on every few phyllo sheets. Repeat until mixture is done and end with four more phyllo sheets. Brush top layer with butter. With sharp, pointy knife, cut triangle or square portions all the way down to the pan (phyllo becomes very crispy and difficult to maneuver when it's cooked). Sprinkle some drops or spray some water to prevent phyllo from overcrisping and curling up. Traditionally, Greeks dig a whole clove into center of each baklava prior to cooking.

④ Bake at 350°F for approximately 30 minutes or until golden brown. (This will vary depending on your oven or if you use a convection oven.) Remove from oven and let cool down.

⑤ In a pot, boil sugar, water, thyme honey, and lemon rind. When syrup visibly coats the back of a spoon, it's ready. When still hot, pour evenly over cooled baklava and let cool completely. If you like it very soaked in as I do, let it sit overnight. Serve at room temperature.

NOV. 18 Vichyssoise Day

If you've ever read any of Anthony Bourdain's books, you know how he refers to vichyssoise as his epiphany moment. The magic is that it's actually served ice cold. It's so good you can serve hot if you want, or even use it as a base for most soups you'd want to make. It's a classic and a good foundation dish that every cook must know how to make. We'll keep things simple, with potatoes, leeks, a little cream, and crispy leeks for texture.

VICHYSSOISE

Serves 2–3

1 medium white onion

2 cups (about 5) leeks (white part only)

Olive oil

2 pounds white potatoes

1 cup heavy cream

2 tablespoons butter

Salt and white pepper

2 egg whites

½ cup all-purpose flour (for dredging)

Oil for frying

Cook's Note

Sweating is cooking something without browning at all; this is a beautiful white soup so you don't want any color.

❶ Clean and cut onion into 1" cubes, then cut bottom half of leeks (the white part) and slice lengthwise to clean dirt out of middle. Hold leek under running water, folding layers back to let water clean out any dirt that might be stuck. Clean remaining leeks and chop white part into 1" pieces. Save leek greens for later.

❷ In an 8-quart pot, sweat onions with leek whites and a little olive oil over medium-low heat. Cook onions and leeks, stirring occasionally, while you peel potatoes. Cut into small cubes (about ½").

❸ Once leeks and onions have wilted and are almost transparent, add potatoes, followed by 6 quarts of water. Cover almost completely (leave a little room for steam to escape so pot doesn't overflow) and raise heat.

❹ Cook for about 20 minutes, until potatoes are cooked through. How do you know when they're done? Eat one. Does it taste good? Then they're done.

❺ Purée soup (I prefer using a hand blender because it's cleaner, but a regular blender works just fine). Add heavy cream, butter, salt, and pepper until yummy.

❻ Slice leek greens thinly, dip them in egg whites, toss them in flour, and fry at 375°F until golden. Another option: Layer leek greens in a baking dish, add olive oil, salt and pepper, a little vinegar, cover with aluminum foil, and cook at 350°F for 20–30 minutes. *Voilà*, braised leeks. Either one of these makes a great side dish with soup.

Carbonated Beverage with Caffeine Day

Beaujolais Nouveau Day

Carbonated beverages are drinks that are effervescent due to the presence of carbon dioxide. Carbonation in these beverages may occur naturally as in spring water or beer, or in the case of soda the bubbles can come from the artificial introduction of carbon dioxide. Joseph Preistly is said to have invented artificial carbonation in England in 1767, and it is partially thanks to him that soda fountains exploded in America in the 1800s. Today, Americans drink upwards of 500 cans of soda a year, and the energy drink market is not far behind. Sugar and caffeine power these drinks. Here we make things a little healthier.

Beaujolais nouveau est arrivé! Beaujolais nouveau est arrivé! *This is the great slogan that has been used to mark the arrival of Beaujolais nouveau wine every year. The line means literally "the new Beaujolais has arrived" and refers to Beaujolais wine, a light and young wine made from the gamay grapes in the region of Burgundy, France. This wine is released on the third Thursday of November, is produced with very few tannins, and should be drank slightly chilled. So I thought, sangria, baby!*

BEAUJOLAIS SANGRIA

Serves 8–10

  2 oranges (thinly sliced)

  1 lemon (thinly sliced)

  2 green apples

  1 gallon Beaujolais nouveau

  ½ cup brandy

  ¼ cup Cointreau

  1 quart fresh orange juice

  ½ cup fresh lemon juice

  ½ cup superfine sugar

  1 quart chilled club soda

  Ice

SPARKLING TEA

Serves 3–4

  3 cups water

  8 tea bags

  4 tablespoons honey

  3 cups sparkling water

❶ Boil water and steep tea bags for 3 minutes, then remove tea bags, squeezing to remove any infusion left inside. Add honey (you may want to add more if you like your tea sweeter), stir until dissolved, and chill.

❷ To serve, combine sparkling water with tea-honey mixture and serve over ice with a lemon slice.

❶ Wash and cut all the fruit into ½" cubes.

❷ Combine all ingredients and serve over ice.

NOV. 21 Gingerbread Day

Gingerbread is a loose term used more to describe a spicy-molasses-honey-ginger flavor than an actual bread. That's why you find gingerbread ice cream, gingerbread cookies, cakes, biscuits, pancakes, as well as bread. For the invention of gingerbread we can thank the Armenian monk Gregory Nicopolis who created it in Europe around 992. He taught the French how to make it, and they taught the Germans, who in turn brought it to Swedish monasteries, but the court of Queen Elizabeth I is responsible for creating the iconic man.

GINGERBREAD COOKIES

Makes about 2 dozen cookies

½ cup butter (soft)

½ cup granulated sugar

3 cups all-purpose flour

¼ teaspoons salt

¾ teaspoon baking soda

2½ teaspoons ground ginger

1½ teaspoon ground cinnamon

¼ teaspoon ground nutmeg

¼ teaspoon ground cloves

1 egg

⅔ cup molasses

❶ Whip butter and sugar until fluffy. Sift dry ingredients.

❷ Add egg to the butter mixture and combine well, then add molasses and mix.

❸ Incorporate flour-spice mix slowly until combined.

❹ Wrap dough in plastic wrap and refrigerate for at least 1 hour.

❺ On a clean, lightly floured surface, roll out dough to ¼" thick and cut out desired shapes.

❻ Bake at 350°F for 8–10 minutes.

❼ Cool slightly and enjoy with an ice-cold glass of milk!

Cook's Note

For extra kick, add a few pieces of dry preserved ginger or ginger candy.

Cashew Day

Did you know that the cashew nut actually comes with a cashew fruit. Yup, not only is it one of the weirdest looking fruits out there, it's one of Brazil's most popular juices. The cashew gets its name from the Portuguese name caju, which in turn gets its name from the Indian acajú, which in turn gets it name from the word anacardium referring to the shape of the fruit, which looks like an inverted heart. Though not as common as the peanut due to its higher prices, cashews are buttery and delicious and make and incredible filling for this pie.

CASHEW PIE

Serves 4–5

Pie Dough (Apr. 28)

3 large eggs

1 cup light brown sugar

¾ cup light corn syrup

3 tablespoons butter (melted)

1 tablespoon vanilla extract

¼ teaspoon salt

3 cups cashews

Perfect Chantilly Cream (Jan. 5)

❶ Make dough, and press into pie tin.

❷ Combine eggs with sugar, corn syrup, butter, vanilla, salt, and cashews. Mix well until batter is smooth. Pour filling into pie crust and bake at 350°F for 55 minutes or until set.

❸ Let pie cool and serve with whipped cream.

Espresso Day

NOV. 23

Everybody needs a shot of good, creamy, intense, invigorating espresso sometimes. Good espresso requires just a few things, but these things must be perfect. First you need a good, fresh, and recently roasted coffee, secondly, you need a good machine. Thirdly you need good water, considering that espresso is mostly water make sure there is a filter attached to your machine. The best part of an espresso? The crema, which is the little emulsified foam that forms on top.

CHOCOLATE-COVERED ESPRESSO BEANS

Makes 1 cup espresso beans

½ cup bittersweet chocolate (melted)

1 cup espresso beans

½ cup cocoa powder

❶ Melt and temper chocolate.

❷ Put beans in a metal bowl and drizzle chocolate, then stir, using a wooden spoon. Refrigerate beans until cold and chocolate is hard. Repeat process several times until a nice thick coat forms on beans. On final coat, toss beans with a little cocoa powder.

❸ Place beans on cookie sheet lined with parchment paper in freezer for at least 30 minutes until chocolate is hard. Serve at room temperature. These are great when you don't have the time for a coffee but need a little afternoon pick-me-up, and they also make great ice cream toppers!

Sardines Day

NOV. 24

Fresh, cleaned, and grilled over crackling wood, then gently peeled off the bone and served on crusty, grilled, and buttered country bread. . . . Right before you bite into it, squeeze a little lemon on top and sprinkle with coarse salt, then take a deep breath, close your eyes, and crunch away . . . hmmm. That is my favorite way to eat sardines. No disrespect to the can, but this is just so much better.

SARDINES ON BUTTERED TOAST

Serves 2

Olive oil

3 fresh sardines (from a reputable fishmonger)

Coarse sea salt (Maldon or Fleur de Sel)

Pepper

Lemon wedges

Crusty country bread

Butter (room temp)

❶ Place pan over medium-high heat and add a little olive oil. Sprinkle sardines with salt and pepper, stuff with a few lemon wedges, and sauté for 2–3 minutes on each side until slightly browned. Remove sardines from pan (or grill).

❷ Toast bread and butter. To serve, place toast on plate. With a knife, slide filet off of sardine and place atop toast, skin-side up. Squeeze lemon juice on top and crunch away!

Cook's Note

These taste best over a grill fired with wood, but if you don't have a grill, don't worry—a good pan works, too. The trick here is to get überfresh sardines, so go to a reputable fish market, and smell them. If they smell fishy, don't do this.

NOV. 25

Parfait Day

What's wonderful about parfaits is that they are not only wonderfully light, but they lend themselves to savory creations as well as the expected sweet treats. When it comes to parfaits, I always recall a rhubarb-strawberry variety I love to make. But since we're coming up on winter, this calls for something a bit heartier. Which for me is simply luscious thick honey with a smooth and rich yogurt parfait.

GREEK YOGURT PARFAIT

1 vanilla bean

1 cup heavy cream

3 tablespoons sugar

1 envelope powdered gelatin

2 tablespoons cold water

One 17.6-ounce tub Greek yogurt

¼ cup thick Greek honey

1 cup your favorite granola

❶ Split the vanilla bean and scrape the insides into the heavy cream, then pour into a small pot. Set the pot over the stove, add the sugar, and bring to a boil (make sure to keep an eye on this, it's a small amount of cream and will boil fast). Once it comes to a boil, turn off the heat, cover it, and allow it to steep for 15 minutes.

❷ Sprinkle the gelatin over the cold water to re-hydrate it.

❸ Remove the vanilla bean from the cream, rinse it, and place it in the oven to dry out for later use (in sugar or vodka is great). Add the gelatin to the cream, whisk until it's completely dissolved, then add the yogurt and whisk together until smooth.

❹ Then pour in the cream mixture into glasses. Refrigerate for at least 3 hours. When ready to serve pour some thick Greek honey on top and top with your favorite granola.

Cake Day

A cake is a gift, either for yourself or for a loved one. They are always baked with good intentions, and that's mostly why they taste so good! Think about it, cakes are a representation of happy thoughts, joy, love, care, all these wonderful emotions all packaged up and wrapped in sugar and butter. Doesn't it sound like someone just loves ya? I made this cake for a friend of mine named Cristina while I was trying to court her, and I think it worked like a charm. So what am I trying to tell you? If you want to win someone over? Bake them a cake.

❶ Sift the flour and baking powder. Make a well in the middle of the sifted ingredients and add the sugar, salt, and egg yolks. Combine until it starts to thicken up, then add the raspberries and lemon juice a bit at a time to create a smooth paste. Continue to add the lemon juice, then add the water and continue whisking slowly until all ingredients are combined. Add the lemon zest and the oil and combine well.

❷ In a clean bowl, whisk the egg whites on medium speed for about 1 minute until they are frothy. Add the cream of tartar and whip on high until it forms soft peaks. Add about ½ of the whites to the rest of the batter and fold gently with a spatula. Add the remaining whites with the rose water and fold until you have a homogeneous fluffy batter.

❸ Spray 2 round cake pans with nonstick spray and coat with a little flour. The pans must be at least 1" smaller than the ring mold, which must be at least 2". Pour the batter in, and bake at 325°F for 25–30 minutes or until a knife inserted in the middle comes out clean. When it comes out of the oven run a sharp knife around the edges to release the cake. Allow it to cool.

❹ Boil the water and sugar, cool, then add the rose water and lemon juice. Taste and set aside.

❺ Place the cake ring on top of a parchment-paper-lined baking sheet that can fit inside your freezer. Coat the sides of the ring with the freshly prepared white chocolate mousse, and with a spatula or spoon coat the sides of the ring, making sure to fill in all the little air holes where the ring meets the parchment. This will give you a smooth cake when you remove the ring later on.

CRISTINA'S CAKE

Serves 6

2 cups all-purpose flour

1 tablespoon baking powder

1½ cups granulated sugar

½ teaspoon salt

8 eggs (separated)

4 raspberries (or 2 tablespoon raspberry purée)

½ cup fresh lemon juice

¼ cup water

Zest of 2 lemons

½ cup vegetable oil

½ teaspoon cream of tartar

1 tablespoon rose water

White Chocolate Mousse (Sep. 23)

Rose Syrup

1 cup water

½ cup sugar

Drizzle of rose water

Squeeze of fresh lemon juice

6. Place one of the cakes in the middle and drizzle a little of the rose syrup on top to moisten it. Top the cake with mousse, making sure to fill in the sides really well to prevent air holes.

7. Now place the second cake on top, and again drizzle or brush with a little of the syrup, and follow with the remaining white chocolate mousse. Smooth out the top of the cake with a spatula, spreading against the edges to make sure you have smooth and sharp corners.

8. Now, this is what we do in professional kitchens to get perfect cakes—freeze it overnight!

9. The following day, remove the cake from the freezer, squeeze the spatula underneath to pull it from the paper, and place it on a coffee canister or any wide container that is at least as tall as the ring itself. Using a hand torch or hairdryer, heat the sides of the ring mold while rotating it slowly. Heat the ring all around so that it peels smoothly and you don't create too much pressure on either side. Once the ring is hot enough, you will feel it begin to slide a little. Stop with the heat and help the ring peel down slowly. Remove your cake and place in the fridge until defrosted (at least 3 hours, you can test this by inserting a wooden stick in the middle).

10. Decorate as you please. I like curls of white chocolate intertwined with bright red rose petals.

Bavarian Cream Pie Day

Back in the day, Sunnyside consisted of mostly farms, but today it's home to the most wonderful donut shop in New York. When my mom used to take us to get doughnuts (the supermarket was close so we had to pass by it), I'd always go after the cream-filled ones. Right below the tray of freshly baked goodies was a sign that read "Bavarian Cream," which may as well have been written in Chinese since I didn't care—all I wanted was to devour my doughnut. If only someone had told me that there was a pie filled with the same cream, we could have avoided some donut casualties.

BAVARIAN CREAM PIE

Serves 4–6

3 tablespoons milk

1 tablespoon powdered gelatin

3 tablespoons cold water

¼ cup sugar

1 cup heavy cream

5 egg yolks

1 teaspoon vanilla extract

1¼ cups whipped cream

2 cups whipped cream

Pie Dough (baked and cooled) (Apr. 28)

1. In heavy-bottomed pot, bring milk to boil over high heat.

2. Hydrate gelatin in cold water for at least 5 minutes.

3. Whip sugar with very cold cream, in a cold bowl, with cold beaters, preferably over ice, on medium speed until stiff peaks form. Set aside and reserve ice bowl.

4. Whisk yolks and set aside.

5. Once milk has come to boil, temper eggs by drizzling hot milk into mixture a little at a time while whisking until you have used up half of milk, then add eggs to pot. Turn heat to medium and cook slowly with a rubber spatula, scraping bottom and removing pot from stove altogether every 30 seconds or so to cook slowly. Once cream coats spatula and you can run your finger through it and the line remains for more than 2 seconds, you're done, now you have what we call Crème Anglaise. Remove pot from stove, transfer cream to another bowl, and place over ice bowl used for whipped cream.

6. Add gelatin to hot milk turned crème anglaise, and whisk until thoroughly dissolved. Add vanilla and whisk in well. Continue whisking mixture over ice bowl until it starts to thicken and is no longer hot. Add half of whipped cream and whisk in well, then add remaining whipped cream and fold everything together with a spatula.

7. Pour Bavarian cream inside cooled pie shell, and top with 2 cups whipped cream. I like to top with shredded coconut for an extra hint of yumminess. Store in refrigerator.

Cook's Note

When it comes to folding, think about folding clothing—what is your hand movement? Hand out flat, palm facing up, under the sleeve, and over to fold it in. Do the same thing to the other sleeve, then fold the bottom up with the same "folding" motion. Now put a spatula in your hand and imagine you are folding clothing. Try it, then go try it in a bowl. See? Same thing.

French Toast Day

NOV. 28

Let's start by asking the important question. Is French Toast really French? And if so, what do they call it in France? Basically just slices of bread soaked in eggs, milk, or cream, and pan-fried, this offers a great option for using up a less-than-fresh, hard crusty loaf. The dish dates back as far as fourth-century Rome, and was initially called German Toast until the First World War. So what do they call it in France? Pain Perdu, which translates into "Lost Bread." Figures.

PANETTONE FRENCH TOAST

Serves 3–4

3 eggs

½ cup milk

½ cup heavy cream

2 tablespoons honey (warm)

2 tablespoons Marsala wine

¼ teaspoon salt

Any spices you might like

Butter

Oil for pan-frying

8 (½") slices Italian panettone

1. Combine eggs with milk, cream, honey, wine, salt, and spices in a bowl and whisk together until smooth.

2. Heat sauté pan with about 2 tablespoon butter and a drizzle of oil over medium-high heat. Dip panettone slices one by one into egg mixture, 10 seconds on each side.

3. Sauté soaked panettone slices for 30–45 seconds on each side until golden. Serve with dollop of Perfect Chantilly Cream (Jan. 5) fortified with a splash of wine.

Lemon Cream Pie Day

Cream pies are classic diner fare. The next time you visit a diner, take a moment to admire all the different pie varieties behind the glass dessert case, just like puppies at the pound waiting for you to take them home. The only other cream pies that come to mind are the iconic clown props used in jokes. There's still nothing like a good pie in the face to make you giggle; ideally, this one would be aimed at your mouth!

LEMON THYME CREAM PIE

Serves 4–5

Pastry Cream (Feb. 20)

2 fresh lemon thyme sprigs

2 tablespoons fresh lemon juice

Graham Cracker Crust

Perfect Chantilly Cream (Jan. 5)

Fresh raspberries

Powdered sugar

Lemon thyme (optional garnish)

1. Prepare Pastry Cream, steeping milk with lemon thyme as well as vanilla. Strain thyme from mixture before cooking cream. Stir in lemon juice when finishing cream.

2. Cool cream and scoop into bottom of prepared Graham Cracker Crust.

3. Top with whipped cream, decorate with raspberries, sprinkle with powdered sugar, and garnish with lemon thyme.

Graham Cracker Crust

1½ cup graham crackers (crushed)

¼ cup sugar

⅛ cup unsalted butter (melted)

¼ teaspoon salt

1. To make crust simply combine all ingredients in a bowl and mix with your hands.

2. Press into pie pan for a cool crust.

Mousse Day

NOV. 30

Mousse in French means "lather" or "foam," the culinary ancestor to modern foams or "espumas" used today. Traditional mousses were made light and foamy by the addition and emulsification of whipped eggs and/or whipped cream. Modern mousses are sometimes made with the addition of dried proteins, gelling agents, and foamers. Mousses can be served savory or sweet and nowadays can even be served warm! Regardless, my favorites remain chocolate and raspberry; classics never die.

RASPBERRY MOUSSE

Serves 3–4

1 cup fresh or frozen raspberries plus ½ cup for decorating

⅛ cup sugar

Zest from ½ lemon

½ tablespoon unflavored gelatin

2 tablespoons cold water

2 cups whipped cream

Mint for garnish

❶ Combine berries with sugar and lemon zest and blend until smooth. In the meantime combine gelatin with 2 tablespoons cold water. Let stand for 2–3 minutes.

❷ Bring raspberry sauce to a boil for 1 minute, then mix in the gelatin and remove from heat. Allow mixture to cool in the fridge until lightly cool, then mix with the whipped cream. Pour into little ramekins and return to the fridge until set about 15 minutes. Serve with a little more whipped cream, some fresh raspberries, and a nice mint sprig as garnish.

DECEMBER

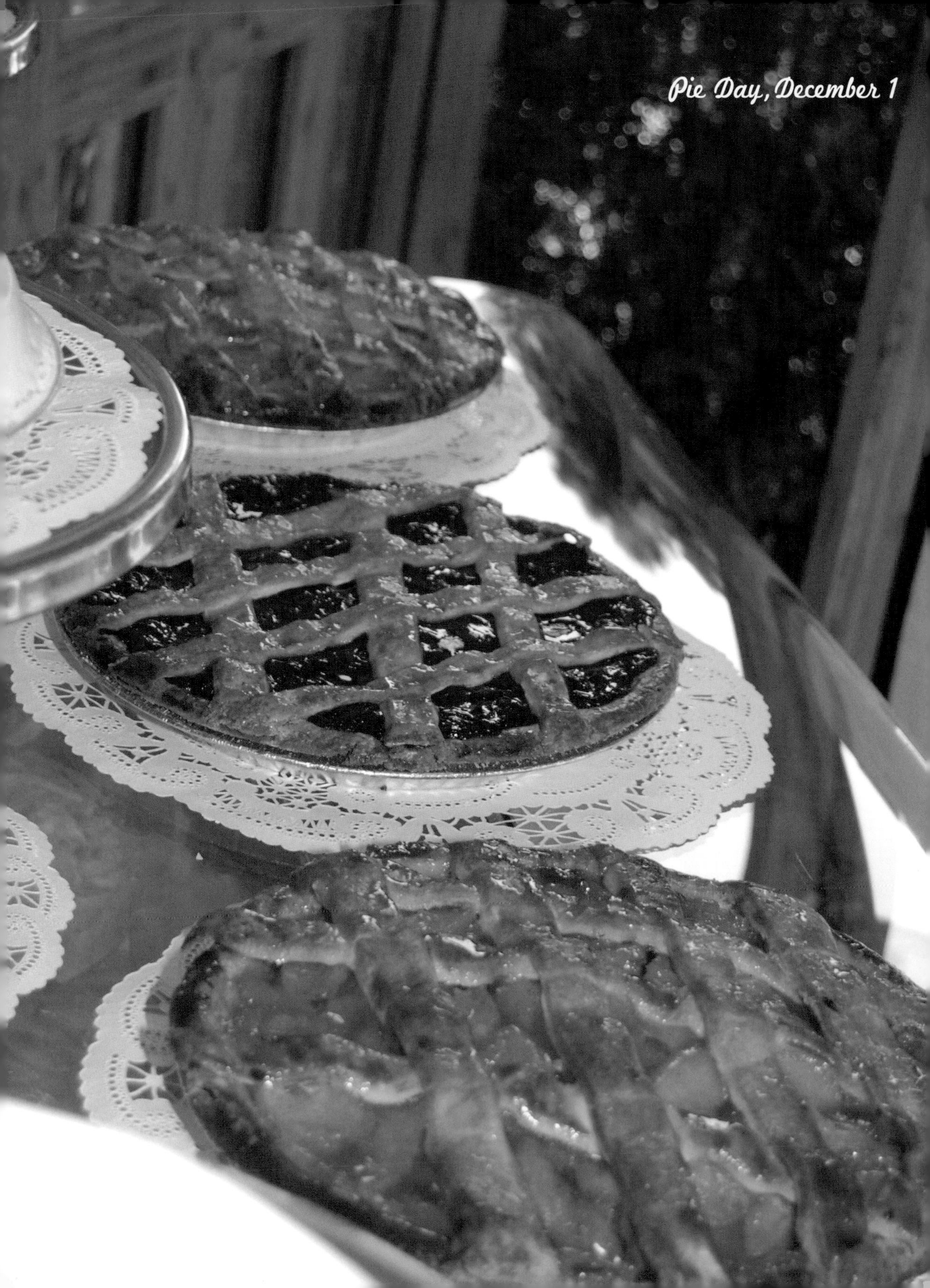
Pie Day, December 1

DEC. 1

Pie Day

My breath started to fog up the window and just for a second I thought of writing my message on the glass: "I want pie." Then I came to my senses and saw the girl behind the counter laughing and signaling for me to come inside. Too excited to feel embarrassed, I raced inside at the opportunity to have a free piece of pie in exchange for my ridiculous display of hunger. I think the girl understood from the drool hanging from my shirt that I was in dire need of a slice. I looked stupid, but what can I say? Pie has that effect on me.

PEAR-WALNUT PIE

Serves 6

Pie Dough (Apr. 28)

1½ pounds Bartlett pears (peeled and sliced ¼" thick)

1 tablespoon sugar

½ cup walnuts

1 egg (for wash)

1 Make dough for crust and allow it to rest. Then roll out and mold inside a pie pan.

2 Add pears in a cartwheel pattern and sprinkle with sugar. Add walnuts.

3 Brush edges of dough with water and top pie with another rolled out piece of dough. Trim, then crimp edges. Or, if you want to get fancy, use a leaf-shaped cookie cutter to cut out pieces of dough, brush edges and arrange them on top of pie leaving a little opening in the middle for steam to escape.

4 Brush pie with an egg wash (1 egg whisked with a little cold water) and bake at 350°F for 30–40 minutes until golden. Serve with Homemade Vanilla Ice Cream (July 23).

Fritters Day

DEC. 2

On a discreet street in Hoboken, New Jersey, there is a wonderful restaurant called Cucharamama. Amongst the thousand dishes that my family was tasting, a little nondescript plate arrived. Through the shadows and flickering of the candles I saw an indistinct silhouette of spiky little things that looked like tiny sea urchins. Unable to control myself, I grabbed hold of one of these crispy little nuggets and tossed it in the air. Crunch, crunch, crunch . . . wow. The chef and owner, Maricel Presilla, calls them chispas, which means sparks in Spanish, and they are shredded green plantains balled up and fried. So I thought of this little number to honor her spectacular little munchkins.

CHISPITAS

Serves 2–3

1 ripe plantain

1 green plantain

Oil for frying

Salt

1 Simple as can be! Grate plantains and combine.

2 Fry at 350°F until golden and crispy. Drain on paper towels and salt as soon as they come out of the oil.

Apple Pie Day

Apple Pies have not changed much over the years. Despite the fact that you can have open-faced pies, closed, or even latticed, they are all mostly composed of the same things: caramelized apples, a little sugar, with the optional cinnamon, and sometimes vanilla nestled in a crumbly crust and served warm with whipped cream or my favorite way—a la mode with a big scoop of vanilla ice cream.

APPLE PIE WITH DEVONSHIRE CREAM

Serves 6

Pie Dough (Apr. 28)

1½ pounds Granny Smith apples (cored, peeled, and sliced ¼" thick)

1 teaspoon cornstarch

2 tablespoon brown sugar

½ tablespoon cinnamon

1 egg (for wash)

❶ Make dough and allow to rest. Then roll out and mold inside a pie pan.

❷ Toss apple slices with cornstarch, sugar, and cinnamon in a bowl, then fill inside of prepared dough in a cartwheel pattern. Brush edges of dough with a little water and top pie with another rolled out piece of the dough and trim, then crimp the edges. Or if you want to get fancy, use a lattice dough cutter to cut out strips of the dough, brush the edges, and arrange them on top in the lattice pattern.

❸ Brush with an egg wash (1 egg whisked with a little cold water) and bake at 350°F for 30–40 minutes until golden. Serve with Whipped Devonshire cream.

Whipped Devonshire Cream

1 cup Devonshire cream (available at specialty food stores)

1 cup heavy cream

2 tablespoons granulated sugar

❶ Keeping creams cold, add sugar and whisk until stiff.

Cook's Note

I love this cream *way* better than just regular whipped cream. Try it on pancakes, waffles, and even ice cream!

Cookie Day

Cookies! Cookies! Cookies! What can be more fun to make, bake, decorate, eat, share, sell, and give than a big basket of cookies? There are thousands of different cookies throughout the world, and who can be surprised? They've existed as far back as any baking was done. Since sugar was not initially available, the first cookies were a little more like dried unsalted biscuits containing nuts and sometimes honey. The modern cookie, and for that matter the name itself, came along with those crafty Dutch and their "koekje," meaning "little cake."

CHOCOLATE CHIP COOKIES

Makes about 2 dozen

- ¾ cup butter (unsalted)
- 1 cup brown sugar
- ½ teaspoon salt
- ¾ cup all-purpose flour
- ½ teaspoon baking soda
- 1 large egg
- 2 cups instant oats
- 1 teaspoon vanilla extract
- 1 cup chopped bittersweet chocolate or chocolate chips
- Coarse salt (I like Fleur de Sel)

❶ Cream butter and sugar for about 8 minutes on high speed until butter is fluffy.

❷ Sift all dry ingredients.

❸ Slow mixer and add egg. Mix for 10 seconds, then add flour in 2 parts.

❹ Combine thoroughly then add oats, then vanilla and chocolate chips. Combine well for at least 10 seconds.

❺ Spoon mixture (if you have a small ice cream scoop of about 1–2 tablespoons, use it) about 1 tablespoon at a time leaving about 1" between each cookie.

❻ Sprinkle with coarse salt and bake at 350°F for 10–12 minutes (fewer for chewy cookies, more for crispy ones).

Sacher Torte Day

DEC. 5

The Sacher Torte is a dense chocolate cake invented by Franz Sacher in 1832. The story begins in Austria, when the prince was to have a gala at the castle. By a stroke of fate, the head chef mysteriously fell ill and the task to create something special fell on the then second-year apprentice, sixteen-year-old Franz Sacher. Years later, after moving back to his hometown in Vienna, Sacher's son Edward improved upon the recipe while working at the Demel bakery and developed it into what we know today as the Sacher Torte.

SACHER TORTE

Serves 6

- 1 pound butter (soft)
- 3 cups granulated sugar
- 4½ cups all-purpose flour
- 1½ tablespoons baking powder
- 6 eggs
- 1½ cup buttermilk
- ½ teaspoon salt
- 1 teaspoon vanilla
- Apricot jam
- Perfect Chantilly Cream (Jan. 5)

❶ Cream butter with sugar on high speed for about 8 minutes.

❷ Sift flour and baking powder. Break all eggs into a bowl and add buttermilk. Add remaining ingredients (except jam and whipped cream) to whipped butter, alternating between eggs and flour, incorporating well between additions.

3. Spray a pan with nonstick spray and coat with flour. Bake at 350°F for 40 minutes or until a knife inserted in the middle comes out clean.

4. Let the torte cool. Using serrated knife, slice the cake in half and spread the middle with the jam. Top the cake with the other half and glaze over a cooling rack with the chocolate glaze. Serve with dried apricots and whipped cream.

CHOCOLATE GLAZE

1½ cups sugar

¾ cup water

6 ounces bittersweet chocolate, coarsely chopped

1. Combine sugar and water in a pot and boil for 5 minutes. Pour over the chopped chocolate and stir until dissolved. Return to pot and cook over medium heat for 1 minute. Then use right away.

Gazpacho Day

C'mon, say it with me: guh-spah-choh! Doesn't it sound exotic? As a matter of fact, it is. It comes from La Madre España, Spain. The gazpacho traces its roots to the Arabs. When they conquered Spain they brought along the soup, which was quickly adapted into the Andalusian diet. Today the word gazpacho has expanded to basically mean any chilled soup and is often made with avocadoes, watermelon, and even summer fruits!

WHITE GAZPACHO

Serves 4

⅛ cup almonds

5 slices crusty country sourdough bread, lightly toasted

2–3 cups water

2 tablespoon Greek yogurt

2 tablespoon olive oil

Salt and pepper

White grapes

Dill

Cucumber, sliced

1. Toast nuts at 350°F for 10 minutes. Soak bread in water. Place nuts in a blender, add ½ the water slowly and blend for 1 minute on high. Add the bread, yogurt, and olive oil. Season with salt and pepper, cover and chill.

2. Serve with sliced grapes, little dill sprigs, sliced cucumber, and a drizzle of olive oil.

Cotton Candy Day

DEC. 7

I got my first cotton candy machine about ten years ago so I could give free cotton candy away to our diners. Except instead of using the store bought flavors, we added mint powder, raspberry powder, cocoa powder, and other flavorings to make the fluff monsters taste amazing.

COTTON CANDY MARGARITAS

Makes 1 colorful drink!

Big handful of cotton candy

1 ounce fresh lime juice

Ice

2 ounces silver tequila

1. Set your table up with a few margarita glasses and fill each with a big cloud of your favorite cotton candy.

2. Then, when ready for the showstopper, combine fresh lime in a shaker with ice and tequila. Shake vigorously for 10 seconds and pour the drink right in front of your guests into the glass with the cotton candy.

DEC. 8 Chocolate Brownie Day

Brownies are America's greatest contribution to the pastry world. Why? Take a cake and condense it, but keep it fudgy, and soft, with little tiny caves of molten chocolate, maybe a few nuts for a bit of crunch . . . . Now, doesn't that sound good? The chocolate brownies we know today actually started as blondies. The first recipes for brownie-like goodies were molasses-based, and can be traced back to honey cakes. It wasn't until the 1900s that brownies took their rightful form as America's favorite chocolate dessert.

BROWNIES

Makes a dozen

- ½ cup unsalted butter
- ½ cup granulated sugar
- ½ cup brown sugar
- 2 eggs
- ⅓ cup unsweetened cocoa powder
- ½ cup all-purpose flour
- ¼ teaspoon salt
- ¼ teaspoon baking powder
- 1 teaspoon vanilla extract
- ½ cup semisweet chocolate chips

1. Melt butter in a sauce pan. Then beat in sugars and eggs. Sift the remaining dry ingredients into sugar-butter mixture and incorporate, whisking thoroughly. Finish by adding vanilla and chocolate chips.

2. Spread into a greased 8" pan and bake at 350°F for 25 minutes.

3. Allow to cool slightly and serve with a big, cold glass of milk!

Pastry Day

Pastries can be traced back to the Mediterranean inching toward the Middle East—there is evidence Egyptians ate pastries—and normally consisted of phyllo dough, thin layers of pastry, layered with nuts and honey. The crusaders brought it back to Europe, then the Renaissance came and chefs transformed the simple pastries into extravagant works of art. Today pastries are widely available in supermarkets across America and in small bakeries. Thanks to our understanding of the chemical requirements to make great pastries, we can now make wonderfully sweet goodies easily at home. I guess practice does make perfect.

RASPBERRY CARAMEL NAPOLEONS

Serves 4

1 gelatin sheet

1 quart heavy cream

½ cup white chocolate

½ cup sugar

1 sheet from 14-ounce package puff pastry, baked into 2½" circles and cooled

2 cups fresh raspberries

½ cup raspberry jam

Coarse salt

① Soak gelatin in cold water.

② Bring cream to a boil, then cover it and set to the side.

③ Melt white chocolate slowly in the microwave.

④ Pour sugar into a heavy-bottomed 4-quart pot, and over high heat melt sugar, stirring slowly with a wooden spoon. While sugar melts, break up clumps with spoon and continue cooking. Once all the sugar has melted, bring the white chocolate close to you and take the lid off of the pot with the cream. This process must be done quickly.

⑤ Continue cooking the sugar until you start to see a little smoke, then wait 10 seconds until it starts to smoke more. If you get a little scared and it starts to smell like burned sugar, don't fear, just turn off heat, add melted white chocolate, and stir until it is dissolved, about 5 seconds, then start to drizzle the heavy cream about 2 tablespoons at a time (be careful, this will bubble and boil furiously; if you add too much cream too fast the cream will boil over). Switch over to a whisk and turn the heat to medium. Continue whisking slowly until all caramel has melted and completely incorporated into cream.

⑥ Squeeze all water out of gelatin and add it to cream, then whisk until dissolved. Strain mixture and chill overnight. The next day, whisk about 2 cups of caramel carefully until fluffy.

⑦ Line edges of the puff pastry "cookies" with raspberries then drizzle raspberry jam around the inside edge of the raspberries, and fill middle with caramel. Sprinkle with coarse salt, then top with a little more salt.

Lager Day

Legend is that beer is actually the reason sailors decided to land on Plymouth Rock. The crew took stock of the beer they had left, and running low, decided that it was better to let the passengers off than to keep them on board and share their dwindling stock. Fast track to today when we use over 15 percent of the world's rice to make beer. But what is beer precisely? Beer is a simple fermented beverage composed of water, brewers yeast, a starch source—such as malted barley, wheat, millet, sorghum, cassava, potato, rice or agave—and sometimes flavoring. The most common flavoring nowadays is hops as it adds a distinctive bitterness and preserves the beers freshness, but before hops beer was normally flavored with roots, herbs, and sometimes honey.

BEER CHEESE

Serves 4

1½ cups beer

8 ounces Monterey jack cheese (shredded)

¼ teaspoon onion powder

¼ teaspoon garlic powder

1 teaspoon hot sauce

❶ Boil beer and pour it into a food processor or blender, then add a little cheese at a time on medium speed until it's a smooth sauce.

❷ Add spices and hot sauce and blend for about 2 minutes on high until thoroughly smooth.

Noodle Ring Day

Think noodle casserole cooked in a ring mold then inverted onto a plate, perhaps fill the middle with some sort of stew or chowder, and then you have a noodle ring. I found a recipe in a book called The American Woman's Cookbook, published in 1848 by the Culinary Arts Institute. These rings were very popular, and there are many recipes ranging from creamed proteins to mixing the noodles with grits and filling with creamed chicken.

NOODLE RING PARMESAN

Serves 6

1 pound noodles

2 eggs

2 cups ricotta cheese

2 cups mozzarella, shredded

¼ cup parsley

2 cups Simple Pasta Sauce (Jan. 4)

❶ Cook the noodles until they are a little less cooked than al dente, drain, and toss in a bowl with the eggs, ricotta, 1 cup mozzarella, half the parsley, and 1 cup sauce.

❷ Grease a ring mold and stuff the pasta inside.

❸ Cook at 400°F for 20 minutes.

❹ Flip onto a plate and top with the remaining pasta sauce and shredded cheese.

❺ Return to the oven until melted and garnish with the remaining chopped parsley.

DEC. 12 — Cocoa Day

The snowflakes fell slowly, each one as big as popcorn kernels, and I sat there wishing they would bounce like them, too. In anticipation I jumped up a little until I just couldn't wait anymore and ran out. Luckily the wind had blown the snow into little mounds that let me build a small but lively snowman. The thing was, I was never one to withstand the cold, and due to my overeagerness to slide around, I always managed to flip and turn into the snow in such ways that snow always stuffed itself down my socks and proceeded to melt and freeze my toes into submission. Besides, I was craving what we all crave after playing in the snow, a nice cup of hot cocoa, one for me and a couple for my siblings.

YUMMY HOT COCOA

Serves 2–3

3 cups milk

1 cup water

½ cup sugar

9 ounces bittersweet chocolate (about 1¼ cups)

Pinch of salt

❶ Bring milk, water, and sugar to a boil.

❷ Add chocolate and whisk on medium heat for 2 minutes.

❸ Remove from the heat, add salt, and blend for 1 minute.

❹ Serve. Its always fun to top hot chocolate with whipped cream (Jan. 5), but try a little cinnamon on top for an extra hint of spice.

Ice Cream and Violins Day — DEC. 13

A violin is a beautifully stringed instrument with four strings tuned to perfect fifths. It is very popular in classical music and indispensable when you want to achieve that "romantic" and regal sound. Now combine that with a little ice cream and you truly have a work of art. So go ahead, turn out the lights, serve yourself a bowl, light some candles, and play my favorite song of all time: J.S. Bach's Air on the G String.

CHAI ICE CREAM

Serves 3–4

1½ cups heavy cream (divided, 1 cup and 1 cup)

1½ cups milk

12 whole allspice

5 whole black peppercorns

4 cardamom pods, opened to seeds

3 cinnamon sticks

2 whole star anise

11 whole cloves

¾ cup sugar

6 egg yolks

Pinch of salt

¼ cup black tea

❶ Bring cream and milk with spices to a boil. Once cream boils, cover and steep for at least half an hour. Strain spices and bring back to a boil over medium heat.

❷ In the meantime, combine sugar and egg yolks and give them a good whisk. Temper eggs by adding a little cream at a time while whisking.

3. Once you have combined about 2 cups of cream into egg mixture, return to pot and cook on low heat while scraping bottom of the pan until you reach 170°F.

4. Remove from heat and strain with a fine strainer. Allow mixture to cool in the refrigerator or in an ice bath if you can.

5. When mixture is cool, add salt and tea, then freeze according to your ice cream machine's instructions.

Bouillabaisse Day

Traditionally every port or seaside community has some sort of fisherman's stew consisting of the seasonal bounty of the sea. In New England you have creamy chowder, in Italy bright red cioppino is the stew of choice, in Brazil its all about Moqueca, Caldeirada is what the Portuguese love, down South its all about Gumbo, but Bouillabaisse—originating from the port city of Marseille—well, that's the mother of all stews. What sets this magnificent stew apart is the intoxicating flavors of fennel and saffron. Serve it big, serve it in a group, and most of all serve it with crispy, crusty country bread to sop up all those wonderful juices.

Cook's Note

Sofito is a great base for lots of Spanish food—it's a mixture of onions, tomatoes, and peppers that are cooked until soft. You can make it yourself, but if you're pressed for time look for it in the Spanish section of your local supermarket.

BOUILLABAISSE

Serves 4–5

½ pound large shrimp

½ pound scallops

10 clams

10 mussels

2 small crabs

2 small lobsters (split into bite-sized pieces)

Garlic powder

Onion powder

Paprika

Cayenne pepper

Salt and pepper

Olive oil

2 cups vegetable stock

1 teaspoon saffron

1 medium Spanish onion

2 garlic cloves

2 tablespoons sofrito

2 cups whole tomatoes in sauce

2 cups white wine

½ cup cognac

Bay leaf

1 cup heavy cream

3 medium calamari (cut in rings)

1. Good things take time, as is so with this stew. Start by making the base for your soup. Shell and devein shrimp (save the shells!) and clean seafood. Season all the seafood with the spices.

2. In a 2-quart pot drizzle 2 tablespoons olive oil and sauté the shrimp over high heat on each side for 30 seconds, then set them in a bowl. Cook scallops for 1 minute and scoop them into the bowl with the shrimp.

3 Add in clams and mussels with ½ cup of vegetable stock, cover and cook until they are all open (about 2–3 minutes). Remove shellfish and add to shrimp bowl.

4 Add shrimp shells along with remaining vegetable stock and saffron to pot. Lower heat to a simmer and cook until you have 1 cup of liquid.

5 In the meantime, grab another pot about 4 quarts in size and set it on stove over medium heat.

6 Clean onion and slice it in half then into ¼" slices. Sauté onions over low heat for 10 minutes stirring often until translucent. Slice garlic thinly and add to onions. Cook until translucent. Add sofrito and tomatoes with the sauce, crushing them in your hand, then add wine with cognac and bay leaf, and cook for 20 minutes barely simmering until you have about 1½–2 cups left.

7 I like my bisque smooth so I like to blend the sauce at this point using a hand blender, but it works just fine in a regular blender.

8 Return sauce to pot, add cream and strain shrimp stock in. Return all seafood to pot and bring to a rapid boil over high heat.

9 Finish by seasoning cleaned and cut calamari and adding to pot. Cook over high heat for 1 minute and you're done!

10 Serve with toasted country bread and rouille as a spread for bread.

ROUILLE

4 large garlic cloves

1 teaspoons kosher salt

1½ tablespoons freshly squeezed lemon juice

Zest of 1 lemon

½ teaspoon saffron threads

¼ teaspoon crushed red pepper flakes

2 tablespoons good olive oil

fresh black pepper

1 tablespoon parsley leaves

1 Purée all ingredients in a blender until smooth. Keep cold.

Cupcake Day

The Great American Bake Sale, since its inception in 2003, has gathered more than 1.7 million people to communally make sure no child grows up hungry in America. It is a simple activity that with your involvement can teach your children to be humanitarians and lend a hand in making the world a better place. So this year, set up a bake sale in your community and join us in the Great American Bake Sale.

ICE CREAM CUPCAKES

Makes 1 dozen

½ gallon chocolate ice cream

1 cup dark chocolate (melted)

1 loaf chocolate pound cake

10 crushed chocolate cookies

1. Take ice cream out of freezer and allow it to soften.

2. In the meantime, melt all chocolate except 1 tablespoon in microwave in 30-second intervals, making sure to stop and stir until smooth and hot.

3. Add remaining chocolate and stir until all dissolved (do not put back in the microwave, let the last bits melt slowly).

4. Line up cupcake papers on a cookie sheet and spray lightly with nonstick spray (don't use flour).

5. Brush inside of cups with melted chocolate, using a pastry brush. Once they are all coated, place in freezer until hard. Take them out and repeat the process.

6. Slice your pound cake in ½" slices and lay them all side by side.

7. With a round cookie cutter (a little smaller than the size of the inside diameter of your cupcake papers), cut out little cake disks.

8. Spoon one tablespoon of softened ice cream into cups lined with hard chocolate. Take back of the spoon and slather ice cream on sides of the cups, creating a well. Place first round of cake disks in center and push down. Add another spoonful of ice cream, and repeat process, alternating cake and ice cream until you reach the top. Freeze until hard.

9. While cupcakes are freezing, make chocolate frosting. Put it in a piping bag with a large star tip. (You might need to soften the frosting a bit by stirring it a few times). Pipe little rosettes on top of the cupcakes.

10. Sprinkle cookie crumbs and serve. You can store these cakes for up to a week, but they are best served right away. Enjoy!

Chocolate Frosting

11 ounces dark chocolate

2 cups unsalted butter (softened)

3 tablespoon whole milk

1 teaspoon vanilla extract

Pinch of salt

Pinch of ground cinnamon

3 cups powdered sugar (sifted)

1. Melt chocolate in a microwave slowly, about 30 seconds at a time, stirring between turns.

2. In a large mixing bowl, beat butter with an electric mixer until light and creamy.

3. Add milk and vanilla slowly; beat until smooth.

4. Add melted chocolate and beat well for about 3 minutes. Add salt and cinnamon.

5. Add sugar slowly and beat on low until completely incorporated and homogeneous. Set aside at room temp.

Chocolate-Covered Anything Day

Of course you can cover anything in chocolate! From savory to sweet, hot to cold, the proper chocolate can accentuate many foods and add a hint of luxuriousness to your favorite recipes. A hint of white chocolate in a gazpacho, bittersweet chocolate on barbecue ribs, cocoa powder in tomato sauce—if you can think of chocolate more like a spice and less like a dessert food, you can really learn to use the subtle notes of chocolate in everyday foods.

CHOCOLATE-COVERED FROZEN BANANAS

Serves 5

5 bananas

2 cups bittersweet chocolate (melted and tempered)

3 cups peanuts or cashews (toasted, cooled, and coarsely chopped)

1 Chop bananas and stick popsicle sticks in them and freeze.

2 Melt and temper chocolate and put in a deep bowl and insert a spoon on side to help you dip. Now set a plate on the side with the nuts. Remove 1 banana at a time from the freezer and dip in chocolate using spoon to help you coat completely, then roll in nuts and set on a clean plate, then place plate in freezer. Repeat process with remaining bananas.

Maple Syrup Day

Native Americans discovered that during the winter maple trees would store starches that were converted into sugary sap to nourish the tree. By tapping the tree, they were able to allow the tree to secrete this sap, removing it and using it to sweeten their foods, making maple the first natural sweetener in America, long before sugarcane sugar.

SPICY MAPLE WINGS

Serves 4

1 package chicken wings (about 20)

1 tablespoon salt

1 tablespoon freshly ground pepper

1 tablespoon onion powder

½ tablespoon garlic powder

½ tablespoon chili powder

¼ cup olive or vegetable oil

1 tablespoon pure maple syrup

2 tablespoon Dijon mustard

1 tablespoon chipotle hot sauce (from the can)

½ tablespoon hot sauce

1 Cut wings into drummets and wingettes. Toss together with spices, add the oil, and toss again. Place on a baking pan lined with a sheet of aluminum foil.

2 Cook wings for 15–20 minutes at 500°F, turning once or twice until golden brown.

3 Combine maple syrup, Dijon mustard, and hot sauces and pour into a bowl.

4 Add wings to bowl, toss, and serve.

Roast Suckling Pig Day

I think its perhaps a primal urge—the raw force of a crackling fire, a whole animal, the tinge of the smoke, the beautiful simplicity of it all—that makes man want to cook whole pigs over a roaring fire. But let's clarify what a suckling pig is exactly. According to the Oxford English Dictionary, a suckling pig is a young pig between two and six weeks old that has only fed on its mothers milk. Due to the feed and its relative age, it tends to be a milder tasting animal full of collagen and gelatin, which makes it wonderful for whole roasting.

ROAST SUCKLING PIG

Serves 6–8

1 10–15 pound suckling pig that fits in your oven

2 cups honey

Brine

10 quarts water

5 cups kosher salt

4½ cups brown sugar

½ cup garlic cloves (crushed)

½ cup vegetable oil, for basting

1 Combine all ingredients and brine pig in a cooler or large garbage bag overnight.

2 When ready to cook, stuff pig with aluminum foil balls to help conduct the heat and prevent it from caving in when roasting. Place pig on all fours and pull the back legs forward and the front legs back under the body. Use as much aluminum as you need to make the pig sit right. Pat skin dry and rub with a little oil.

3 Roast at 250°F for about 3 hours until the internal temperature reaches 125°F.

4 Remove foil, baste with oil and honey, pump the oven up to 400°F

5 Cover ears and snout with foil and cook for 45 minutes basting every 15 minutes until the pig reaches 160°F in a thick part.

Hard Candy Day

When you think about it, it's almost magical the wonderful things one can do with a little sugar, coloring, and a little know-how. Candy has been made for thousands of years and was very popular in medicine because it tends to dissolve slowly. Candy ranges from soft and gummy to slimy and syrupy, creamy soft, creamy semihard, and the topic of the day, hard. Hard candy is older candy. It takes its time. It allows you to ponder and think. It teaches you patience. Unless you're the candy around the tootsie pop, and then it teaches you to stay the hell out of the way of chewy candy, or you see what happens.

HARD CANDY

Makes about 2 dozen candies

3¾ cups granulated sugar

1½ cups light corn syrup

1 cup water

3 drops vinegar

1 tablespoon flavored extract

Food coloring

① Combine all ingredients except vinegar, flavoring, and coloring, and cook on medium until candy boils.

② Boil candy to 300°F, turn off heat, and add vinegar, flavoring, and coloring. Give it a good stir then dip bottom of pot into warm water (this will stop sugar from cooking further).

③ Pour sugar into candy molds or pour into heat-proof pan to harden.

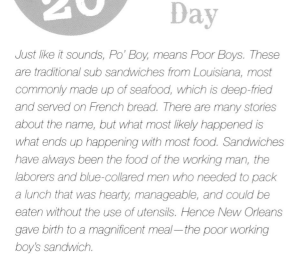

DEC. 20
Fried Shrimp Day

Just like it sounds, Po' Boy, means Poor Boys. These are traditional sub sandwiches from Louisiana, most commonly made up of seafood, which is deep-fried and served on French bread. There are many stories about the name, but what most likely happened is what ends up happening with most food. Sandwiches have always been the food of the working man, the laborers and blue-collared men who needed to pack a lunch that was hearty, manageable, and could be eaten without the use of utensils. Hence New Orleans gave birth to a magnificent meal—the poor working boy's sandwich.

SHRIMP & CHIPOTLE PO' BOY

Serves 2

Old Bay seasoning

2 cups flour

15 medium-sized shrimp (peeled, and deveined)

2 eggs (lightly beaten)

Oil for frying

French baguettes

Shredded lettuce

Sliced ripe tomatoes

Lemon wedges for garnish

① Add a little Old Bay to flour and whisk together. Dredge shrimp in flour, toss in egg mixture, then toss in flour again. Shake off excess.

② Fry in 350°F oil until golden. Remove from oil, drain on paper towels, and shake some Old Bay seasoning on top.

③ Slice bread and lightly toast in the oven, then open it up and spread about 1–2 tablespoons of the Chipotle Mayo on both sides, fill with the lettuce and tomato slices, top with fried shrimp, and serve with a few lemon wedges on the side.

CHIPOTLE MAYO

4 tablespoons mayonnaise

2 tablespoons sour cream

2 chipotles in sauce

① Combine all ingredients and blend until smooth.

Hamburger Day

Google "burger" and you will get over 41 million hits. Are we really that obsessed with the almighty burger? I know I am. Steak tartare was a popular dish in Europe as early as the twelfth century. As meat got a little older, people started cooking it. In the 1800s commercial meat grinders were starting to be used, and that's really what gave rise to the great American burger. Then in NYC to attract German customers, restaurants started serving steak in the style of Hamburg, which was America's introduction to the popular term. So yes my friends, "hamburger" simply means steak made in the style of Hamburg.

① Burgers are all about proportion. The right amount of fat to meat (70/30), a good amount of crust, and a juicy rare center (that's how I like it), which will lead us to technique. Toss meat together lightly with the salt, pepper, and liquid smoke. Cook a little piece and see if it's good, then proceed.

② Heat a sauté pan over high heat to super scorching. Open a window, turn on the hood fan, and set the fan near an open window.

③ Grab a ball of meat about 2½" thick. Flatten it a little and form it so you have smooth sides. Once the pan is screaming hot, place patty in and press it down slowly and lightly (I find that a 10-ounce can of chicken stock is just the right weight).

④ Cook on high heat for about 1 minute, then flip it. Cook for another minute and continue to do this until you have a nice crust on both sides. (According to noted food scientist Harold McGee, by flipping the burger repeatedly, the juices get evenly distributed, which cooks the burger more evenly and faster. I tested this and it's absolutely true.)

⑤ Remove the patty and rest it on its thin side for at least 30 seconds. (When you rest the patty on its flat side, the bottom side becomes soggy as some of the fat and juices run out. By resting it on its thin side, both flat sides remain dry and crispy. Cool, huh?)

⑥ Season with salt and serve on a lightly toasted potato roll with your favorite sauces, fresh lettuce, ripe tomato slices, and pickles. I LOVE my burgers with a handful of crushed potato chips inside—the crunch is incredible.

SIMPLE BURGERS

Makes 5–6 mouthwatering burgers

1 pound chuck steak (double ground through a fine meat grinder and always kept cold)

1 pound brisket (double ground through a fine meat grinder and always kept cold)

2 tablespoons salt

1 teaspoon black pepper

Couple of dashes of good quality liquid smoke (try Deep South Natural Hickory or Mesquite)

Cook's Tip

I LOVE my burgers on the grill, but I also like a nice crust on my meat from the griddle. So what's one to do? The reason I love open grill burgers is the smoky flavor the charcoal or wood lends to the meat. There's something very primal about fire and smoke with meat. By adding a little liquid smoke you impart that smokiness to the burger, just don't overdo it!

Date Nut Bread Day

I never met James Beard, but I think we could have been friends. I've been to his house many times, and walked by many more. It used to be a place of solace where I would reflect and think about cooking, and life. I started reading his books recently, and though his food is pretty cool, it is his spirit that I love. To me he is the Zen Buddha of the food world: wise, generous, and funny as hell! Anyway, I found one of his recipes and made it. With a couple of my own modifications, it gave way to this recipe. This is for you, my friend.

JIM'S BREAD

Serves 4–5

½ cup butter (soft)

½ teaspoon salt

1 cup brown sugar

2 cups flour (sifted)

1 teaspoon baking soda

½ teaspoon baking powder

2 eggs

1 cup bananas, puréed (about 2 ripe)

3 tablespoons buttermilk

½ cup dates (chopped)

½ cup walnuts (chopped)

1 Cream butter with salt and sugar for 4 minutes until fluffy. In the meantime sift flour with baking powder and baking soda.

2 Add eggs to butter and mix, then add a little of the flour mixture to smooth out.

3 Add bananas and mix well.

4 Alternate adding buttermilk and flour until you have a smooth batter.

5 Add dates and nuts, mix well, and pour into a buttered and floured loaf pan.

6 Bake at 350°F for 30–40 minutes until a knife inserted in the middle comes out clean. If the top starts to get too brown, simply cover with foil and continue baking.

7 Allow to cool, cut, and serve.

Pfeffer-nuesse Day

DEC. 23

The story of Santa Claus starts with holy St. Nicholas, because it was his custom to give little gifts to children. In his honor you have Sinterklaas, which is celebrated on the fifth or sixth of Dec. every year, depending where you are. Pfeffernuesse is a traditional cookie made for this festival—and enjoyed throughout the Christmas season. In German, Danish, and Dutch, pfeffernuesse translates into pepper nuts and are named such because it is made up of nuts with a bit of spice.

PFEFFERNUESSE

Makes about 2 dozen nuggets

⅛ cup butter

⅛ cup shortening

½ cup granulated sugar

⅛ cup brown sugar

¼ teaspoon salt

2 cups all-purpose flour

¾ teaspoon baking soda

½ teaspoon ground cardamom

½ teaspoon ground nutmeg

½ teaspoon ground cloves

½ teaspoon ground ginger

1 teaspoon ground cinnamon

½ teaspoon allspice

½ teaspoon ground black pepper

½ teaspoon ground white pepper

1 egg

⅛ cup honey

¼ cup molasses

1 cup confectioners sugar

❶ Whip butter and shortening with sugar and salt until fluffy. Sift flour with baking soda and spices. Add egg, honey, and molasses to butter mixture and combine well. Follow up with flour and spice mixture and combine well.

❷ Form dough into a log, wrap it in plastic wrap, and refrigerate for at least an hour or overnight if you can.

❸ Preheat oven to 325°F and roll out ¾" balls and plop them on a parchment-paper-lined cookie sheet. Using your thumb, press down slightly and bake for 10–15 minutes. Remove and immediately but gently place them in powdered sugar and roll around. Cool, then roll them in sugar again and serve.

Eggnog Day

DEC. 24

Ponche crema. Kogel mogel. Su~a hô.t gà. Advocaat. Zabaglione. Coquito. Eierpunsch. Rompope. Cola de mono tamagozake. No, I'm not talking gibberish here. I'm simply trying to covey the love the world has for eggnog. All of the above mentioned drinks are egg based, enriched with cream or milk, always spiked with some sort of liquor, and often jolted with a bit of spice. Traditionally, Eggnog is a holiday drink, mostly served in a self-serve punchbowl to entertain guests. But the name? Well, lore tells us that it's a simple evolution from "Egg and Grog" the latter a colonial term for rum.

CHOCOLATE EGGNOG

Serves 4

3 cups milk

1 can condensed milk

1 cup heavy cream

2 vanilla beans

5 yolks

¼ teaspoon freshly ground cinnamon

¼ teaspoon freshly ground nutmeg

1 cup bittersweet chocolate

1 cup rum

❶ Combine all milks and cream with vanilla beans (split and scraped) and bring to a boil.

❷ Combine eggs and spices, then temper by adding hot cream a little at a time. Return to stove and cook on low heat until thick and creamy. Remove from heat, add chocolate, and stir until melted. Strain and chill rapidly.

❸ Add rum and serve, top with chocolate shavings.

Pumpkin Pie Day

Pumpkin pie. Soft and creamy nestled in a flaky crust, just a hint of salt, and sparkling with different notes from the spices that are sprinkled throughout. Served cold or warm with a dollop of cold and smooth whipped cream, that's really all you need sometimes. Traditionally served during pumpkin harvest time, which just happens to coincide with Halloween and Thanksgiving. Sometimes things just line up right.

PUMPKIN PIE

Serves 6

1¼ cups pumpkin purée (canned)

¼ cup light brown sugar

¼ teaspoon salt

1 teaspoon all-purpose flour

2 eggs

1 cup condensed milk

3 tablespoons milk or heavy cream

½ teaspoon vanilla extract

¼ teaspoon ground ginger

1 teaspoon ground cinnamon

Pie Dough (Apr. 28)

❶ Purée all ingredients in a blender (except pie shell), pour into pie shell, and bake at 400°F for 15 minutes, then lower the heat to 350°F and continue to cook for an additional 30 minutes or until set.

❷ Remove from oven, allow it to cool, then serve it up!

Candy Cane Day

Candy was being made throughout Europe in the seventeenth century. At the time they were simple white candy sticks. Then lore tells us that a choirmaster one day bent the sticks and started giving them to children to represent God the Shepard. Nobody really seems to know why, but it wasn't until the twentieth century that candy canes started appearing with the red striping, which coincidentally is when the candy cane got its peppermint flavor. Coincidence? Hmm . . . I smell a great candy cane conspiracy.

CANDY CANE COOKIES

Makes about 2 dozen cookies

1 cup butter (unsalted and soft)

1 cup sugar (brown or white)

3 cups flour

1 teaspoon baking soda

2 large eggs

1 teaspoons pure vanilla extract

Zest of 1 lemon

White chocolate (melted and tempered)

Candy canes (crushed)

❶ Cream butter and sugar until fluffy.

❷ Sift dry ingredients and add them to butter mixture along with eggs, then finish with vanilla and lemon zest.

❸ Wrap dough into a block and refrigerate for at least 2 hours.

❹ Roll out dough to ¼" thickness on a clean, well-floured table and cut into candy cane shapes using a cookie cutter.

⑤ Lay cookies on parchment paper and bake at 350°F for about 8 minutes.

⑥ Dip cookies into white chocolate or lightly brush them, then sprinkle with crushed candy canes.

⑦ Place cookies in freezer for 10 minutes to harden chocolate, then remove and keep in a sealed container at room temperature so the candy doesn't melt.

Cook's Note

You can also make these with dark or even milk chocolate!

DEC. 27 Fruitcake Day

Thump! went the package as the mailman dropped it on my porch smiling. "Sign here please," he said. Perplexed, and freezing, I took the package and analyzed it, hoping it wasn't some sort of holiday joke. I held the package and it felt alarmingly heavy and dense, then, against my will, I did what most people in my profession and most dogs tend to do when encountering a foreign object. Sniff. Sniff. Sniiif . . . hmmm . . . cinnamon, vanilla, cloves, allspice, ginger. I felt my fear just melt away. I smiled back at the mailman and signed. This recipe will change your perception of fruitcake. Just think of a warm, buttery, and crumbly fruitcake rich in spice and molasses. Yum!

FRUITCAKE CUPCAKES

Makes 1 dozen cupcakes

¼ cup butter

½ cup brown sugar

¼ teaspoon salt

1 cup all-purpose flour

¼ teaspoon cinnamon

¼ teaspoon nutmeg

⅛ teaspoon cloves

¼ teaspoon ginger

½ teaspoon baking soda

¼ teaspoon baking powder

3 tablespoons buttermilk

1 banana

1 egg

1 teaspoon vanilla

2 tablespoon molasses

1 cup of each dried apricots chopped, raisins, and cranberries

1 cup nuts (I like pecans and walnuts coarsely chopped)

Grand Marnier or orange rum

① Cream butter with sugar and salt. Sift dry ingredients.

② Blend buttermilk with banana until smooth and set aside. Add egg to butter mixture and combine well (it will separate and look weird, don't worry). Alternate adding flour and buttermilk until batter is smooth. Add vanilla and molasses, mix, follow with fruit and nuts and mix again until smooth.

③ Spray cupcake or muffin tin with nonstick spray and dust with flour. Shake the excess off and fill the tins all the way up, then bake at 350°F for 15 minutes until a knife inserted in the middle comes out clean.

4 As soon as they come out, use a toothpick to poke little holes on the top of fruitcakes, and glaze with about ½ teaspoon of the orange liqueur. Allow to cool and wrap in plastic.

DEC. 28 Chocolate Candy Day

Chocolate making is a wonderful and delicious art. It is a medium that is easily explored since the rules are simple; once mastered, the sky's the limit. Not to mention that chocolate is friggin' delicious, makes all your worries melt away, is good for your health, and heals mind, body, and soul! My friend Mehdi of Chellaoui Chocolates is lucky enough to have a zeal for working with chocolates. He makes the most amazing little morsels. I reached out to him when I heard about Chocolate Candy Day, and knowing my passion for, um, passion fruit, this is what he sent me.

PASSION FRUIT TRUFFLES

Makes about 2 dozen

½ cup heavy cream

1 tablespoon honey

12 ounces bittersweet chocolate (finely chopped)

3 tablespoons unsalted butter

¼ cup passion fruit purée

Coarse salt (Fleur de Sel is my choice)

½ cup Dutch process cocoa powder for coating truffles

1 In a heavy pot, bring cream and honey to a boil. Pour boiled cream into chocolate and let stand for 1 minute. Whisk thoroughly then add the butter, and once dissolved, the passion fruit purée, and whisk again. Pour everything into a baking dish so that the mixture is at least 1" deep. Refrigerate for 1 hour until firm.

2 Using a melon baller, scoop out as many balls as you can, working fast and somewhere cool. Sprinkle the balls with a little salt and refrigerate for at least 30 minutes to 1 hour.

3 Melt and temper the chocolate, and set up another baking dish with cocoa powder. One by one, drop the truffles into the chocolate, roll it around, then toss it in the cocoa powder. (This works much better with two people.) Have the second person use two forks to toss the chocolates around coating them completely in the cocoa powder. Repeat the process with all the truffles and refrigerate for at least 30 minutes.

Pepper Pot Day DEC. 29

The most incredible stews in the world are not made with the best ingredients available. As a matter of fact, the main reason stews, soups, chowders, and such were made was to try and utilize the leftover scraps during hard times. Pepper Pot was created out of necessity during the long cold winter of 1777. Legend goes that because there was nothing to eat at Valley Forge, George Washington and the Continental army had to survive on a thick stew of beef tripe, vegetables, and pepper through the whole winter. Lucky them!

PEPPER POT

Serves 4–6

Olive oil

2 pounds veal bones or veal neck bones (chopped into 1" pieces)

1 large Spanish onion

2 medium carrots

3 celery stalks

2 pounds beef tripe (cleaned)

Small bunch of thyme

2 bay leaves

1 tablespoon black peppercorns

Salt

❶ In a big pot over high heat, drizzle a little olive oil and sauté veal neck bones for about 10–15 minutes until toasty brown.

❷ Peel vegetables and cut into 1" pieces.

❸ Now slice tripe and rinse in cold water.

❹ Remove veal pieces and place in a bowl.

❺ Sauté tripe for 5 minutes until some of the juices deglaze the pan.

❻ Return meat and add vegetables and aromatics and bring to a boil. Once boiling, reduce heat and simmer for 1½–2 hours. Skim constantly removing foam from on top to create a clear broth.

❼ Once 3 hours have passed, adjust salt, and add lots of fresh black pepper, garnish with chopped parsley or cilantro

❽ Serve with little lemon or lime wedges and crusty bread.

Bicarbonate of Soda Day

DEC. 30

Bicarbonate of wha? Bicarbonate of soda, or $NaHCO_3$, or sodium hydrogen carbonate, or perhaps its simpler in its natural form called Nahcolite? Ring any bells? I'm talking about the common indispensable ingredient, the chameleon of household chores, the humble baking soda. It's many uses can be traced back to the Egyptians who mined a compound called Natron, consisting of about 17 percent baking soda, and used it like soap.

IRISH SODA BREAD

Serves 4–6

3½ cups all-purpose flour

1 teaspoon bicarbonate of soda

½ teaspoon baking powder

1 rosemary sprig (leaves only, chopped finely)

1 teaspoon salt

½ teaspoon sugar

1 cup sharp Cheddar (shredded)

1½–1¾ cups buttermilk

❶ Sift flour and baking powder and baking soda into a bowl then make a well in the center. Add rosemary, salt, sugar, and cheese.

❷ Slowly add buttermilk while mixing with your hand until you have a solid but sticky ball. *Do not overmix.* It is okay if it looks lumpy. Form dough into a ball, dust with flour all around, and place on a cookie sheet, pizza stone, or inside a preheated cast iron pan with a lid. Using a sharp knife, make a 1" deep cross at the top.

3 Bake bread for 10 minutes at 450°F, then drop to 400°F and cover (you can do this with an inverted bowl or lid of the pot).

4 Bake until golden brown (about 30–35 minutes).

DEC. 31 Champagne Day

It's finally Dec. 31. New Year's Eve. Time for bubbly. Champagne, a sparkling wine produced in the Champagne region of France, is traditionally made with either chardonnay, pinot noir, or pinot meunier grapes and gets its bubbles from a secondary fermentation that occurs within the bottle with the addition of a little yeast and rock sugar. Then the bottles are turned upside down and allowed to ferment. The sediment slowly "sinks" to the top of the bottle, where it is then frozen and "popped" while you sing "Auld Lang Syne" This old Scottish poem-turned-song is translated and sung in just about every language in the world—and it goes perfectly with champagne. So, I leave you with this:

CHAMPAGNE TOWER

Coffee beans

Cranberries

Raspberries

Sparklers

Pop Rocks

Champagne

1 On a serving platter place a glass bottle with a small opening on top. Fill the bottle with coffee beans, cranberries, raspberries, and/or fir sprigs.

2 Set a sparkler inside and place in the middle of a serving platter. Stack champagne flutes all around the bottle. Place 1 raspberry and 1 teaspoon Pop Rocks in each glass.

3 Gather everybody around, light the sparklers, and pop your champagne then pour it freely into the glasses; the bottom ones will fill up as the top ones fill up.

Should old acquaintance be forgot,
and never brought to mind?
Should old acquaintance be forgot,
and old lang syne?

CHORUS:
For auld lang syne, my dear,
for auld lang syne,
we'll take a cup of kindness yet,
for auld lang syne.
And surely you'll buy your pint cup!
and surely I'll buy mine!
And we'll take a cup o' kindness yet,
for auld lang syne.

CHORUS
We two have run about the slopes,
and picked the daisies fine;
But we've wandered many a weary foot,
since auld lang syne.

CHORUS
We two have paddled in the stream,
from morning sun till dine;
But seas between us broad have roared
since auld lang syne.

CHORUS
And there's a hand my trusty friend!
And give us a hand o' thine!
And we'll take a right good-will draught,
for auld lang syne.

Index

Yvan Lemoine likes to play with food. Born in Caracas, Venezuela, he is a chef and mixologist in New York City. Together with his brother, he owns iFoodStudios, a creative food studio where he consults with bars and restaurants, provides food styling and photography, and leads media tours. Yvan has appeared on The Food Network's *Challenge*, competing against "The Ace of Cakes" Duff Goldman, and on *Chopped*. He started his career at fourteen at the famed La Caravelle restaurant in Manhattan and went on to work with Jacques Torres, Rocco Dispirito, Sam Mason, and Jahangir Mehta. Yvan is the host of a monthly cooking and entertaining segment on Univision called *El Toque de Lemoine*. He has made chocolate dresses for Kelly Ripa on *Live! with Regis & Kelly*, designed cocktails for Angelina Jolie at the Santa Barbara International Film Festival, and been featured in the *New York Times*, *Food Arts*, the *Daily News*, *Food & Wine*, *El Diario*, and numerous national morning shows. He is an active member of the United States Bartender Guild and Slow Food USA. Yvan has joined First Lady Michelle Obama in the "Let's Move" campaign to provide healthier food in schools and make healthier, more affordable food available in every part of our country. Fresh, fun, and irreverent, Yvan believes food has its own language—all you have to do is listen up.